ROMANTICISM

By the same author

MOTOWN AND THE ARRIVAL OF BLACK MUSIC
PERSPECTIVES ON ROMANTICISM: A Transformational
  Analysis

ROMANTICISM
A Structural Analysis

David Morse

First published 1982 by
THE MACMILLAN PRESS LTD
London and Basingstoke
Companies and representatives
throughout the world

First published in the USA 1982 by
BARNES & NOBLE BOOKS
81 Adams Drive
Totowa, New Jersey, 07512

MACMILLAN ISBN 0–333–28297–3
BARNES & NOBLE ISBN 0–389–20165–0

Printed in Hong Kong

To my Mother and the Memory of my Father

Contents

Preface

Since *Perspectives on Romanticism* and this book together make a continuous work the obligations which I acknowledged there are of equal relevance here. However I would like to thank those friends and colleagues who discussed the project with me, offered comments on sections of the manuscript or were otherwise helpful: Henry Thomas, Cora Kaplan, Alan Sinfield, Frank Gloversmith, Peter Stallybrass, Jonathan Dollimore, Peter Nichols, Gerald Moore, Douglas Tallack. I would also like to thank members of a faculty discussion group at which a paper based on the second section of this book was first presented. Evidently they bear no responsibility for what now appears.

As before I have cited passages from foreign-language works in translation, but have tried to preserve the original titles.

I am young, I grant, and know but little of the barbarity which is pretended to be universal. I cannot think the accusation true. Or, if it be, I am convinced it must be the result of some strange perversion of what may be called the natural propensities of man.

Thomas Holcroft, *Anna St Ives*

He who lives according to the highest law is in one sense lawless.

Emerson

Postscript by way of an Introduction

Although this discussion can usefully serve to introduce the reader to some of the salient features of a general argument about Romanticism contained in this book, it is, perhaps, more properly viewed as a postscript. That is, like most introductions, as I should surmise, it was written last and therefore has the character of a drawing together of threads and a retrospective viewing of the implications of the Romantic discourses here analysed, rather than of an introductory fanfare or provisional adumbration. It is no more a summation or substitute for the book than the book is a summation or substitute for the Romantic literature it discusses. If certain general propositions about Romantic literature are put forward here, they are offered as neither unproblematic nor exhaustive and they should be understood in relation to the analysis of particular genres that follows. If the reader will subsequently return to the beginning he will be in a position to understand rather better the issues to which this postscript as introduction addresses itself.

The analytical approach to Romanticism is structuralist because it is concerned to represent Romanticism as a series of characteristic intellectual structures rather than as a climate of opinion, an ambience or sea through which the individual authors as fishes move. Romanticism is by no means an accidental subject for a structuralist methodology, for it is both source and exemplification of the majority of assumptions that continue to underpin the practice of literary criticism and which this work is specifically designed to rebut. If I am happy to to designate it 'structuralist', despite the many possibilities for misconstruction that that introduces, it is because no word better indicates my intellectual distance from the assumptions and practice of the 'New Criticism', a

1

movement ostensibly buried and yet a perennial *revenant*. A cardinal axiom of Romanticism was that of the uniqueness, singleness and particularity of everything in the universe, and such an assumption has pervaded modern literary criticism with consequences so catastrophic that they verge on deliberate mystification and anti-intellectualism. On this view every artist is an entirely original and unique genius who creates a wholly idiosyncratic perceptual field that we name Blake, or Wordsworth, or Lawrence, or James, and which we interpret as the construction of a personal identity. The artist is a miraculous source who consults no other oracle than that of his own inner light. Every literary work is a unique organisation of words that can never be reproduced in any other organisation of words, nor is it strictly comparable with any other – even earlier drafts of a similarly designated work. The task to which literary criticism addresses itself is a tracing and retracing of the internal relations of these words, the recurrence of symbols, metaphors, figures. The mystic object invoked is the irreducible artwork, which as unique eludes all possible explanations and reductions, so that all such explanations and reductions have the same validity/non-validity. That is, no interpretation can give the whole meaning, but every such interpretation is a part of a totality of meaning that is always present in the work itself and always absent in our endlessly faceted discussions of it. Moreover, even to speak of meaning is simplistic, because no discussion of meaning can represent the work's specific literary or aesthetic qualities, which in discussion must necessarily be liquidated. In such a discrimination of unique particulars general designations must necessarily falsify. So Lovejoy in discriminating Romanticisms questions Romanticism, and, more generally, many critics who nevertheless use Romanticism as a convenient shorthand may nevertheless feel that it is more or less supererogatory so long as they can designate real entities such as Keats, Wordsworth and Blake.

Therefore to speak of Romanticism at all is perhaps in some way to be committed to a view that there are collectively constituted forms of organisation in society and that there is rather more to the history of literary activity than the self-defining, self-confined, self-sufficient, self-expression of individuals. It is to suggest that the artist is not simply a source but also has his sources; that his literary activity is always inserted into particular fields of literary discourse that themselves define the nature of what can be and what is said; that he will share many thoughts, feelings and preoccupations with other writers and with those who have never put pen to paper; that we understand his literary productions not as and how we like but within the parameters of the discourses in terms of which they are constructed. To do so is not to liquidate subjectivity and individual action but to understand more accurately how we should speak of them.

In this book the major genres of Romantic literature are discussed: the Gothic, the historical drama of Goethe and Schiller and the historical novel of Scott, the German *Märchen* or folktale and the major texts of English Romantic poetry. However, the forms adopted in the Romantic period are viewed not as intriguingly shaped bottles that can contain an almost infinite variety of liquids, but as distinctive fields of discourse with their own particular concerns and subject-matter. The Gothic is a field of discourse saturated with political connotations and addressing itself to issues raised in the work of Godwin and Paine: the incompatibility of reason and humanity with a society based on domination and fear; the critique of secrecy and the insistence that a healthy society must be based on frankness, openness and sincerity; the suggestion that in a society governed by despotism and permeated by religious hypocrisy and bigotry natural human impulses will become warped and distorted; the conviction that relationships between individuals on any basis other than that of freedom and equality must necessarily be alienating, even for – perhaps especially for – those who coerce and manipulate. It is on psychological grounds that a critique of an authoritarian and mystified society is presented. The genres of historical drama and historical novel are showed to be anchored in the political sociology of Montesquieu and Adam Ferguson and as having special pertinence to problems of Germany and Scotland as backward countries that are both provincial and economically and politically weak. Integral to these discourses is a strong critique of the centralising power of the modern state that suppresses variety and difference, ruthlessly destroys ancient traditions and folk-ways and replaces customary and unwritten rights that serve to protect the individual from arbitrary power with written laws and statutes designed to oppress him. In so far as this also implies a hostility to subordination there is common ground with the Gothic, but in the historical genres there is an oscillation between critique and nostalgia, for the freer world from the past that is invoked is either lost or irrevocably passing away. The German *Märchen* and English Romantic poetry can be regarded as forming a common field of discourse that addresses itself to the position of the artist, as an individual separated from his fellow men by a commitment to the visionary, yet under a moral constraint, negatively, not to cut himself off from them, and, positively, to communicate with them. This discourse of the artist reflects the contradictions in the emergent role of author as a person dependent on his income from selling his work to an unseen and unknown public and who is both obliged and not obliged to satisfy their expectations as to what he will write.

These fields of discourse are organised around particular figures and motifs. In the Gothic the central figure is that of the hypocrite, a man who loses touch with the sources of his identity through the acting out of a particular social role. Linked with the hypocrite is a double, who serves both as a marker of the individual's inauthenticity and alienation and as a destructive consequence of it. In the historical genres the crucial figure is that of the anachronistic hero, representative of an older and nobler world who survives into a world that has lost integrity and honour and who serves as a reminder of other possibilities and other values. The anachronistic hero either is an outcast himself or linked with the figure of an outcast; both point to the intolerance of 'progress' as variety, plurality and difference are suppressed. The *Märchen* and the poetry of English Romanticism characteristically put in the foreground either the figure of the artist himself or a figure who represents the artist. A characteristic motif is that of the 'lost vision'; for, since the visionary is precisely that which opposes itself to the everyday world, it could not be brought back to the world entire without liquidating the vision itself. Frequently the artist's vision is represented by the maiden, a beautiful girl whose symbolic and elusive character may be emphasised through metamorphosis and transformation as woman/flower (Novalis), woman/watersprite (Fouque), woman/snake (Keats, Hoffmann).

Though all these discourses have a distinctive focus, there are nevertheless numerous points of contact between them, significant areas of overlap and, in their later development, distinct indications of convergence. As a historical novelist, Scott was strongly influenced by his Gothic predecessors and contemporaries and there are elements of the Gothic in almost every novel he wrote. *The Heart of Midlothian* is a crucial intersection point: it is completely permeated by the figures, symbols and intellectual assumptions of the Gothic, yet this does not in any way derogate from or undermine its character as a historical novel. Hoffmann's work marks the transition from Gothic to the tale of the artist, since he wrote in both genres. He pursued the theme of a shift from ideal beauty to the real, which he took over from Lewis, in his tales of the artist and never failed to give its articulation, as in *Der Sandmann*, a characteristically Gothic *frisson*. Similarly, Hölderlin's Hyperion is both a symbol of the artist and an anachronistic hero who attempts to revive the values of ancient Greek culture in a world too late to receive them. Novalis's Augsburg and other parts of his unfinished novel *Heinrich von Ofterdingen* also invoke the idea of a more beautiful and radiant world where peace and serenity ruled, where the poet was prophet, lawgiver and king. All of these discourses contain the elements of a social critique. Each involves a hypothetical place to stand from which the world can be bracketed, qualified and relativised, a place that is no place. The polarities are given in the alternative titles of two novels of the period, William Godwin's *Caleb Williams* and Robert Bage's *Hermsprong*: respectively, 'Things as They Are' and 'Man as He Is Not'. It is misleading to suggest that writers of the period *believe* in the natural goodness of man or to erect a division between those who do and those who do not; rather they posit or hypothesise that man can be something other than what society and civilisation, political domination and religious hypocrisy have made him, and their optimism or pessimism or indecision depends on the degree to which they find it possible to sustain such an hypothesis. Ultimately the whole hypothetical nature of Romantic literature raises questions about the status of that literature itself. The good and

innocent heroes and heroines of the social and Gothic novels
of the early 1790s (and it is my contention that they form a
common field of discourse) seem unnaturally pure in relation
to the corrupted world in which they move. But, contrariwise,
it is never clear whether the perverted and distorted characters of later Gothic could ever be other than what they are.
The reader's ambivalent reaction to them, despite the evident
evils for which they appear responsible, is that they are both
blamed and not blamed. In the historical drama and historical
novel the past is invoked as an alternative source of values –
perhaps not better pure and simple, since every period and
every form of society has its own characteristic deficiencies as
well as its blessings; yet the past seems to exemplify values that
the present might well emulate. On the other hand, if, as
Ferguson suggested, all aspects of a given society are bound
together as an ensemble, it is perhaps unrealistic to expect
that, say, anything resembling a feudal code of honour should
be found anywhere other than in a feudal type of society. The
question is doubly academic, for if in the inexorable course of
modernisation and historical development early types of
society and social organisation must necessarily pass away the
values associated with them can only be the subject of
nostalgia. So the past, in the end, can never really be a source
of alternatives. The same problem affects the artist's transcendent vision. He may dream of an actualisation of that
vision – and some Romantic writers (Blake, Hölderlin, Novalis,
Shelley – to mention only a few) certainly hoped that it might
come about – yet the visionary, virtually by definition, is not
the real. The visionary is that which the real world resists.
In his attempts to communicate his vision to the world the
artist faces the problem that the vision, because hypothetical,
lacks credibility; the artist has no credentials that can validate
his claims to prophetic status; in the act of communication
itself the vision becomes warped, fragmented and distorted,
while there is equally the danger that the artist was mistaken
and that his vision was nothing more than a delusion, and a
dangerous and destructive one at that. The artist veers
between megalomania in his intoxication with his own ideas
and impotence and despair at his inability to maintain his own
sense of the visionary and to bring it into some kind of
meaningful relationship with the everyday world. The

Romantic protagonist, whether anachronistic hero, artist or hypocrite, becomes a law unto himself. Estranged from the world and at variance with it, he has no choice but to assume that he is right and that the world is wrong. He increasingly figures as a Superman – a man who moves beyond ordinary criteria of good and evil and enters a world of moral relativity in which he knows no law but that of his own will. A multiplicity of misrecognitions are generated in which he misrecognises the real world just as the world misrecognises him. The curious pessimism that is found in such late Romantic works as Hogg's *Justified Sinner*, Scott's *The Fair Maid of Perth* and Hoffmann's *Kater Murr* is bound up with their sense of a tangled world, where no obvious distinctions apply, where communication has become so distorted that there is no real prospect of anyone understanding anyone else's point of view, a world so mixed up that there seems to be no possible way of unscrambling it. Romantic discourses seem to converge on their recognition of a relativism from which there is no way out.

What is also notable about Romantic discourse is that it is much more critical and aware of its own presuppositions than is the thought of our own time. Concepts of self and society and of self and relation to society, of human nature and civilisation, of reason, the imagination and the unconscious, that in Romantic discourse never lose their problematic character have in the twentieth century been used in a completely unquestioning way, deployed as if there were no past and no tomorrow, taken for granted as entities, and put to work on problems as if they were solutions and not symptoms of disorder in themselves. Thus Romantic discourse only hypothesised a free and autonomous self, uncontaminated by social influences, it did not imagine that such was actually the case. It did not imagine, as did much later fiction, that you could take such a desocialised individual and then insert him back into the world in a narrative that was at the same time a portrait of society, as if this constituted an ineluctable *rite de passage*. Romantic literature is aware of its own character as a discourse about the world that both relativises that world and holds it in question. The holding apart of the hero as individual and society is an artistic strategy that does not construct these as existing and self-evident facts of life. But the thought of our own day is a science of myths or myths of science, in which science studies its own mythic object with its own mythic discourse. Take the 'unconscious', for example. A careful study of Gothic fiction cannot evade the fact that it is importantly concerned with unconscious and involuntary behaviour. The notion of the unconscious is produced by a chain of theoretical reasoning. That is, a hypocrite will be unable adequately to know his own mind, because his persistent misrecognition of his own behaviour and motives in falsely representing himself to others makes it impossible for him to carry through the task of self-examination. Moreover, such behaviour is seen as produced by a civilisation that leads to a denial of the authentic self. Yet at the same time the speculative and reifying determinism of Freudian psychoanalysis – that the unconscious is an entity, that repression is an inevitable consequence of civilisation, that censorship is inescapable in the workings of the mind, that the unconscious is the site of the authentic – is absent. For the necessity is not the necessity of civilisation but a theoretical necessity that will ground the concepts and their relationship in the first place. Freud could not regard his constructions as being hypothetical or open to question. The conceptual framework thinks for itself, bound by its own iron laws, and there can be no gap between what is and what is posited. To bracket any one of Freud's key terms could involve nothing less than a disaster.

The most difficult problem raised by this study is that of structural determination. That is to say, a structural analysis, like most contemporary types of explanation, exhibits relations between various phenomena, but it does not attempt a causal explanation of an earlier type, where the existence of such and such a state of affairs is explained by showing that it was the result of x or y or z. Rather phenomena are seen as multiply determined and understood not as results but as complex changes of state. This in turn reflects an analysis of the past in the human sciences that is oriented towards structures rather than events, to feudalism rather than the battle of Hastings, to imperialism rather than the relief of Mafeking – though events, of course, are by no means precluded. But there can be no doubt that structures are privileged over events in that structures would appear to determine not particular events but the particular type of events that would or could happen. Certainly I, at any rate, would be prepared to embrace this somewhat daunting conclusion, even if to do so might seem somewhat unprofitable, since it is hard to know quite what the implications of commitment are. For it does seem to me that the Romantic discourses do in some way constrain, confine and dictate what is sayable within them. Moreover, it seems to me that a readiness to recognise certain overall types of structuration and structuring of signification in a field of discourse must involve an acceptance of the principle of symbolic equivalence. That is, just as Propp in his *Morphology of the Folktale* suggested a basic structure for Russian folktales in which certain slots or functions could be filled in different ways, so that the return of the hero, for example, might be effected by a magic carpet or magical steed, so it seems to me that Keats's 'Lamia' and 'Isabella', Scott's *Waverley* and *Redgauntlet* must be regarded as symbolically equivalent. This means not that they are of equal aesthetic value, or that their precise significance is the same, but that there is present in them a certain generalised level of meaning that is given by the constituted field of discourse itself, though each work gives it its own characteristic inflection.

The suggestion I have put forward, that the Romantic discourses converge on the figure of the Superman and a recognition of relativism, also implies structural determination, since it does imply that this is implicit in the nature of the discourses themselves and that these implications are simply actualised by the writers concerned. The 'inescapable' movement of categories, both here and in my *Perspectives on Romanticism*, may appear all too reminiscent of Hegel's philosophy of history. However, the notion of structural determination put forward here is somewhat different. The appropriate analogy might be a chess game, where the first half-dozen or so moves serve to establish the character of the opening, the next dozen give the game its general character and produce a position, where retrospectively it is possible to analyse how certain moves structured the game in a certain way, thus leading almost inevitably to the defeat of Black or White or to a particular type of endgame. The same general perspective is relevant to the discourses examined here.

Individual initiative is by no means ruled out. Goethe more or less invented the historical genre; Lewis redefined the Gothic, which had itself been reoriented politically by Charlotte Smith and Ann Radcliffe. At the same time, however, the field of discourse does establish certain integral dispositions. But the writer always has open to him a whole range of options: to continue in a field of discourse, to attempt to reorient it, to construct a new one or to revive one that has fallen into desuetude. But genres and fields of discourse are not free-floating; they are complexly bound up with other discourses in society; the way in which they are articulated involves an address to contemporary issues. If they are exploratory it is not just an examination of consciousness but a struggle with intellectual and social contradictions. But, despite Romanticism, there are no individual ways of looking at the world; collective ways are the only ways we have.

PART I

Gothic

1 The Social Novel and the Gothic

The ease with which the Gothic can be gestured towards as a phenomenon, the readiness with which it can be identified through the isolation of recurrent motifs such as the haunted castle or the criminal monk, has the unfortunate effect of rendering the genre non-problematic at the very moment when we focus our attention upon it. The confidence with which we assume a tradition of Gothic from Horace Walpole to Beckford and Clara Reeve prevents us from asking why Gothic should have developed so rapidly in the last decade of the eighteenth century and, more particularly, why it should have succeeded the Sentimental novel, with which it has certain affinities. There is no real continuity and we must rather explain why novelists should have closed their *Sir Charles Grandison* and reopened their *Clarissa*, and why even writers who were certainly influenced by Rousseau, such as Anne Radcliffe and Charlotte Smith, should nevertheless have eschewed the model of *La Nouvelle Héloïse*.

Moreover, the very clarity of Gothicism as a phenomenon becomes blurred when we examine the fiction of the 1790s more closely. It would be easy to make a distinction in the period between the earnest social criticism of a Godwin, a Holcroft or a Bage, on the one hand, and the escapist entertainments of Mrs Smith and Mrs Radcliffe, on the other. But both Mrs Smith and Mrs Radcliffe have a perspective on society that is worked out in their novels, while there are strong Gothic overtones to the attempted rape scenes in *Barham Downs* and *Anna St Ives*, not to mention the scenes in *Hugh Trevor* when Hugh as a boy is left alone with a woman weltering in blood, or, later, when, with his friend Clarke, he stumbles unwittingly into the dissecting room of an anatomist at night and feels 'a cold, dead, hand, between my fingers'.[1]

13

The connection between politics and terror is not accidental but fundamental: it stems from the fact that the radical political thinkers of the period saw democracy and reason, tyranny and the irrational, as linked and antithetical terms. Behind its trappings and mysteries the Gothic novel presents a powerful critique of arbitrary power.

To put it another way, the sublime has a political dimension. That Burke should have been both a theorist of the sublime and the leading conservative political theorist of his day has a certain logic; for his position on both issues stems from his belief in the limitations of reason. The sublime is not created by man's ratiocinative processes but rather serves to signal their limitations: it occurs at the moment when man is overwhelmed by feelings of awe, wonder and terror on confronting aspects of the universe which go beyond his comprehension and which simultaneously reveal the grandeur of God and his own limited place in the divine scheme of things. This is all of a piece with Burke's traditionalism, which links piety towards God with piety towards institutions – 'We fear God – we look with *awe* to kings – with affection to parliaments – with duty to magistrates – with reverence to priests, and with respect to nobility'[2] – and which at the same time implies that this traditional institutional fabric is a structure which should simply be accepted and which lies beyond the scope of rational inquiry.

For Burke's radical opponents, on the other hand, there could be no more terrible spectacle than that of a power that attempts to set itself above reason. For them authority is the very antithesis of reason and therefore evil. Authority means power, power means coercion and violence, the use of deceit and mystery to maintain an unjust state of affairs. Paine angrily attacks 'the base and false idea of governing men by terror, instead of reason'[3] and deplores 'the attempt to govern mankind by force and fraud'[4], while for Godwin coercion of itself constitutes injustice and he insists that 'coercion has nothing in common with reason'.[5] Thus, the exercise of arbitrary power is by definition irrational and opposed to reason. For Godwin, reason is essentially democratic. In a perceptive passage he observes, 'he that would reason with another, and honestly explain to him the motives of the action he recommends, descends to a footing of equality. But he who undertakes to delude us, and fashion us, to our purpose by a specious appearance, has a feeling that he is our master'.[6] For Godwin, monarchy and aristocracy are bad not simply because no checks are placed on the use of power, but also because the 'blind submission to authority'[7] leads to man's alienation from his fellow men, whom he can neither trust nor communicate with, and from his own latent intellectual powers. The same situation that sets some men up as being more than men, when in reality they are men and nothing more, simultaneously blocks others off from their full humanity. As Paine points out in *The Rights of Man*,

It is by distortedly exalting some men, that others are distortedly debased, till the whole is out of nature.

A vast mass of mankind are degradedly thrown into the background of the human picture, to bring forward, with greater glare, the puppet-show of state and aristocracy.[8]

Thus the struggle of the individual to achieve self-consciousness, to grasp his full humanity as an active, independent thinking being is simultaneously a struggle against domination, authority and arbitrary power. It is precisely such a struggle that is at the heart of the renascent Gothic novel: in *Emmeline*, *The Old Manor House* and *The Mysteries of Udolpho*. Godwin insists that 'All coercion sours the mind';[9] but Emmeline, Monimia and Emily profit from 'the school of adversity' in the only way that Godwin thinks possible: 'by finding resources in their own minds, enabling them to regard, with an unconquered spirit, the violence employed against them'.[10]

The aptness of Godwin's words is striking, but, of course, these novels are inspired not by the theories of Godwin, whose *Political Justice* only appeared in 1893, but by the example of Richardson. Yet Charlotte Smith and Anne Radcliffe go further than Richardson, and, if neither is his equal as a novelist, they see the abject predicament of woman more clearly: in place of the social climbing of Pamela, the Christian resignation of Clarissa, we are explicitly presented with a struggle against manifold forms of bondage. Both Mrs Smith and Mrs Radcliffe know that such a situation is not due to the malignity of a Mr B or a Lovelace but is simply the objective

consequence of the position of woman in society – a chattel
to be bought and sold in marriage, which is, as Charlotte Smith
observes in *Desmond*, 'the most dreadful of all fetters' (or, at
least, a bad marriage is).[11] The stylisation of the Gothic is a
way of presenting this psychological situation with all the
intensity that is subjectively felt, while simultaneously masking
the force of its social critique. In *The Mysteries of Udolpho* Emily
understands that Montoni has sold her to Count Morano and
then arbitrarily changes his mind. Marriage to Morano offers
the possibility of escape from Montoni, but this means
'submitting herself to the protection of this man, with whom
evils more certain and not less terrible appeared'.[12] Montoni
and Morano are demonic incarnations of the figures of father
and husband; both seek to possess her without acknowledging
her as a person, and what is threatening about them is
generated by her sense of her own powerlessness. The
mystery that surrounds Montoni signifies the inscrutability of
absolute power, while the vastness, obscurity and sublimity of
the castle of Udolpho make it an even more fetishised symbol
of the way in which domination appears simply as a marvellous fact, impenetrable to perception and resistant to inquiry.
The castle cannot be taken in at a glance, partly because of its
sheer size and partly because of the gloom that surrounds it.
Emily attempts to judge 'the heavy strength and extent of the
whole'[13] from the gigantic courts and towers that are presented immediately to her perception, but the ramparts
extend to further towers, which are lost in the distance and in
the obscurity of twilight. Udolpho is sublime because it
appears beyond human comprehension, but this very characteristic that makes it sublime is also what makes it threatening.
If Udolpho suggests to Emily 'even more terrors, than her
reason could justify'[14] this also involves the recognition that
the context of Udolpho is spiritually demoralising partly
because of her own state of mind; it is not altogether an objective fact but rather serves as an emblem of a form of consciousness, which Emily herself must strive to overcome. From
this standpoint the customary objection to Mrs Radcliffe's
fiction, that she diminishes the horror and poetry of the
events which she describes by supplying the reader with
excessively delayed and highly prosaic explanations, loses
much of its force. While it is true that Mrs Radcliffe's

disposition to illuminate her subject with the factuality of a Clare Reeve is always in danger of suggesting that the subject itself was relatively factitious, it is important to grasp that this act of clarification is psychologically necessary. The struggle against obscurity is a struggle against domination and the attempt on Emily's part to free herself from the power of Montoni and the mysteries of Udolpho is at the same time her attempt to realise her identity as a free and autonomous individual. As Emily grows in self-confidence, so she is more capable of presenting resistance to Montoni's threats. As his motives and processes of thought become more obvious to her, so does his ability to oppress her diminish. Montoni's power is symbolically broken in the scenes in which he tries to compel her to submit, for his fervour betrays the weakness of his own position, while his very preoccupation with Emily serves to endow her thoughts and actions with an importance that they have hitherto lacked. Mrs Radcliffe makes the connection between the spiritual development of Emily and the diminishing of Montoni quite explicit, after a scene in which Montoni has notably failed to make Emily subject to his will:

> To her own solitary chamber she once more returned, and there thought again of the late conversation with Montoni, and of the evils she might expect from opposition to his will. But his power did not appear so terrible to her imagination, as it was wont to do: a sacred pride was in her heart, that taught it to swell against the pressure of injustice, and almost to glory in the quiet sufferance of ills, in a cause which had also the interest of Valancourt for its object. For the first time she felt the full extent of her own superiority to Montoni and despised the authority which, till now, she had only feared.[15]

Emily has learned the great lesson preached by radical and Jacobin thought, that Montoni, like any king, tyrant or oppressor, is *only a man*. Freed from her psychological thrall, it is appropriate that Emily should now effect her physical escape from the castle and that Udolpho should play no significant part in the remainder of the narrative. The unreality of Gothic here appears as a reflection of particular

states of mind – just as the unreality of Kafka's story 'The
Judgement' communicates the impotence of the protagonist
before his omnipotent father, an omnipotence which appears
true in so far as it is subjectively felt.

Although the novels of Mrs Smith are not worked towards
such a high degree of stylisation as those of Mrs Radcliffe, Mrs
Radcliffe only developed and intensified to a point that we
now characterise as 'Gothic' themes that were present in Mrs
Smith's work. At first sight such novels as *Emmeline* and *The Old
Manor House*, with their mysterious old houses, helpless
orphans and lost wills, appear as banal cliches, of so little
interest that it is tempting to make an absolute distinction
between them and such novels as *Desmond*, where the subjection of woman and her struggle against it is explicitly linked
with the French Revolution. But such a conclusion would be
short-sighted. For all literary themes and motifs have a
meaning, even though this may occasionally be lost sight of;
and perhaps what characterises melodrama is not simply the
use of certain plots but rather the process of 'forgetting' just
what it is that they mean. For *Emmeline* and *The Old Manor
House* have a high political content and they deal with the
principal social evils of the day as these presented themselves
to radical opinion. The castle or old manor house is a
polyvalent symbol. In the first instance, it is for Emmeline and
Monimia a place of imprisonment, and perhaps the greatest
legacy of Sentimentalism had been to make the prison, or even
cage for a caged bird, an embodiment of everything that was
most repugnant to the human spirit. If anything characterises
Romantic literature as a whole, it is a rage against prisons,
from Blake's 'A robin redbreast in a cage/Sets all Heaven in a
rage' to Beethoven's *Fidelio*. But the castle also suggests the
massive strength and intransigence of power and authority
and the way in which the past can oppress and stifle the living.
The solidity of the castle and the weakness of the heroine
communicate in vivid metaphorical form the power of institutions over the lives of individuals; it dramatises the enormous
obstacles that stand in the way of the individual's self-
realisation. By implication, imprisonment is not a special
punishment imposed upon malefactors, but, rather, a normal
way of life for the majority of people in society, who find their
existence circumscribed with a multitude of constraints.

When Monimia in *The Old Manor House* is not allowed to attend Mrs Rayland's grand ball but is confined to her room, it is quite clear that this confinement is that of confinement to a particular social class: she may not mingle with or even see persons of a higher social standing than herself. If the fortunes of Emmeline and Orlando and Monimia are ultimately restored, this is not mere plot mechanics but has considerable moral force, involving as it does both the righting of ancient wrongs and the victory of truth over the determined opposition of power and privilege. In *The Rights of Man* Paine drew attention to the evils of primogeniture and the injustice and unfairness that followed from this institutionalising of privilege within the family. He pointed out that 'Every aristocratic family has an appendage of family beggars hanging round it, which, in a few ages, or a few generations, are shook off, and console themselves with telling their tales in almshouses, work-houses and prisons. This is the natural consequence of aristocracy.'[16] The Somerives in *The Old Manor House* are just such a family and their inferior and dependent position leads them into endless humiliations: not least the fact that the young daughter Isabella is expected to marry the elderly General Tracy – an alliance which because of the vast difference in their ages and because of her very natural repugnance verges on the obscene – simply on account of his wealth. The lost will, which serves to delegitimise established power and authority, serves to question power and authority themselves, especially when the same power and authority are shown actively opposing and thwarting the discovery of truth. Mrs Smith's heroines have to struggle against the bondage that society imposes on them and she is perfectly clear that marriage, far from being the delightful consummation aspired to by a Pamela or a Fanny Price, is simply the most obvious form of this.

Emmeline is a *Werther* written from Charlotte's point of view, but the transpositions of sex and social status produce a completely different meaning. Lord Delamare, the passionate young lover, is a less appealing figure than his prototype, because he seeks to appropriate Emmeline without fully acknowledging her as a person. Emmeline's wisdom in persistently rejecting her valuable 'catch' is underscored by the fate of her friends Mrs Stafford and Lady Adelina, who

have both made rash marriages to selfish, inconsiderate and
profligate young men which they have lived bitterly to regret.
Marriage, indeed, in the novels of both Mrs Smith and Mrs
Radcliffe, appears most often to be a dreadful fate. The
consequences of giving up one's freedom and of placing
onself entirely in the hands of a husband emerge most
piteously in the cases of Lady Adelina, Mrs Roker and
Madame Montoni: the first two are driven to the point of
madness, while the latter pays for her imprudence by a
lingering death in the castle of Udolpho. In every case the
woman is treated by her husband not as a fellow human being
but as a chattel to be abused, manipulated and exploited. The
torments of Gothic convey in a heightened form the predicament of woman in contemporary society. Their thoughts,
wishes and feelings are not considered. If Emmeline is a
cypher to her social superiors, if her status as a person is
invisible to virtually everyone, this is a statement not about
'orphans' but about the position of women in general.

Although the castle is usually described as being located in
some remote and desolate spot, it nevertheless serves to
encode a multiplicity of references to civilisation: its role in
confining and oppressing the innocent signifies the constraints which society serves to impose upon the individual.
This is most apparent in *The Mysteries of Udolpho*, where Emily,
after her innocent upbringing in La Vallee, where she is
exposed to the beneficent influences of nature, is only brought
to Udolpho, after the death of her parents, through the
influence of her aunt, Madame Cheron, in whom all the vices
of polite society – the concern with social position, conspicuous consumption, a behaviour characterised by envy, vanity
and selfishness – are prominently displayed. The considerations that lead her to reject Valancourt as a suitor for Emily
and yet accept Montoni as a husband for herself are shown by
Mrs Radcliffe to have disastrous consequences. Udolpho is, as
it were, the hell for those who have been corrupted by society;
for here the masks that normally veil behaviour in polite
society are removed to reveal brutal egoism, unscrupulous
greed, machination, manipulation and violence. Moreover,
the behaviour of Montoni and his associates is marked by the
envy, resentment and competitiveness that Rousseau had
noted and deplored in Paris. The castle, like the madhouse,

expresses the truth of social existence: that it imposes pains and tribulations on the human spirit that are almost greater than it can bear. If madness figures prominently in the Gothic, it is not simply because madness can be deemed sublime, but rather because madness is the supreme testimony that the individual pays an intolerable price for his initiation into culture. Culture is shown to represent a milieu of deception and intrigue that it is too much for innocence to bear, yet, because it would not be fitting to presume the heroine herself to be subject to madness, the Gothic creates a structure of surrogates and doubles, through which the punishment is displaced. This is clearly demonstrated in *Emmeline*, where the sequence Emmeline – Mrs Stafford – Adelina makes us realise that the torments of Adelina are those that Emmeline herself might have endured – indeed, the very name Adelina seems to signify 'mad Emmeline'. Similarly, their implication in their husbands' malignant intrigues precipitates, through a kind of poetic justice, the fate that seemed designated for the heroine. Michel Foucault has pointed out that in eighteenth-century fiction confinement was believed to produce madness, and he also observes,

> It is sufficient to remember the value, both moral and medical ascribed at about the same period to country air (bodily health, spiritual vigour), to realise the whole complex of contrary meanings, conveyed by the corrupt air of hospitals, prisons, houses of confinement. By this atmosphere laden with maleficent vapours, entire cities were threatened whose inhabitants would be slowly impregnated with rottenness and taint.[17]

The Gothic novel of Mrs Smith and Mrs Radcliffe manipulates whole sets of oppositions of this type, which can be set out schematically as follows:

Nature	Culture
Simplicity	Corruption
Truth	Falsity
Being for oneself (self-esteem)	Being for others (honour, glory)
Liberty	Confinement

| Health | Sickness |
| Tranquillity | Madness |

Thus, if the heroine is an orphan, this has the effect of placing her beyond the corrupting influences of culture. Mrs Smith continually emphasises 'the extreme simplicity'[18] of Emmeline's appearance, 'her perfect ignorance of fashionable life and fashionable accomplishments',[19] 'the naivety of her manners'.[20] If Godolphin finds in Emmeline 'a native dignity of soul, an enlarged and generous heart, a comprehensive and cultivated understanding, a temper at once soft and lively, with morals the most pure, and manners simple, undesigning and ingenuous',[21] this is because her upbringing has been such as to insulate and protect her from the decadence of civilised society. London is presented by Mrs Smith as a scene of moral enervation and corruption. Emmeline finds it disagreeable: 'the melancholy, deserted houses in the fashionable streets, and the languor that appeared in the countenance of those who were obliged to be in town, offered no amusement or variety to compensate for the loss of pure air she had been accustomed to breathe'.[22]

In the work of both Mrs Smith and Mrs Radcliffe nature is a continual solace and consolation. Moreover, for both novelists the world of nature is the locus of the heroine's best self: it is associated symbolically with the parents whom the orphan has lost. For Emily in *The Mysteries of Udolpho* the influence of landscape is intimately connected with memories of her father, St Aubert, who frequently remarked 'while tears of pleasure trembled in his eyes'[23] that the hours spent in the country provide 'moments infinitely more delightful than any passed amid the brilliant and tumultuous scenes that are courted by the world'.[24] Her love of nature proves to be a source of moral strength when she is transported to the sinister setting of Udolpho. The contemplation of natural beauty, the spectacle of the setting and rising of the sun are for her a deep source of pleasure in the midst of her troubles and anxieties: they serve as the endless renewal of a promise that her freedom and peace of mind will ultimately be restored to her. Emmeline learns of her own legitimacy and her consequent claim to the estates of Mowbray castle from an old French servant who had once served her father in the setting of the most picturesque French countryside between Marseilles and Toulon. Mrs Smith describes the rocky landscape with its aromatic plants and shrubs, its purple heather and summits of fir, larch and pine before which Emmeline pauses in admiration as a significant prelude to this denouement. Since she alone enjoys this scenery, while her companions are engrossed in other matters, the discovery of the truth about her past at this particular point seems to constitute a privileged moment, at which nature assets its claims over the entrenched privileges of culture. Nature is connected with the deepest sources of identity. In this respect there is a significant parallel between the work of Mrs Smith and Mrs Radcliffe and that of Jean-Paul Richter in Germany. In Richter too nature is a source of comfort and consolation. In *Der Titan* he speaks of his hero, Albano, cooling his heart 'in the tide of nature',[25] while nature also serves to awaken him to revelations of the grandeur of his own spirit: 'O then arose his inner colosseum full of silent, godlike forms of spiritual antiques and the torch-gleam of Fancy glanced round upon them like a play of a moving magic life.'[26] Implicitly in both Richter and Mrs Radcliffe, society serves to repress the individual, who can only discover his full potentiality in solitude and through exposure to the sublimity of natural objects. Wordworthianism in this sense is well established before Wordsworth himself appears on the scene.

In British social fiction of the 1790s a contrast between the decadence of fashionable European society and a spirit of freedom, innocence and honesty to be found in the newly independent American colonies is frequently drawn. America naturalises the concept of naturalness and makes it possible to see the concept of the noble savage not as some bizarre and improbable fiction, but as a living historical reality that can be confidently gestured towards. In Holcroft's *Anna St Ives* Frank Henley is so doubtful about the possibility of advancing the cause of truth in a European context, where prejudices are so deeply ingrained that he seriously considers leaving England for the New World:

I think of sailing for America, where I may aid the struggles of liberty, may freely publish all which the efforts of reason can teach me, and at the same time may form a society of

savages, who seem in consequence of their very ignorance to
have a less quantity of error, and therefore to be less liable
to repel truth than those whose information is more multifarious.[27]

A stay in America is invariably shown as having beneficial and
life-transforming consequences. In Charlotte Smith's *Celestina*
the young Count de Bellegarde describes how his 'residence in
America, had awakened in my mind a spirit of freedom',[28]
while in *The Old Manor House* Orlando, though finding the
American wilderness psychologically demoralising, finds in
Wolf-Hunter, the Indian chief with whom he has established
'The secret sympathy between generous minds',[29] a more
genuine and loyal friend than any that he has encountered in
England. When he returns home to discover that Monimia has
disappeared and that he himself has been dispossessed of his
inheritance, he is demoralised to find that his inquiries make
so little headway and to discover at the Fleet prison such an
absence of trust:

> But mistrust seemed universal in that scene of legal
> wretchedness; and, with a heart bleeding at the thoughts of
> there being such complicated miseries, and that man had
> the power to inflict them on his fellow-creatures, he almost
> wished himself again among the cypress swamps and
> pathless woods of uncultivated America.[30]

This formulation indicates how the generous sympathies and
radical political views of the social novels very naturally
inclined towards Gothic modes of expression; for what is the
Gothic but a prolonged demonstration of the perversity of
human nature as a result of the conditioning processes of
culture, an exhibition of 'complicated misery' which could
never occur in the setting of the New World?
    The belief that truth and integrity are the first casualties in
the advance of culture is one that is shared by Mrs Radcliffe.
In *The Romance of the Forest* the innocent Adeline, to whom 'the
arts and practice of dissimulation were hitherto equally
unknown',[31] finds through her exposure to corruption that
she is forced to practise them for her own self-preservation.
The partial fall of Adeline symbolises the fall of man into

society; like her predecessor Emmeline, she has been protected from decadence by the fact that she is an orphan.
Education, far from being beneficial, is seen as a process that
prevents man from acting generously and spontaneously:
'Truth is often perverted by education. While the refined
Europeans boast a standard of honour, and a sublimity of
virtue, which often leads from pleasure to misery and from
nature to error, the simple, uninformed American follows the
impulse of his heart and obeys the inspiration of wisdom.'[32]

Such virtuousness is exemplified by Robert Bage's hero
Hermsprong. Hermsprong was 'born a savage'[33] and his
education among the American Indians has developed in him
the 'uncourtly obduracy'[34] of always speaking the truth. Bage
makes it clear that the great virtue of such an upbringing is
that is encourages self-reliance and independence of thought
and action: man is freed from the pressure to conform to the
expectations of his superiors or peers. Hermsprong exclaims
to Miss Fluart,

> I cannot, I fear, submit to be fettered and cramped
> throughout the whole circle of thought and action. You
> submit to authority with regard to the first, and to fashion
> with regard to the last. I cannot get rid of the stubborn
> notion, that to do what we think is right to do is the only
> good principle of action. . . . Servile compliance is a crime,
> when it violates rectitude; and imbecility, at least when it
> is prostituted to folly. When it has become habitual, what
> a thing it has made of man.[35]

Man and society are seen as being inevitably and necessarily at
odds.

Although Mrs Radcliffe is not normally thought of as a critic
of society, this theme serves to articulate the structure of
virtually all her work. On the one hand there is the beauty and
sublimity of nature which arouses man's noblest feelings; on
the other the artificial environment of the city, which corrupts
him and destroys his finer feelings. This contrast is well
brought out in a scene in *The Romance of the Forest*. Confronting one of Mrs Radcliffe's characteristic spectacles Adeline
enthuses, 'The stillness and total seclusion of this scene . . .
those stupendous mountains, the gloomy grandeur of these

woods, together with that monument of faded glory, on which
the hand of time is so emphatically impressed, diffuse a sacred
enthusiasm over the mind, and awaken sensations truly
sublime.'[36] Later in the book M. Verneuil observes that such
delights are incompatible with ordinary social existence. The
'romantic' is precisely defined in opposition to society, and
society, by this epithet proclaims its own opposition: 'Yet the
world, sir, would call the pleasure of which you speak,
romantic... for to be sensible of this pure and exquisite
delight requires a heart untainted with the vicious pleasures of
society – pleasures that deaden its finest feelings, and poison
the source of its truest enjoyments.'[37] This view of society led
Mrs Radcliffe to place great emphasis on the changeableness
of human nature. In *The Romance of the Forest* La Motte
appears initially as a person of good character. He is progressively corrupted by exposure to various immoral influences,
but at the end of the novel he is offered the prospect of
redemption by Mrs Radcliffe: 'His former habits became
odious to him and his character gradually recovered the hue
which it would probably always have worn, had he never been
exposed to the tempting dissipations of Paris.'[38]

A similar metamorphosis is undergone by Valancourt
in *The Mysteries of Udolpho*. The happiness of Emily and
Valancourt is associated with the world of nature and La Vallee.
When they are separated, Emily's ordeal at the castle of
Udolpho is paralleled by Valancourt's corruption in Paris.
Since Emily is sustained through all her dreadful experiences
by her memories of Valancourt, the discovery of his 'un-
worthyness'[39] is doubly shocking. The remainder of the novel
centres on the prospect of Valancourt's redemption. Valancourt asks Emily if she will be ready to hope for his reformation, but both he and she are tormented by the thought of
their former goodness and innocence, which seem to be lost
irrecoverably. For Emily it is a terrible and terrifying thought
that even such a great and noble nature as that of Valancourt
could be corrupted by exposure to the customs of Paris: '"And
such a mind", said she, "such a heart, were to be sacrificed to
the habits of a great city!"'[40] Like Fitz-Edward in *Emmeline*,
Valancourt is identified as the mysterious figure who has been
wandering about the house at night. These ghostly appearances have a symbolic function: in both cases they suggest

that the character is a 'lost soul' who wanders because he cannot find rest or peace. He is an outcast because he has sinned, yet he is still capable of atonement. It appears that Valancourt's conduct has been represented as being worse than it actually was – significantly, 'though his passions had been seduced, his heart was not depraved'.[41] Valancourt is restored to Emily's favour and their marriage returns them to the rural scenes of their former love. The nightmare from which Emily and Valancourt are trying to awake in *The Mysteries of Udolpho* is the nightmare of civilisation.

The novelists of the 1790s took over from Richardson the theme of the struggle between oppressor and oppressed, between aristocrat and commoner, but in their hands it acquired a more explicitly political significance. They used it not merely to propound the superiority of virtue to rank but also to show the iniquity of all domination and arbitrary power. They were always conscious of the connection between authority in the family and authority in the political sphere. The power that a father wielded over his daughter or a husband over his wife (and there they significantly differed from Richardson) was essentially despotic because it sought to exact claims of obedience on the basis not of reason but of tradition and social position; in the presentation of such situations the analogy with the relationship between a king and his subjects was never very far away. Neither Thomas Holcroft's *Anna St Ives* nor Robert Bage's *Hermsprong* is a Gothic novel in conventional parlance, which directs our attention towards such phenomena as apparitions and creaking doors, yet both have great affinities with the symbolic world of the Gothic. They present the reader with a world in which good, virtuous and kindly people are subjected to malignant machinations at the hands of people who enjoy a high social position and in which incarceration and confinement become both the dramatic high-point of the novel and, at the same time, a focus of moral indignation against those who seek to impose their will on others in this barbarous way. The imprisonment of Pamela is repeated over and over again as if it were the novel's primal scene. In *Anna St Ives* both Anna and Frank Henley, her virtuous and lowly born lover, are imprisoned by the aristocratic Coke Clifton, who is filled with uncontrollable resentment at the preference which Anna shows for Frank Henley. Fittingly, she is subjected to the latest instruments for the control of deviance, the straitjacket and the madhouse. In *Hermsprong* the tyrant is Lord Grondale, and Robert Bage acknowledges the affinity of his theme with that of the Gothic, through his ironic introductory description of the noble peer's country seat:

> Above this ruin, on the summit of a hill, are the remains of the castle of Grondale. One tower is left, and enough of the battlements to show how a savage grandeur once fortified its own tyranny against the tyranny of others. But the most pleasing of all the objects now under my view, is a stately structure of the Gothic kind, half modernised, once the seat of friendship and hospitality – now of Lord Grondale.[42]

Despite his genial tone, Bage's wit is pointed. The edifice is only 'half modernised', a reference which points to a discrepancy between inner and outer, so characteristic of the Gothic: the castle *appears* pleasing and to have changed with the times – but in reality and within it is just as much the seat of despotism as ever it was. To prevent the marriage of his daughter Caroline Campinet to Hermsprong, the mysterious and wealthy young man who has been brought up among the American Indians and who is impatient of the constraints and shibboleths of English society, Lord Grondale confines her within the castle and tries to force her to marry the more suitable Sir Philip Chestrum. This scheme, however, is triumphantly foiled by Miss Fluart, to whom Lord Grondale would readily become attached were it not for her independence of mind: she takes the place of Caroline at the ceremony and then, with admirable *sang-froid*, exits, pistol in hand! This scene parallels an earlier instance, in Bage's *Barham Downs*, where Lord Winterbottom imprisons Annabelle Whitaker in an inn in Milan, overpowers her with drugs and effects a forced marriage without her knowledge. For Bage, as for Richardson, will and consciousness coincide, and both must be extinguished at one and the same time. The torments, tribulations and suspensions of consciousness to which the heroine is subjected in Gothic fiction only serve to emphasise the unshakability, steadfastness and intransigence of consciousness itself. The Gothic is, as it were, *The Pilgrim's Progress* rewritten in terms of personal identity, for it is this, above all, that has to be saved. The Gothic affirms the superiority of virtue; but its deeper subject is the sanctity of personality. The individual is something so precious that society must never be allowed to violate it.

But although the heroine is important in both *Anna St Ives* and *Hermsprong*, Holcroft and Bage diverge from the Richardsonian model by turning a dualism into a triad: by introducing a male hero, Henley and Hermsprong, who simultaneously struggles against society and against the villain and who serves as a positive focus for the author's social critique. Frank Henley and Hermsprong stand outside society; their strength and their freedom from corruption stem from this. In their perfection, their very flawlessness, they point to the fallen and enfeebled state of civilised man. Henley and Hermsprong are prototypes of the Superman. The heroine, Anne St Ives or Caroline Campinet, is still an important figure, since it is for her that hero and villain struggle, but, whereas one seeks to liberate her the other seeks to oppress her: the liberation of woman becomes the indispensable criterion by which moral worth is to be assessed. In Richardson the women is the true possessor of value and virtue and she must struggle against a social situation in which value is only ascribed to the man. In Holcroft and Bage, the fact that the heroine is already a person who enjoys a favourable social position makes her clear preference for the Superman figure all the more significant, since she freely chooses him over persons of appropriate social rank and in the face of parental opposition. Hero and heroine simultaneously confer value on one another in a gesture that represents a deliberate turning-aside from the degraded social world. The blurring, the inmixing of moral and social criteria that we find in Jane Austen's *Mansfield Park*, so that sound judgement and moral courage are seen as the indispensable precondition for an *entree* into the aristocratic world – such a confusion is unthinkable in the radical vision of Holcroft and Bage. They hold fast to the truth that, since aristocracy involves assertions as to the superiority of rank and birth, this indicates not so much the existence of moral criteria as their complete and necessary absence. On Coke Clifton in his final letter before his repentance Holcroft enforces the ultimate ignominy: to recognise the discrepancy between his aristocratic pretentions and the baseness of his own nature: 'I am all fiend! – hell born! – The boon companion of the foulest miscreants the womb of sin ever vomited on earth! The arm in arm familiar of them! In the face of the world! This it is to be honourable! I – I am a man of honour, a despiser of peasants, an assertor of rank!'[43] The purpose of the novel is to demonstrate precisely how little such an assertion means. In *Hermsprong* Bage is concerned to draw a distinction between the two different senses of honour; to insist on a higher estimation for moral worth, which comes from within, than for the social position that calls for gestural recognition. When Hermsprong has had the estates of Lord Grondale restored to him – they are his rightful inheritance since he is the only son of Lord Grondale's elder brother – he writes that, should he find Lord Grondale in a more contrite and repentant mood, he would, 'not pay you exterior marks only of respect, but those interior ones, which cannot become your due but by contrition and true respectability'.[44] Moreover, this formulation itself points to a transvaluation of values: respectability is to be construed not socially but morally. The inner self is given absolute priority over public identity.

Hermsprong and Frank Henley differ in so far as Hermsprong, as it is later disclosed, is a person of noble birth – a concession doubtless dictated, like Hermsprong's attempts to dissuade rioting workers, by the fact that the novel appeared four years later than *Anna St Ives*, in 1796, when the Reign of Terror was at its height. Nevertheless, both characters are presented in essentially similar terms: they are full of good deeds, of an unimpeachable moral character, indifferent to the punctilios of civilised society, possessed of remarkable physical strength, sincere, fearless and brave. The concern with good deeds, of course, is part of the heritage of Sentimentalism, but, in Holcroft in particular, the concern with them is especially striking – his principal rival, doubtless, is Horatio Alger, but, whereas the Alger hero has his eye on the main chance, Holcroft's heroes proclaim by their actions their altruism and feeling for humanity. Frank Henley's generosity is even-handed. Having saved Anna and her father from highwaymen, he later redeems the highwayman himself and persuades him to embark on a new life. Given a £20-note by Anna, Henley uses it to rescue a young man from a debtor's prison and to restore him to his wife and child (an episode very reminiscent of *Werther*), and, when Coke Clifton tries to impress Anna and a French nobleman by leaping into a lake from a high rock, Henley magnanimously jumps in after him and saves him. He also saves Anna and her father from drowning when they have to land from their boat in rough seas at Deal, and he extricates Anna's brother from the clutches of a professional gambler. Hermsprong saves Caroline Campinet from certain death when he seizes the reins of her horse as it careers towards some cliffs. He aids Mrs Garnett and a servant, both of whom have incurred Lord Grondale's displeasure. He saves Miss Sumelin from a rash and precipitous marriage. Both men are possessed of quite remarkable physical strength and agility. Henley astonishes the assembled company when, having saved Clifton, he slings his body over his shoulder and races into the house ahead of the rest of them. On another occasion he surpasses Clifton by twice leaping across a ha-ha in the park of Villebrun in Paris, when Clifton had previously impressed everyone by jumping it on horseback. Hermsprong follows a morning walk of forty miles by demolishing two pounds of beef in a twinkling. His upbringing among the Indians has given him remarkable physical prowess, although he admits that they are his superiors. At a crucial point in the novel he humiliates his rival for Caroline's hand, Sir Philip Chestrum, by gently lifting him over a fence! As Sir Philip later remarks, 'the fellow is cursedly muscular'.[45] Such feats demonstrate that Henley and Hermsprong are free from the effeteness of fashionable society.

Henley and Hermsprong win their respect from others not by accident of birth but by virtue of their extraordinary merits. At an early point in *Anna St Ives*, Frank Henley is described as a secular saint, who is far superior to the impostors and pseudo-miracle workers of the Church. His superiority is continually insisted on. Louisa Clifton writes that 'His unshakeable patience, his generosity, his forgiveness, his courage, his perseverance are inimitable proofs of his superiority',[46] and Anna describes him as 'a man whose benevolent heart, capacious mind and extraordinary virtues are above my praise, and I almost fear beyond my attain-

ment'.[47] Anna cannot understand why it is that Coke Clifton
will not acknowledge Frank's virtues – 'how can Clifton be
willfully blind to such courage, rectitude of heart, understanding and genius?'[48] – but even Clifton, who is deeply resentful
of Henley, because of his lowly origins and because of the
esteem Anna has for him, is finally forced to acknowledge his
merit, despite the desperation with which he has struggled
against this recognition. Holcroft in effect transposes Shakespeare's *Othello*. Clifton is a Iago figure who instead of
destroying honesty and integrity is himself crushed by the
example of moral righteousness and reborn in a new identity.
In the final scene he acknowledges Henley as the divine man,
who can awaken like divinity in others: 'I have had a glimpse,
and begin to know you – the soul of benevolence, of tenderness, of attention, of love, of all the divine faculties that men
make deities, infuses itself and pervades you.'[49] Henley is the
moral Superman by virtue of his will, which refuses to
succumb to notions of human weakness: 'Man is weak because he is willing to be weak.'[50] Hermsprong has a similar
exemplary character. He is equally free from the infirmities of
purpose that afflict men subject to the conformist pressures of
society:

> 'It was imposed on me as a duty by my father,' Mr.
> Hermsprong answered, to speak, when I did speak, with the
> spirit of conscious truth; and to act when I did act, with the
> spirit of conscious justice. I have obeyed my father; and
> hope I have been rewarded as he promised me I should, by
> a proper portion of firmness and intrepidity. If this, as I
> suspect, has the appearance of boasting, I answer, that to
> the weak and enervating, humility of thinking or pretend-
> ing to think, worse of myself than I deserve, I am and desire
> to be a stranger. . . .
> 'I have energies, and I feel them; as a man, I have rights
> and will support them: in acting according to principles I
> believe to be just, I have not yet learned to fear.'[51]

Implicit in this account is a theory of alienation. The man who
fully knows himself and relies upon himself and is conversant
with his own capacities is strong. But social existence teaches
men to distrust themselves and to place too much importance

on the estimation of others. They live on the surface and play out an assigned social role without ever fully discovering themselves ('the stranger within' of Young). They will tend to underestimate themselves and to feel weak and helpless when they measure themselves against others. Mrs Clifton offers similar advice to her son Coke:

> The weak hearing their worth or talents questioned, are too apt to swell and assume; and I have heard it said that the strong are too intimately acquainted with themselves to harbour doubt. I believe it ought to be so. I believe it to be better that we should act boldly and bring full conviction upon ourselves when mistaken, than that a timid spirit should render us too cautious to do either good or harm.[52]

Coke, indeed, is a weak character – not of necessity – but because his social position is the only basis for his identity. His very position as an 'assertor of rank' is a fatal obstacle that stands in the way of self-discovery and leaves him merely seething with feelings of inferiority, envy, jealousy and impotence that are discharged in the most damaging and destructive manner. Yet, as Anna points out, he is only intensifying his own torment, and every action that he performs only serves to tighten the screw still further: 'Poor depraved, mistaken man! It is himself he injures! Every effort he makes is but a new assault upon his own peace! It is heaping coals of fire upon his own head, which it has long been the wish of my heart to extinguish!'[53] Clifton's redemption is possible only when he can free himself from the illusions of grandeur connected with his rank; can dig down beneath the husk and shell of social identity to the discovery of his own soul. Clifton says that Henley is trying to be a Pygmalion and infuse a soul into marble, but Henley answers, 'There is no need: you have a soul already; inventive, capacious, munificent, sublime!'[54] Henley's injunction 'Feel yourself a man!'[55] implies that the individual must see himself as a man rather than as a social role: the communication that a man opens up with himself is, at the same time, the moment that brings him closer to others.

In the fiction of Holcroft and Bage the contrast between frankness and openness on the one hand, secrecy and manipulation on the other, assumes great moral importance.

Honest actions, by definition, do not require the cover of darkness. Truth and freedom of discussion are intimately connected. Anna writes to Louisa Clifton, 'I trust in the frankness of my heart for the proof of its sincerity. My determination is to have a clear and unspotted conscience. Purity of mind is a blessing beyond all price and it is that purity only which is genuine or of any value.'[56] She does so although such openness makes her vulnerable before Clifton, who exults, 'She has herself given me my clue: she has laid open her whole heart.'[57] Anna St Ives, Frank Henley and Hermsprong all believe in speaking plainly without regard to the consequences, either for themselves or for others. Hermsprong acknowledges that frankness is his 'vice' and insists, 'I hold a manly freedom of thinking and speaking among the most estimable qualities of man.'[58]

By the same token, secrecy is to be avoided. Not the least reason why Hermsprong is opposed to Miss Sumelin's elopement is that it is immoral because clandestine. Anna does not hesitate to tell Coke Clifton that she believes Frank Henley to be his superior because 'the proceedings of rectitude never can be dark, hidden, and insidious'.[59] In an image that makes explicit the connection between such an attitude and the Protestant hostility to curtains, which imply that the user may have something to hide, Anna writes,

> Secrets are indeed absolutely contrary to my system. 'Tis pride or false shame that puts blinds to the windows either of the house or of the mind. Let the whole world look in and see what is doing; that if anything be wrong, it may have an opportunity to reprove; and whatever is right there is some hope it may imitate.[60]

The hypocrite is a man who does not permit such scrutiny. He will not allow inspection of himself, since this will reveal the discrepancy between inner and outer. It is symbolically appropriate that James's arch-hypocrite Gilbert Osmond in *The Portrait of a Lady* lives in a villa closed off from the inspection of the world. But the hypocrite does more than refuse the truth. He uses his hypocrisy and deceit as a way of manipulating others. Coke Clifton pretends to Anna that he is a convert to her way of thinking since he feels that his own doubleness places him in the position of superiority. The brute force that Lord Grondale and Coke Clifton finally resort to is the inevitable outcome of their particular system of behaviour. They have chosen not to reason with others or to communicate openly with them but to impose their will upon them. Hypocrisy, fraud and force are simply tools with which to control others. To treat people freely and openly is to eschew manipulation. The model of human relations that we find in the social novel and the Gothic is always charged with political implications. For, if secrecy corrupts ordinary inter-personal relationships, how much more must it corrupt proceedings of the state? In the secret workings of Vatican or monastery, council or cabal, the Protestant and Romantic imagination discerns the unspeakable presence of Antichrist!

In *Anna St Ives* and *Hermsprong* the heroines recognise that it is morally wrong for them to abdicate their right of judgement to the authority of a father or husband. The emancipation of woman is simply part of the general emancipation of mankind from tyranny and arbitrary power. To Coke Clifton Anna writes, 'You think no doubt that the lover ought to yield, and the husband to command; both of which I deny. Husband, wife, or lover, should all be under the command of reason; other commands are tyranny. Reason and not relationship alone can give authority.'[61] By the same token it is by placing human relationships on a rational basis that confusions and misunderstandings can be swept away. The title of Jane Austen's famous novel can be attributed with some confidence to the passage in *Hermsprong* where Bage observes of Caroline and Hermsprong that 'the tender interest they had in each other was torn asunder by pride and prejudice'.[62] For Bage at least, such prejudices and pride are the product of social relations. Before the upraised lamp of reason they will vanish.

The hypocrite is a man who violates a social contract based on openness and reason. Clifton commits what is perhaps the greatest of all moral wrongs – to proclaim a change of heart that is feigned. He pretends to Anna that he is genuinely converted to her progressive principles when in fact he seeks to mock them and revenge himself by transforming their discussions into parody and theatre. His performance de-monstrates how treacherous the world of appearances can be. Epistemological scepticism had already figured prominently in *The Mysteries of Udolpho* – for the nightmarishness of Udolpho is intensified by the fact that Emily is unable to find confirmation for many of the sights and spectacles that she witnesses. The world appears just as treacherous in *Anna St Ives*. For how is one to distinguish being from seeming, appearance from reality, the false conversion from the true? Frank Henley, confronted with Clifton's arrival on the scene as a suitor for Anna's hand, finds it difficult to read the intentions of the participants from their behaviour: 'Looks, words, appearances, daily events are all so contradictory, that the warfare of hope and fear increases and becomes violent, almost to distraction.'[63] Yet his own father, Abimilech, chief gardener to the father of Anna, provides a comparable enigma. Abimilech constantly assures Sir Arthur that he is his humble servant, yet behind the cloak of amiability and complaisance he is steadily transferring assets from Sir Arthur to himself. Such deceptions render experience treacherous in the extreme and cast a shadow over all attempts at human communication. Confronted with Clifton's deceit Anna asks, 'What! Can guile so perfectly assume the garb of sincerity? Can hypocrisy wear so impenetrable a mask? How shall we distinguish? What guide have we?'[64] Yet Clifton relishes this duplicity of appearance that gives him power over others:

> And who is it inspires that dread? It is I! They seem to have discovered that all circumstances, all incidents wear a double face; and that I am the malignant genius who can make what he chooses the true one – Yes, I am with them! I send the Incubus that hag-rides them in their dreams! They gasp and would wake, but cannot![65]

Thus, Clifton believes that the master of appearance is simultaneously master of reality. But, although Holcroft wishes to show how much deception corrupts, he also insists that it cannot prevail. Henley warns Anna against Clifton and in language saturated with biblical overtones Anna writes to him from her place of confinement, 'His most secret machinations could not have withstood thy searching spirit. Thou wouldst have been here? These bolts would have flown, these doors would have opened, and I should have seen my saviour.'[66] It is not the virtuous who are finally confused, but rather those, such as Clifton, who are alienated from virtue. They wander through a maze into which their perversity has led them. Thus Holcroft adopts a Shaftesburian position: evil is not so much a thing in itself as a vacancy, an unreasonable refusal of the good, a denial of the normal social feelings which leads to a state in which a man is cut off from his fellow men. And such is the consequence in Coke Clifton's case: he writes, 'I feel, Fairfax, as if I had taken my leave of hope, joy and human intercourse! I have a quarrel with the whole race, for having been forced into existence and into misery.'[67] Clifton's repentance, proved sincere by his action in saving Frank Henley by killing his assailant the murderous MacShane, whom he himself had hired, reopens his communication with others and restores him to the human race. His exemplary reformation is a sign that the individual can peel away the layers of social identity until he reaches his authentic self.

Anna St Ives has little of the iconography of the Gothic novel, but it does possess a demonology. Notions of diabolical possession are frequently invoked. In the final scene Henley calls on Clifton to 'Exorcise the foul fiend.'[68] Clifton relishes the sense of having Henley and Anna in his power; he tries his hardest to make their life intolerable:

My spirit at present is haunting them, never leaves them, girds at and terrifies them at every instant, during their amorous dalliance! I know it does! They cannot get quit of me! I am with them, weighing them down, convulsing them! They feel they are in my grip! – Ha! The thought is heart's ease.[69]

But the converse is also true. The image of Frank Henley, his moral superior, oppresses Coke Clifton. He says of Frank, 'he seems born to cross me'[70] and in a letter describes him as his 'familiar' in a punning sense. 'Our censor in private, and in public our familiar: like a malignant demon, no respect, no place, no human barriers could exclude him.'[71] Frank serves as a perennial reminder for Clifton of the unworthiness of his existence. Yet his feelings are also deeply contradictory – he could 'kiss him one minute and kill him the next'[72] – his envy and resentment are the tribute that vice pays to virtue. In the

novel Clifton has two doubles that represent different roles of
morality for him: on the one hand, Frank Henley, whom he
could emulate if he would; on the other MacShane, who
represents baseness in himself that he can release if provoked.
Clifton's espousal of MacShane is presented by Holcroft as a
Faustian contract: 'The very master-devil that I wanted has
appeared to me and we have signed and consigned ourselves
over to the great work of mutual vengeance.'[73] In saving
Frank Henley from MacShane, Clifton simultaneously, in
symbolic action, rescues his own 'best self' and destroys his evil
'shadow self'. These doubles point to the discrepancy between
different parts of the self. Holcroft's dramatisation of this
process of internal conflict shows great psychological
subtlety – so that Marilyn Butler's claim that he shows no
interest in 'psychological processes'[74] seems quite astonishing
even though it depends on a well-established prejudice that
psychology and politics are incompatible.

In his other major work, *The Adventures of Hugh Trevor*, the
first part of which appeared in 1794, the year of his imprisonment in connection with charges of high-treason, the
second in 1797, Holcroft made equally striking use of the
double motif to dramatise the distinction between social and
authentic being. But in *Hugh Trevor* he was concerned not to
present the hypocrite as a characteristic type but to show
hypocrisy pervading all the major institutions of society.
Successively Hugh Trevor comes into contact with Oxford
University, the Church, political activity, the theatre and the
law. In every case he finds corruption and sham. At Oxford
there is no genuine concern with learning but only pettiness
and malevolence on the part of the fellows, idleness and
profligacy on the part of the students. On going down he
writes sermons for a famous bishop, who behind his distinguished exterior is lustful, gluttonous and unscrupulous. He
writes articles for the Earl of Idford, who similarly exploits
him and who, after· having encouraged him to attack the
government for a while, instructs him to change his line when
it becomes expedient to do so. In the theatre he finds that a
talented playwright, Wilmot, has met with such persistent
discouragement that he even attempts suicide. Enamoured of
justice Hugh takes up the study of law, but finds – a truth
insisted on also by Godwin and Bage – that the law is only an

instrument of class oppression. Moreover, as his friend Turl, who attempts to give Hugh some moral perspective on the compromised activities to which he devotes himself, says, the evils of the law have a deeper source in 'the system of property, of which law is the support'.[75] Holcroft sees society as systematically opposed to truth. The arch hypocrite, Glibly, admits as much: 'To tell the truth would be to overturn all order.'[76] In *Desmond* Mrs Smith placed a similar dictum in the mouth of the reactionary Mr Cranbourne: 'We know that *truth is not expedient*, and that it is the business of government to enforce obedience.'[77] For Hugh society is 'systematic selfishness, systematic hypocrisy and systematic oppression',[78] a continual process that has the effect of destroying man's finer impulses and feelings; for 'Men are rendered selfish and corrupt by the baneful influence of the systems under which they live.'[79]

The simple opposition of Henley/Clifton is dramatically broadened in *Hugh Trevor* so that on the one hand we have the figures who support the existing reactionary order – the Bishop, the tutor Glibly, the Earl; on the other the small band of people – Turl, Clarke, Olivia, Mr Evelyn, Wilmot and Hugh himself – who are struggling against it. The progressives agree that social existence enforces harmful and hurtful compromises on the individual so that, under the prevailing order, moral behaviour is virtually precluded: 'manners, customs, and laws, obliged us to conform to many things which were odiously vicious; and . . . to live in society and rigidly observe those rules of justice which would best promote the general happiness was, speaking absolutely, a thing impossible'.[80] There can be no doubt but that Holcroft sees the conflict between self and society in an absolute, apocalyptic perspective taken over from Christianity: to acquiesce in social hypocrisy is to lose one's soul, to fight against it is to save it. And for Holcroft, who had been imprisoned without trial, as a public enemy, that fight was very real.

Hugh Trevor draws heavily on the puritan tradition of the examined self. This duty is enforced on him from the very outset by his mentor Mr Elford, who writes 'Above all things first examine yourself.'[81] Later Hugh acquires another mentor, Turl, in effect his best self, who points out how he is building an existence that is based on falsity and deception. By lending himself to the doubtful schemes of others Hugh himself is no less guilty. A persistent theme of the book is the change of heart, the experience of conversion and beginning anew. Hugh himself makes many such beginnings – as when he brutally defeats a carpenter, Clarke, in a fist fight, a man he has falsely accused of stealing his handkerchief. The effect of this episode, since he is later befriended and compassionately treated by Clarke, is to purge him of the haughtiness and false pride (cf. Coke Clifton) which, for Holcroft, are all too characteristic of a class society. Yet for other characters, too, such a change of heart is necessary. Olivia, whom Hugh Trevor loves, has to learn to oppose prejudice, 'to assert the dignity of truth'[82] and 'to speak in defiance of that hypocrisy which inculcates the silence that intends to deceive, and which teaches females that sincerity is an unpardonable vice'.[83] The involvement in the cause of human progress is presented by Holcroft as one that calls for and inspires a religious fervour, analogous to a Methodist conversion. Clarke is described as being 'in a state similar to those religious converts who imagine they feel that a new light is broke in upon them';[84] while later, 'He discovered that there is a disinterested grandeur in morality, of which he had no previous conception, he was in a new world; and a dark room, with barred windows, was heaven in all its splendour.'[85] As the soul is liberated from the confinement of its social prison, the world becomes radiant and transfigured. The capacity for change in human nature provides an unshakable ground for optimism and hope.

In *The Adventures of Hugh Trevor* the apostate figure is Wakefield/Belmont, who, amongst his other crimes, marries Hugh's widowed mother and robs her of what little money she has. Wakefield is always playing a part. He appears in the novel with two separate identities, both as the sinister Wakefield and as the apparently genial and affable Belmont, with whom Hugh becomes acquainted, without realising that this man is his deadly enemy. Belmont's cynical conception of the world, his delight in role-playing, is significantly expressed through a theatrical metaphor: he warns Hugh,

Mark my words; the day will come, Mr. Trevor, when you

will discover that there are greater jugglers in the world than your players, wonderful as their art of transformation is. The world is all a cheat; its pleasures are for him who is most expert in legerdermain and cajolery; and he is a fool indeed who is juggled out of his share of them.[86]

Wakefield/Belmont's double nature points on the one hand to the treacherousness of appearances, the danger of taking anything on trust, but on the other to the possibility that even in the most depraved individual there may be a better self. In his capacity as Belmont he does a number of good deeds: it is he who points out to Hugh that Clarke has not been responsible for the theft of his handkerchief, and he returns £20 that he has won from Hugh when, after the fight with Clarke, he lies injured and penniless. If Wakefield is involved in Hugh's unjust imprisonment – 'I have been one of the infernal instruments to bring you here'[87] – he also repents what he has done and is instrumental in securing his release. At an earlier point in the novel Belmont comes close to confessing his true identity to Hugh: 'Let us suppose, Mr Trevor, a whimsical, or if you please a strange coincidence between the man with whom you have been so angry and myself. I mean Wakefield. What if he felt some of the sober propensities toward which I find a kind of a call in myself?'[88]

The correlation between a radical political vision and a Gothic mode of presentation characterises all the major novelists of the 1790s, but it was William Godwin himself, in his *Caleb Williams* (1794), which bears the provocative alternative title 'Things as They Are' – a clear-enough indication that the domination that Godwin describes is not to be taken as mere fiction – who produced the most powerful articulation of the social nightmare of a class society. Indeed, in reading this novel we can scarcely avoid the connection between religious and political dissent, for Godwin was brought up in a Sandemanian environment and his novel is offered not as mere entertainment but as a discourse that is directly relevant to real life, a translation into more immediate terms of the principles of his *Political Justice* – though it is, of course, not simply to be regarded as a political–philosophical comic strip. In his Preface Godwin insisted that his purpose was both didactic and down-to-earth:

What is now presented to the public is no refined and abstract
speculation; it is a study and delineation of things passing in
the moral world. It is but of late that the inestimable
importance of political principles has been adequately
apprehended. It is now known to philosophers that the
spirit and character of government intrudes itself into every
rank of society. But this is a truth highly worthy to be
communicated to persons whom books of philosophy and
science are never likely to reach. Accordingly it was pro-
posed in the invention of the following work, to comprehend,
as far as the progressive nature of a single story would allow,
a general review of the modes of domestic and unrecorded
despotism, by which man becomes the destroyer of man.[89]

But Godwin's formulation is far from crude. It indicates a new
type of fictional purpose: the delineation of a particular type
of value system and a representation of the ways in which
domination becomes institutionalised, legitimised and endlessly extended so that it reaches into the remotest corners of
society, carrying its contagion everywhere with the relentless
thoroughness of a plague. So provocative did this intention
appear that Godwin was forced to withdraw it for the first
edition of 1794. In *Caleb Williams* we find a more complex
social vision and social critique than in any other Gothic novel,
or in the other works of Godwin himself. For Godwin's
criticism is not directed purely and simply at individuals, but is
also directed at the social circumstances that determine the
pattern of their actions. *Caleb Williams* is thus a determinist
novel, but this term is not to be construed in any fatalist sense:
for Godwin, determining circumstances can also generate a
sense of freedom, as his description of the psychological
processes of Caleb Williams testifies. But Godwin did believe
that men were deeply influenced by their environment and
the values and pressures by which they were surrounded. For
this reason his thought, though characterised by great optimism about the possibility of human progress, to which he
assigns no limit, is often unexpectedly pessimistic when it
comes to a more immediate prognosis. In the section of
Political Justice in which Godwin shows how men are influenced
by their environment, and, in particular by the nature of
political organisation, he writes,

Political institution, by the consequences with which it is pregnant, strongly suggests to everyone who enters within its sphere, what is the path he should avoid, as well as what he should pursue. Under a government fundamentally erroneous he will see intrepid virtue proscribed, and a servile and corrupt spirit uniformly encouraged. But morality itself is nothing but the calculation of consequences. What strange confusion will the spectacle of that knavery which is universally practised through all the existing classes of society produce in the mind? The preceptor cannot go out of the world, or prevent the intercourse of his pupil with human beings of a character different from his own.[90]

The connection between a social and political system where manipulation, intimidation and the brutal exercise of power are not the exception but the rule and the circumstances that affect the lives of every single individual is a constant if largely implicit thread running through the narrative of *Caleb Williams*. It is brought out most explicitly by Godwin in the section of the novel where, after Caleb Williams has learned from Mr Falkland's own lips of his murder of the domineering Tyrrell and thereafter has found life under the watchful eye of his master intolerable, he runs away to the house of the apparently friendly Mr Forester. But there, when Falkland accuses Caleb, quite falsely, of stealing property of his to a considerable value, including money, gold watches and diamonds, Caleb finds that his protestations of innocence count but little; for in any conflict of opinion Mr Forester is naturally disposed to believe a member of his own class rather than a servant. The injustice to which Hawkins, a yeoman farmer who has been wrongly charged with Mr Falkland's own crime, has been subjected is now compounded by the commitment of Caleb. This evokes the following reflections:

It was not much longer before everything was prepared for my departure, and I was conducted to the same prison which had so lately inclosed the wretched and innocent Hawkinses. They too had been the victims of Mr. Falkland. He exhibited, upon a contracted scale indeed, but in which the truth of delineation was faithfully sustained, a copy of

what monarchs are, who reckon among the instruments of
their power prisons of state.[91]

The argument of the novel is thus generalised through a
series of parallels and analogies: Caleb's fate mirrors and is
directly connected with that of Hawkins; while even the
apparently kindly and well disposed Falkland comes to echo
both the tyranny of Tyrrell and that of powerful rulers.
Justice is therefore shown to be not an objective quality but a
function of class position: 'justice' is used against *some* (the
weak and poor) by *others* (the rich and powerful). For this
reason also, Caleb Williams's period of imprisonment is far
more than a transitory moment in the narrative. For Godwin
and for his Romantic contemporaries the prison, though a
place which few voluntarily visit and whose operations remain
obscure to the majority, is nevertheless a crucial focus of moral
indignation, because it simultaneously exemplifies both the
torments to which one man can subject another and the
heartless manner in which a man can be deprived of the use of
the very faculties and abilities that make him what he is.
Godwin at this point is able to show with the utmost clarity how
meaningless is the chauvinistic complacency with which
Englishmen are wont to congratulate themselves on the
unique reasonableness of their institutions:

> Among my melancholy reflections I tasked my memory,
> and counted over the doors, the locks, the bolts, the chains,
> the massy walls and grated windows that were between me
> and liberty. These, said I, are the engines that tyranny sits
> down in cold and serious meditation to invent. This is the
> empire that man exercises over man. Thus is a being,
> formed to expatiate, to act, to smile and enjoy, restricted
> and benumbed. How great must be his capacity or heed-
> lessness who vindicates this scheme for changing health and
> gaiety and serenity, into the wanness of a dungeon and the
> deep furrows of agony and despair!
>   Thank God, exclaims the Englishman, we have no
> Bastille! Thank God, with us no man can be punished
> without a crime! Unthinking wretch! Is that a country of
> liberty where thousands languish in dungeons and fetters?
> Go, go ignorant fool! and visit the scenes of our prisons!

witness their unwholesomeness, their filth, the tyranny of their governors, the misery of their inmates! After that show me the man shameless enough to triumph, and say, England has no Bastille![92]

Again, it is patent that religious imperatives help to formulate and give edge to Godwin's social criticism. Man has been formed for freedom, and therefore to imprison him and to deprive him of his capacity for action is not simply gratuitous, immoral and cruel: it is a violation of the pattern of divine providence. The prison embodies the truth of modern culture and parodies all dreams of social justice and progress:

> For myself I looked round upon my walls, and forward upon the premature death I had too much reason to expect; I consulted my own heart that whispered nothing but innocence; and I said, This is society. This is the object, the distribution of justice, which is the end of human reason. For this sages have toiled, and the midnight oil been wasted. This![93]

For 'justice', as institutionalised, is the very thing that negates *justice* – the most crucial, for Godwin, of human values.

But the prison also has a further significance for Godwin. Godwin belongs to the intellectual tradition of Shaftesbury, which laid great stress on man's social impulses, which are the source both of his moral capacity and of his disposition to expand and develop that capacity. But, when a prisoner is placed in solitary confinement in order to 'educate' and 'reform' him, the methods by which this is to be achieved are, in fact, calculated to achieve exactly the reverse:

> Shall we be most effectively formed to justice, benevolence and prudence in our intercourse with each other, in a state of solitude? Will not our selfish and unsocial dispositions be perpetually increased? What temptation has he to think of benevolence or justice, who has no opportunity to exercise it? The true soil in which atrocious crimes are found to germinate, is a gloomy and morose disposition. Will his heart become much either softened or expanded, who breathes the atmosphere of a dungeon?[94]

This cascade of rhetorical questions from *Political Justice* makes
it indisputably clear how great an evil imprisonment is for
Godwin. But in *Caleb Williams* the notion of imprisonment is
vastly expanded. For Godwin shows that in their different
ways both Falkland and Caleb Williams become prisoners,
because they are cut off from free communication of their
thoughts and feelings to others. Falkland, because of the
crime that he has committed and because of his failure to
confess it, is locked up within himself in an agonising interior
solitude that places him beyond the beneficent sphere of
human communication. And, even when he is finally brought
to the point where he has to reveal the whole story to Caleb
Williams, his decision loses its virtue, because he insists on
binding Caleb at one and the same moment to an oath never to
disclose what his master has told him. From this action many
evils flow. Falkland himself continues to be tortured by guilt,
remorse and, above all, anxiety that at some point or another
Caleb will eventually reveal everything to persons who may be
inclined to believe him. Consequently he employs the sinister
and implacable Gines to pursue Caleb and to watch and
observe his every action. Caleb's own existence becomes
equally intolerable, since he is forced to adopt a variety of
disguises and to flee from place to place; like Falkland before
him, he cannot afford to open his heart to others, since any
such action would only be one step towards his downfall.
Disguise, for Godwin, heir to a puritan tradition, is a false
mode of being, a dangerous step into inauthenticity and
deceitful seeming – indeed, one of Caleb Williams's later
comments on the subject seems somewhat extreme: 'There
was one expedient against which I was absolutely determined,
disguise. . . . Life was not worth purchasing at so high a
price.'[95]

But, in fairness, it must be added that Godwin has already
shown the price that Caleb has paid for his various subter-
fuges and the torment of his continual loneliness and distrust.
The point is that Caleb, like Falkland, forces himself to go
against nature (to invoke the phrase that in French symbolism
was later to acquire such resonance, though with more
positive connotations), for at every moment when he yields to
ordinary and normal human feelings he finds himself betrayed. For example, he is alone one night at his lodgings when

he hears a knock at the door; in the belief that it must be his landlord, Mr Spurrel, who has no key, 'A gleam, a sickly gleam! of the social spirit came over my heart. I flew nimbly down the stairs and opened the door.'[96] But he has been betrayed: Spurrel is there, but his companion is Gines! Indeed, perhaps the most interesting part of the novel is this depiction of Caleb Williams's frantic inner world in the closing stages of the narrative, which, while designed to show the agonies of internal isolation, has the paradoxical side-effect of showing the very processes of consciousness as a form of torture. This may well be Godwin's deepest and most enduring fictional legacy. After Godwin it was scarcely possible to show men thinking calm, lucid and appropriate thoughts: the representation of consciousness from Poe to Dostoevsky and Kafka became rather a matter of frenzied leaps, switches and jumps, of thought doubling and redoubling upon itself, of ideas flooding recklessly and pell-mell into the mind, the revelation of a chaotic inner world. This is all of a piece with Godwin's views on the changeableness of human nature. In *Political Justice* he writes,

> ideas are to the mind nearly what atoms are to the body. The whole mass is in a perpetual flux; nothing is stable and permanent; after the lapse of a given period not a single particle probably remains the same. Who knows not that in the course of a human life the character of an individual frequently undergoes two or three revolutions of its fundamental stamina? The turbulent man will frequently become contemplative, the generous changed into selfish, and the frank and good-humoured into peevish and morose[97]

and again: 'Everything in man may be said to be in state of flux; he is a Proteus whom we know not how to detain.'[98] Thus the dramatisation of the processes of consciousness is at the same time the most vivid and exemplary dramatisation of the possibility of freedom.

In *Caleb Williams* there is no necessity that Falkland or Caleb Williams play the part of hypocrite or of false seemer; there is nothing inherent in the role or the position. It is rather society that creates it through the possibility it affords for one man to

dominate and oppress another; because in the absence of a
spirit of freedom and equality between all men there is also
necessarily lacking an openness and sincerity in their mutual
dealings. The doubling of Falkland and Caleb Williams has
the effect of generalising the theme of the novel and of
showing that the issue is not one of an unchangeable human
nature that makes one man a hypocrite and another a miser,
but rather of a particular form of social organisation which
has the effect of isolating men from one another and of
rendering their attempts to communicate with one another
dubious and unstable, even destructive. But in this novel
Godwin opened a fictional Pandora's box, which was to have
repercussions spreading far beyond his own particular
philosophy. For he initiated a whole series of novels in which
men enter into mutual confidences and are oppressed by
mysterious and enigmatic others, in which hypocrisy and an
appearance of public righteousness are exposed by the
mechanism of the double. The couple of the hypocrite and the
double haunts Romantic and post-Romantic literature because of the very facility with which these fictional devices can
speak the unspoken or unspeakable. These motifs are so
popular because they lend themselves to a spirit of irreverence
and bitter mockery: they expose the falsity and the hollowness
of man in his public and social roles and point to deeper and
more complex psychological realities which society cannot
permit, and which even the individual may be reluctant to
scrutinise too closely. At the same time the whole tradition of
the examined self of the individual's scrutiny of his own
motives becomes more and more problematic. The mind
offers no certainties. As Godwin points out in *Political Justice*,

Self-deception is of all things the most easy. Whoever
ardently wishes to find a proposition true, may be expected
insensibly to veer towards the opinion that suits his incli-
nation. It cannot be wondered at, by him who considers the
subtlety of the human mind, that belief should scarcely ever
rest upon the mere basis of evidence, and that arguments
are always viewed through a delusive medium, magnifying
them into Alps, or diminishing them to nothing.[99]

The Gothic becomes, *par excellence*, the genre of uncertainty:

devoted not simply to an epistemological scepticism at a parade of fantastic and delusionary appearances, leaving the spectator baffled and bemused by puzzling and contradictory evidences; but, far more significantly, throwing into question the very reliability of the mind that scrutinises those appearances, and displaying the mind itself as fraught with division and contradiction. Freudianism is simply the inheritor of this Gothic legacy – retaining, as did the nineteenth century, the fascination with unconscious and subconscious mental processes, but shedding the social critique to which the Gothic once emphatically gestured.

2 The Transposition of Gothic

The publication of *The Monk* by Matthew Lewis in 1796 marked a decisive turning-point in the development of Gothic. Other writers of the 1790s, such as Radcliffe, Bage and Holcroft, had taken over a genteel literary tradition and attempted to open it up by broaching within its parameters themes of personal and political liberation. Since their paramount value was reason, they felt obliged to maintain a consistent moral perspective in their work. Oddly, *The Monk* too is written from a rationalistic point of view and there is much in it that is consistent with the radical temper of the times, but it is marked off from its predecessors by its unequivocal character as a work of popular literature, by its frank espousal and even exultation in the erotic, in violence, in the horrors of the supernatural. Where Mrs Radcliffe presented mysterious happenings and then explained them away, Lewis presented the satanic as real; where she hinted at illicit sensuality and gestured towards obscure crimes, Lewis openly presented and described. What made the book all the more disturbing was the equivocal attitude which Lewis took towards his subject: behind a genteel deploring of such nefarious goings-on can be discerned a humanistic point of view, similar to that Diderot, which sees the religious and ascetic life as unnatural because it contradicts the essential nature of man; but at the back of that is the implication that man is most truly himself when most utterly perverse: that is to say, when he follows deep and unexplained impulses within him. *The Monk* reflects the intellectual ferment and confusion in the aftermath of the French Revolution: its clearest message is the disintegration of all traditional moral values and one which the Gothic iconography is able to present with the utmost force.

50

Virtually all the paradoxes of *The Monk* are linked with its
pretensions to be a polemic against the Catholic Church.
Lewis can write about Catholicism with confidence, secure in
the knowledge that his Protestant readers will be only too
ready to concur in his condemnation, without examining too
closely the standpoint from which the condemnation is made.
Lewis alternates between an indictment characteristic of the
Reformation period, in which the church is seen as a decadent
and morally corrupt institution, propagating mystifying doctrines to deceive the people while licensing practices that are
morally abhorrent, and a more contemporary view in which
the church is seen as violating man's natural instincts. Significantly anti-Catholic literature of the Reformation and
post-Reformation period, dealing with licentious monks and
so forth, was an important source both for Lewis himself and
for other writers of the Romantic period. Lorenzo, in *The
Monk*, though a Catholic in Spain during the period of the
Inquisition, adopts towards the church the stance of a good
Protestant:

> Universal silence prevailed through the crowd, and every
> heart was filled with reverence for religion – every heart but
> Lorenzo's. Conscious that among those who chanted the
> praises of their God so sweetly, there were some who
> cloaked with devotion the foulest sins, their hymns inspired
> him with detestation at their hypocrisy. He had long ob-
> served with disapprobation and contempt the superstition
> which governed Madrid's inhabitants. His good sense
> had pointed out to him the artifices of the monks, and the
> gross absurdity of their miracles, wonders, and supposititious
> relics. He blushed to see his countrymen the dupes of de-
> ceptions so ridiculous, and only wished for an opportunity
> to free them from their monkish fetters. The opportunity,
> so long desired in vain, was at length presented to him.
> He resolved not to let it slip, but to set before the people, in
> glaring colours, how enormous were the abuses but too
> frequently practised in monasteries, and how unjustly
> public esteem was bestowed indiscriminately upon all who
> wore a religious habit. He longed for the moment destined
> to unmask the hypocrites, and convince his countrymen that
> a sanctified exterior does not always hide a virtuous heart.[1]

There is also much in Lewis's criticism of the church that is consonant with the views of Godwin and other radical contemporaries. The novel points to the dangers of absolute and irresponsible use of power, so that the prioress can commit murder (or contemplate it) without fear of retribution and can even deny a papal bull. Hypocrisy and lack of openness are identified as the gravest of moral crimes. The dangers associated with closed institutions and the excessive practice of secrecy are insisted upon. Like Godwin, Lewis also shows that justice or the lack of it is bound up with one's position in society: Agnes can have the severest punishments inflicted upon her, while Ambrosio and the prioress can act with complete impunity. The irrational is displayed as the means by which arbitrary power is masked and veiled. For Lewis everything that is connected with the institutional is false; it is therefore fitting that the novel should reach its climax with the destruction of the convent of St Clare. Since many religious institutions were similarly invaded during the French Revolution, it is difficult not to see Lewis as associating himself with the destruction of an irrational and oppressive past – its replacement by a society based more securely on the principles of human nature.

Critical discussions of *The Monk* tend to focus obsessively on the character of Ambrosio; yet it is crucial to any understanding of the novel to recognise both its polycentric character and the intricacy of its construction. In particular it is clear that the story of the Bleeding Nun, or the History of Don Raymond, as it is known, is not an exotic interpolation but is the motif that underlies everything else, as it is subjected to various permutations. Lewis took the theme of the Bleeding Nun from traditional German literature, but there can be little doubt but that Lewis clearly understood its erotic significance – the repression of female sexuality. For Lewis's purpose it was necessary to show that convents, as much as monasteries, were unnatural places and that the confinement of women within them involved the denial of their libidinal instincts as well as their capacity for bearing children. The myth of the Bleeding Nun is built around a structural opposition between the fact that the nun is veiled and the fact that she is bleeding. The veil stands for the traditional chastity ascribed to women, the fact that their charms are traditionally covered, the belief that sex does not and need not concern them. The symbol of the veil is contradicted by the symbol of blood, which implies both the defloration of the virgin and the menstrual flow, which is a perpetual sign of a woman's capacity to have children. Significantly, in the story of the Bleeding Nun, Beatrice has been early confined in a convent, but her highly sexed nature cannot be concealed and she exchanges the role of nun for that of mistress. Her death at the hand of her lover Otto and her repeated and regular reappearances strongly suggest that the sexual nature of woman cannot be denied: she will keep returning to haunt a world that refuses to give it a place and truly acknowledge it. In the case of Matilda the nature of the veil becomes completely explicit:

> Oh, since we last conversed together, a dreadful veil has been rent from before my eyes. I love you no longer with the devotion which is paid to a saint; I prize you no more for the virtues of your soul; I lust for the enjoyment of your person. The woman reigns in my bosom, and I am become a prey to the wildest of passions.[2]

At this moment, the meaning of 'woman' becomes transvalued.

Thematic doubling is a notable feature of literature of the Romantic period and *The Monk* is no exception. Lewis lays great stress on the idea of the erotic woman, and all the female characters in the novel are shown to be highly sexed – in fact, the women characteristically take the initiative. Baroness Lindenberg presses her attentions on Don Raymond in a way that he finds embarrassing. Marguerite, who aids him when he is in danger from brigands, describes her nature as being 'licentious and warm'.[3] When it is suggested that Agnes be confined within a convent, Lewis refers to this as 'a fate so contrary to her inclinations'.[4] Ambrosio is initiated into the delights of sex by Matilda in a way that strongly recalls the corruption of Adam by Eve. Even the beautiful Virginia de Villa Franca is induced to give up the veil by the fact that Lorenzo's 'person pleased her'.[5] The only woman character whose modesty is stressed is Antonia, but even here Lewis hints at the passion that lurks behind her reserved de- meanour. In the opening description of her on her appear- ance at the church of the Capuchins in Madrid – where she is

significantly veiled and refuses to unveil (a veiling paralleled
by the early appearance of Matilda as Rosario, who always
keeps her head muffled in a cowl) – Lewis notes, 'She appeared to be scarcely fifteen; an arch smile, playing round her
mouth, declared her to be possessed of liveliness which excess
of timidity at present repressed.'[6] Her age is, of course, highly
pertinent: she is just at the point of becoming conscious of
herself as a woman and of her own sexuality. This is betrayed
by her constant blushing, which is insisted upon by Lewis at
virtually every point in the narrative. Her cheeks are 'suffused
with blushes'[7], 'a deep blush'[8] spreads across her cheek, her
cheeks are 'suffused with Crimson'.[9] This only confirms the
veil–blood opposition of the narrative: Antonia though veiled
nevertheless has erotic feelings, which are disclosed by the
appearance of blood in her cheeks. The whole novel can be
seen as a struggle between those who conceal or deny the
nature of feminine sexuality and those who seek to bring it out
into the open. For this reason it is symbolically appropriate
that Agnes after her terrible sufferings should finally be freed
from the convent of St Clare and enabled to marry Don
Raymond; for Agnes has become identified with the Bleeding
Nun and her liberation signifies the ending of the nightmare
induced by the false and unnatural ideal of chastity.

The motif of the veil that conceals feminine sexuality is
doubled and paralleled by the mask of sanctity that covers the
uncontrollable desires of Ambrosio. This symmetrical relation is apparent from the opening scene in the church of
the Capuchins: Antonia is introduced as the veiled woman,
Ambrosio as 'the man of holiness'[10] – a transparent disguise,
since as soon as he is alone he 'gave free loose to the
indulgence of his vanity'[11]; humility is only a 'semblance'[12],
pride the reality. This first chapter announces, in the manner
of an overture, the principle themes of the novel: Antonia's
reluctance to unveil, even in church as is customary, can be
seen as symbolically contradicting the assumption that there is
nothing to offend a woman's modesty in church, while both
Lorenzo's dream and the gypsy's prophecy suggest that in a
future confrontation between Ambrosio and Antonia all such
cultural concealments of the nature of sexuality will be thrown
aside. Indeed, the theme of the picture strongly suggests that
Ambrosio's religious fervour is a deflection from the path of

normal profane love. Matilda, who has presented her image to Ambrosio in the masked form of a Madonna hopes that when Ambrosio gazes upon it a response may be kindled by it that goes beyond mere piety: 'With what pleasure he views this picture! With what fervour he addresses his prayers to the insensible image! Ah, may not his sentiments be inspired by some kind of secret genius, friend to my affection? May it not be man's natural instinct which informs him – ?'[13]

Ambrosio's progress through the novel is not from sensuality to spirituality, but from the spiritual to the sensual; but, what is still more important, Lewis suggests that Ambrosio as a model of religious piety, as a man who does not even know the difference between the sexes, can only be bogus; when erotically obsessed, he is most completely genuine. Moreover, Lewis is perfectly clear that it is culture that prevents the free expression and fulfilment of his desires: 'The danger of discovery, the fear of being repulsed, the loss of reputation – all these considerations counselled him to stifle his desires.'[14] Nevertheless, Lewis suggests that because of his education within religious institutions Ambrosio's sexuality has become warped. His heart has been corrupted by a thoroughgoing Catholic education, so that it is no longer possible for him to respond in a completely spontaneous and authentic manner. His education has been an initiation into moral iniquity:

His instructors carefully repressed those virtues, whose grandeur and disinterestedness were ill-suited to the cloister. Instead of universal benevolence, he adopted a selfish partiality for his own particular establishment: he was taught to consider compassion for the errors of others as a crime of the blackest dye; the noble frankness of his temper was exchanged for servile humility; and in order to break his natural spirit, the monks terrified his young mind, by placing before him all the horrors with which superstition could furnish them; they painted to him the torments of the damned in colours the most dark, terrible and fantastic, and threatened him at the slightest fault with eternal perdition. No wonder that his imagination, constantly dwelling upon fearful objects, should have rendered his character timid and apprehensive. Add to this, that his long absence from the great world, and total unacquaintance with the common dangers of life, made him form of them an idea far more dismal than the reality. While the monks were busy in rooting out his virtues and narrowing his sentiments, they allowed every vice which had fallen to his share to arrive at full perfection. He was suffered to be proud, vain, ambitious, and disdainful: he was jealous of his equals, and despised all merit but his own: he was implacable when offended, and cruel in his revenge.[15]

The position that Lewis adopts is one very characteristic of the Enlightenment. Since man's natural inclinations are good, it is only necessary to give them scope for expression; in contact with others and with the opposite sex, in an expanded commerce with the ordinary world, his benevolence and sympathy for others can expand and flourish. The passions, when acknowledged and given latitude, can also be directed and controlled. A religious education, on the other hand, denies a man's essential nature, cuts him off from his fellow men, develops irrational prejudices and partial sympathies. *The Monk* is a lesson in the catastrophic consequences of such an education: desires that under other circumstances would be natural in Ambrosio become perverse and are deflected from their appropriate forms of expression: erotic tenderness is transformed into sadistic negativity and violence.

That Ambrosio represents the working out in a perverse form of normal human desires is clearly demonstrated by a counter-plot of Don Raymond and Agnes: just as Matilda/Rosario pursues Ambrosio into the monastery and attempts to awaken his natural impulses, so Don Raymond follows Agnes and attempts to secure her release from the convent. Don Raymond's disguise as a gardener's assistant repeats Matilda's disguise as a religious novice. However, there is a very crucial difference between the two cases: Ambrosio has been so long cut off from a pattern of normal relations between the sexes that his desires, when awakened, can find no adequate object; it is his tragedy that his self-discovery necessarily leads him on a downward path of self-destruction.

The conflict between *eros* and the Catholic Church in *The Monk* also has the form of a conflict between life and death. The church is associated with rottenness, putrescence, decay:

the transformation of life into death. Indeed this, for Lewis, is precisely the function fulfilled by the monastery or convent. The church is unnatural, for, instead of acknowledging that the living and the dead are mutually exclusive categories, in its preoccupation with the dead and in its denial of life, it represents the means whereby the world of the living is invaded by the world of the dead. That the church is an institution which contradicts human nature is emphasised by Lewis in the opening lines of the novel: 'The audience now assembled in the Capuchin church was collected by various causes, but all of them were foreign to the ostensible motive. The women came to show themselves – the men, to see the women.'[16] Sexual attraction, not religiosity, is the real motive for the gathering; but, while normal human instincts can express themselves through the forms prescribed by religious convention, the church also has a sinister significance: as a mechanism whereby the living are transformed into the dead. Ambrosio, by a process of religious instruction, is made into a monster of virtue, a man made unnatural as well as hypocriti-cal by the pretence that he is not touched by human feeling. Significantly, his sexual awakening is also associated with revival from death: it is only after Matilda has sucked the venom from a deadly snake bite and after he is restored to consciousness that he also becomes aware of her nature as a woman and his initiation into the erotic takes place. The struggle between *eros* and death is also worked out in the theme of the Bleeding Nun and through its relation to Agnes. The denial of *eros* in the case of Beatrice with catastrophic consequences is nearly repeated with Agnes, who is thwarted in her attempt to escape with Don Raymond, her lover, through the fact that her own impersonation of the Bleeding Nun is inverted, when the spectre of the Bleeding Nun is thought by Don Raymond to be Agnes. The appearance of the Bleeding Nun – herself a symbol of the cultural repression of female sexuality – represents an invasion of the world of the living by the world of the dead. As a result, Agnes is confined within a convent, proclaimed dead, given what is apparently poison, and then discovered in the subterranean vaults in a state that can only be described as half alive. Simultaneously Don Raymond himself has endured a severe illness and been on the point of death. Thus the restoration of both to health and to each other represents a fitting negation of the negation. This state of being between life and death is paralleled by Ambrosio and Antonia. The multiple symbolic deaths of Agnes also befall Antonia: first rendered insensible by mysterious powers, then buried in a state of suspended consciousness, from which she revives only to be slain by Ambrosio. Although Antonia is the most modest and virtuous feminine character in the book, her death figures symbolically as a punishment both of Lorenzo, her lover, and herself for their denial of *eros*. Their relations become so veiled and so oblique as to become virtually non-existent:

> Having thrown a veil over her face, she ventured to look out. By the light of the moon, she perceived several men below with guitars and lutes in their hands; and, at a little distance from them, stood another wrapped in a cloak, whose stature and appearance bore a strong resemblance to Lorenzo's. She was not deceived in this conjecture: it was indeed Lorenzo himself, who, bound by his word not to present himself to Antonia without his uncle's consent, endeavoured, by occasional serenades, to convince his mistress that his attachment still existed. This strategem had not the desired effect. Antonia was far from supposing that this nightly music was intended as a compliment to her. She was too modest to think herself worth such attentions; and, concluding them to be addressed to some neighbouring lady, she grieved to find that they were offered by Lorenzo.[17]

Lorenzo's obedience to social norms of behaviour leads to the masking of both his own and Antonia's feelings. In this scene she is veiled, while he adopts a disguise. The bashfulness of both means the fulfilment of Lorenzo's nightmare at the opening of the novel – not his dream. The appropriation of life by death is most distinctly articulated in the case of Ambrosio himself. His relations with Antonia assume a perverse form, in which he can only deal with her as an inert object – not as a living human being. Ambrosio's erotic impulses are totally transposed into an obsession with death:

> By the side of three putrid half-corrupted bodies lay the

sleeping beauty. A lively red, the forerunner of returning animation, had already spread itself over her cheeks, and, as wrapped in a shroud she reclined upon her funeral bier, she seemed to smile at the images of death surrounding her. While he gazed upon their rotting bones and disgusting figures, who perhaps were once as sweet and lovely, Ambrosio thought upon Elvira, by him reduced to the same state. As the memory of that horrid act glanced upon his mind, it was clouded with a gloomy horror; yet it served but to strengthen his resolution to destroy Antonia's honour.[18]

At this point all the implications of Lewis's opening quotation from *Measure for Measure*,

> Lord Angelo is precise;
> Stands at a guard with envy; scarce confesses
> That his blood flows, or that his appetite
> Is more to bread than stone

are symbolically realised. In Shakespeare's terms Ambrosio is shown to be homologous with *both* bread and stone: he has the feelings and desires of a normal man but expresses them in a perverse form, so that his eroticism has no more appropriate setting than catacombs, filled with decaying bodies. This is the price that Ambrosio pays for his long-standing suppression and hypocritical denial of sexuality. It is a particular irony of the book that Lewis should actually suggest that Ambrosio's principal mistake was to choose an unsuitable setting for his advances: 'The aspect of the vault, the pale glimmering of the lamp, the surrounding obscurity, the sight of the tomb, and the objects of mortality which met her eyes on either side, were ill calculated to inspire her with the emotions by which the friar was agitated!'[19] Ambrosio possesses absolute power over Antonia: 'Resistance is unavailing, and I need disavow my passion for you no longer. You are imagined dead; society is forever lost to you. I possess you here alone; you are absolutely in my power.'[20] She is assigned to the world of the dead – like Agnes: a terrorism only possible within the closed institutions of the church. It is the church which sanctions such dominance and which denies women freedom and autonomy as human beings. Ambrosio's perverted sexuality, which can only express itself as violence, as wounding and bruising, is an inevitable consequence of a society in which sexual relations assume repressed and mystified forms.

Nevertheless, Lewis is not an unqualified sexual libertarian. Lewis recognised that a free and spontaneous sexuality necessarily implied the acknowledgement of feminine sexuality, and he saw the harm caused by its denial; but when it came down to it he was as fearful of opening this Pandora's box as anyone else. Indeed, *The Monk* can also be read as an allegory of the rejection of female sexuality by Monk/Lewis! Ambrosio is at first delighted to be initiated into sexual mysteries by Matilda, but he quickly tires of her because she always takes the initiative and assumes a dominant and demanding role:

> But a few days had passed since she appeared the mildest and softest of her sex, devoted to his will, and looking up to him as to a superior being. Now she assumed a sort of courage and manliness in her manners and discourse, but ill-calculated to please him. She spoke no longer to in-sinuate, but to command: he found himself unable to cope with her in argument, and was unwillingly obliged to confess the superiority of her judgement. Every moment convinced him of the astonishing powers of her mind; but what she gained in the opinion of the man, she lost with interest in the affection of the lover.[21]

It is in response to this threatening reversal of sex roles that Ambrosio reverts to a more passive and acceptable form of femininity – the chaste and gentle Antonia. Ambrosio is in fact in an erotic double bind, from which there can be no escape: he could enjoy liberated sexuality with a woman whom he finds intimidating and therefore not erotic, but he is attracted towards a woman with whom erotic fulfilment is not possible – indeed, the eroticism of Antonia is connected with taboo, the transgression of which would also destroy the erotic, as the rape scene itself clearly demonstrates. The erotic appears itself as a phantom, forever intangible, forever out of reach. The demonic conclusion of *The Monk* has a certain psychological truth, if Lewis himself is far from the moral pietism which it notionally invokes: the dream of freedom and fulfilment has turned into a nightmare.

Although Lewis sealed Ambrosio's fate with terrifying retribution and punishment, he nevertheless did write *The Monk* very much from the point of view of his demonic hero – so much so that there can be little doubt that the longing for erotic liberation, and the anxiety which the prospect induces, is Lewis's own. Lewis ostensibly deplored the duplicity and sensuality of Ambrosio, but his manner of exhibiting Ambrosio's awakening has powerfully amoral overtones. For Ambrosio could only be moral as long as he was not acquainted with his own erotic drives, and, if his consciousness of them left him no alternative but to follow them, there could only be one conclusion: that the appearance of morality could only be hypocritical and inauthentic, that the strength of a man's impulses becomes for him at once truth and nemesis. *The Monk*, for contemporary readers, was shocking simply in the garishness of its surface details, but it also disconcerted at this deeper level. For, although Lewis had retained damnation, he had nevertheless very effectively disposed of morality!

The new orientation which Lewis gave to the Gothic is clearly written in the subsequent development of the genre. It emerges with particular clarity in the case of Mrs Radcliffe's *The Italian*, published in 1797. Although there is a definite continuity with her earlier *The Mysteries of Udolpho* in the way in which a feminist point of view is linked with the critique of arbitrary power, there is also – in Russian formalist terms – a distinct shift in the nature of the *dominant*. Innocence is still for Mrs Radcliffe, as it was not for Lewis, a meaningful and realisable value, but the opposition between innocence and madness is transposed into a contrast between innocence and hypocrisy. It is also important to note that Mrs Radcliffe's attitude towards reason undergoes some modification. Her earlier novels were concerned to show how crucial was the role of reason in the struggle against the forces of oppression and irrational domination and such an emphasis continues to be felt in *The Italian*. It is important that Vivaldi, Ellena's lover, should have an understanding 'sufficiently clear and strong to teach him to detect many errors of opinion, that prevailed around him, as well as to despise the common superstitions of his country',[22] and it is equally significant that Schedoni, the hypocritical monk and dominant figure in the

novel, should be shown as alienated from truth, to which both
reason and feeling should lead. But Schedoni also exemplifies
the tortuousness of reason, its ability to become alienated
from itself through the very complexity and deviousness of its
own workings:

> The elder brothers of the convent said that he had talents,
> but denied him learning; they applauded him for the
> profound subtlety which he occasionally discovered in
> argument, but observed that he seldom perceived truth
> when it lay on the surface; he could follow it through all the
> labyrinths of disquisition but overlooked it, when it was
> undisguised before him. In fact he cared not for truth, nor
> sought it by bold and broad argument, but loved to exert the
> wily cunning of his nature in hunting it through artificial
> perplexities. At length, from a habit of intricacy and
> suspicion, his vitiated mind could receive nothing for truth,
> which was simple and easily comprehended.[23]

Here is a great paradox. The Gothic novel shows a new
awareness of the intricacy of mental processes that represents
one of its most significant claims on our attention, yet what it
exhibits it also deplores. The truth is there, open and
transparent, yet man in his perversity cuts himself off from it.
The most crucial and fundamental moral issues become badly
blurred. Schedoni criticises the Marchese, Vivaldi's father, on
the grounds that he cannot distinguish virtue from vice at the
very moment when he and the Marchese are discussing plans
for the murder of Ellena, whom they regard as an unworthy
object for the affections of Vivaldi. At which Mrs Radcliffe
applies the same criticism to them:

> A philosopher might, perhaps, have been surprised to hear
> two persons seriously defining the limits of virtue, at the
> very moment in which they meditated the most atrocious
> crime; a man of the world would have considered it to be
> mere hypocrisy; a supposition which might have disclosed
> his general knowledge of manners, but would certainly
> have betrayed his ignorance of the human heart.[24]

Thus, in *The Italian* Mrs Radcliffe is more disposed to see evil in the world as connected with faults in human nature. She still criticises evils and injustices and is conscious of their social and institutional basis, but there is notably greater element of pessimism in her work, which doubtless registers the impact on her of the Reign of Terror in France. In *The Italian* she is highly critical of the injustice, arbitrariness and anti-democratic mystifications of the procedures of the religious Inquisition, but it becomes for her an exemplification not simply of the corruptness of civilisation, but also of human irrationality:

> While meditating upon these horrors, Vivaldi lost every selfish consideration in astonishment and indignation of the sufferings, which the frenzied wickedness of man prepares for man, who, even at the moment of infliction, insults his victim with assertions of the justice and necessity of such procedure. 'Is this possible!' said Vivaldi internally, 'Can this be in human nature! – Can such horrible perversions of right be permitted! Can man, who calls himself endowed with reason, and immeasurably superior to every other created being, argue himself into the commission of such horrible folly, such inveterate cruelty, as exceeds all the acts of the most irrational and ferocious brute? Brutes do not deliberately slaughter their species; it remains for man only, man, proud of his prerogative of reason, and boasting of his sense of justice, to unite the most terrible extremes of folly and wickedness!'[25]

The Inquisition is itself a form of perversity: it sanctions the most awful crimes in the name of reason. Instead of assuming that it is only through culture that man is alienated from nature, the possibility has to be faced that man himself becomes, or has become, alienated from the natural. Thus the notion of hypocrisy as the embodiment of a socially generated false consciousness begins to acquire an internal dynamic of its own: it opens up the prospect of perennially false sets of relations – a hall of mirrors, of distorting mirrors, from which it is impossible to escape.

Nevertheless, although influenced by the new mood of irrationalism, Mrs Radcliffe does remain faithful to her belief in the goodness of human nature and in the value of spontaneity. She contrasts the frankness, sincerity, love of justice and generosity of Vivaldi with Schedoni, who 'saw only evil in human nature'.[26] To see only this evil is to be guilty of partiality and excessive despondency, to align oneself with the forces of death against the forces of life. In this respect Mrs Radcliffe shows herself influenced by the symbolic language of *The Monk*. Throughout *The Italian* she is conscious of the difference between those who 'render life a blessing or a burden'.[27] This also appears as a contrast between the sacred and the secular, between those, such as Paulo, who love life and wish to enjoy themselves, and those, such as Schedoni, whose tortuous spirits prevent them from living in anything other than a negative and malignant fashion. In *The Italian* 'enthusiasm' is seen as the greatest of all virtues: a generosity of spirit that contrasts with the meanness and narrowness fostered by the church. The antithesis appears with great clarity in the dialogue between Vivaldi and the Abate of the abbey in which Ellena has been confined:

'And can you endure, holy father,' said Vivaldi, 'to witness a flagrant act of injustice and not endeavour to counteract it? not even step forward to rescue the victim when you perceive the preparation for the sacrifice?'

'I repeat, that I never interfere with the authority of others,' replied the Superior, 'having asserted my own, I yield to them in their sphere, the obedience which I require in mine.'

'Is power then,' said Vivaldi, 'the infallible test of justice? Is it morality to obey when the command is criminal? The whole world have a claim upon the fortitude, the active fortitude of those who are placed as you are, between the alternative of confirming a wrong by your consent, or by preventing it by your resistance. Would that your heart expanded toward that world, reverend father!'

'Would that the whole world were wrong that you might have the glory of setting it right!' said the Abate, smiling. 'Young man! you are an enthusiast, and I pardon you. You are a knight of chivalry, who would go about the earth fighting with everybody by way of proving your right to do good; it is unfortunate that you are born somewhat too late.'

'Enthusiasm is the cause of humanity' – said Vivaldi, but

he checked himself; and despairing of touching a heart so hardened by selfish prudence, and indignant at beholding an apathy so vicious in its consequence, he left the Abate without other effort.'[28]

The whole discussion is striking in the note it adopts. It is unexpected to find the arguments rehearsed at the Nuremburg trials and at the trial of Adolf Eichmann, positions which it is often assumed are peculiarly modern, occurring in a work such as this. But it should not really surprise us. The radical tradition of the times laid great emphasis on the evils of institutions, so it is only fitting that Mrs Radcliffe should insist on the importance of combating injustices that are so strongly and so institutionally entrenched and argue that in relation to them apathy is just as much an endorsement of a malignant system as positive complicity. Oppression figures prominently in the argument of the novel. Vivaldi sees Ellena as 'oppressed'[29] and his own father as a 'haughty oppressor',[30] while Ellena herself regards the Abbess and the other nuns responsible for her enforced captivity as guilty oppressors. However, Mrs Radcliffe does qualify her anti-clericalism to some degree, by presenting in volume III, chapter 4, a good convent where no coercion is used, thus providing a positive contrast with the one shown earlier in the novel. Even so, it does not significantly shift the frame of reference. For Mrs Radcliffe argues so strongly for enthusiasm and generosity of spirit that she even questions the conduct of her heroine: in Ellena's own eyes she appears as

an unjust and selfish being, unwilling to make any sacrifice for the tranquillity of him, who had given her liberty, even at the risk of his life. Her very virtues, now that they were carried to excess, seemed to her to border upon vices; her sense of dignity appeared to be narrow pride; her delicacy weakness; her moderated affection cold ingratitude; and her circumspection, a little less than prudence degenerated into meanness.[31]

These are the moral faults which the religious life tends to engender, intensifying them through mystery, intimidation and coercion. Through the novel Ellena's life is blighted by the spectre of Schedoni, while Vivaldi is subjected to the sinister procedures of the Inquisition. The church appears as a gloomy shadow cast over the secular forms of human life – which is dispelled by the fête of the final chapter and Paulo's cries of 'O! giorno felice!'

In *The Italian* as in *The Mysteries of Udolpho* it is the natural world and the contemplation of scenery that is marked by sublimity and grandeur which constitutes a crucial and saving moral resource. In the first section of the novel Ellena is seized by unknown ruffians and taken on an obscure and frightening journey, of the purpose or direction of which she can have little conception, since she is travelling in a carriage with closed blinds, above which she can see only 'the towering tops of mountains', 'veiny precipices' and 'tangled thickets'.[32] As they pass through highly dramatic mountainous scenery the blinds are raised; but Ellena, far from being oppressed with any sense of terror or of her own personal helplessness, instead experiences a revival of confidence and a creative expansion of her own subjectivity. Her spirits are 'gradually revived and elevated by the grandeur of the images around her'[33] and she says to herself,

> If I am condemned to misery surely I could endure it with more fortitude in scenes like these, than amid the tamer landscapes of nature! Here, the objects seem to impart somewhat of their own force, their own sublimity, to the soul. It is scarcely possible to yield to the pressure of misfortune while we walk, as with the Deity, amidst his most stupendous work.[34]

There follows a passage in which the full splendours of the Radcliffian sublime are unveiled: precipices, torrents, the setting sun, gloom and darkness are brought together in a thunder of hyperbole. But the Radcliffian sublime, unlike that of Burke, does *not* convince the spectator of his insignificance, but rather has a reassuring and tranquillising effect:

> It was when the heat and the light were declining that the carriage entered a rocky defile, which shewed, as through a telescope reversed, distant plains, and mountains opening beyond, lighted up with all the purple splendor of the setting sun. Along this deep and shadowy perspective a river, which

was seen descending among the cliffs of a mountain, rolled with impetuous force, fretting and foaming amidst the dark rocks in its descent, and then flowing in a limpid lapse to the brink of other precipices, whence again it fell with thundering strength to the abyss, throwing its misty clouds of spray high in the air, and seeming to claim the whole empire of this solitary wild. Its bed took up the whole breadth of the chasm, which some strong convulsion of the earth seemed to have formed, not leaving space even for a road along its margin. The road, therefore, was carried high among the cliffs, that impended over the river, and seemed as if suspended in air; while the gloom and vastness of the precipices, which towered above and sunk below it, together with the amazing force and uproar of the falling waters, combined to render the pass more terrific than the pencil could describe, or language can express. Ellena ascended it, not with indifference but with calmness. . . .[35]

It is through descriptions such as this rather than through Austenian character analysis that the development of subjectivity is presented: the progressive revelation to Ellena of herself as a free and autonomous human being rather than a helpless and abject dependant. Soon after her confinement – which is to say, imprisonment in the convent – she climbs a flight of winding stairs to find, at the top, a small turret, which has the most magnificent view. Looking out of the windows she sees 'a landscape spread below, whose grandeur awakened all her heart. The consciousness of her prison was lost, while her eyes ranged over the wide and freely-sublime scene without.'[36] The sublime thus presents itself as a reminder of the possibility of freedom. The turret and its discovery become 'an important circumstance',[37] since here Ellena can find the strength of character that will enable her to endure her persecutions with fortitude. The contemplation of nature elevates the mind and softens 'the asperities of affliction'.[38] Even in her darkest hour, when she is under the sinister guardianship of Spalatro, she overcomes her intense fears in the contemplation of a sea illuminated by moonlight and is finally able to sleep. For Ellena, as for Wordsworth, nature is guardian, guide and nurse.

In contrast with Ellena, the evil characters in the novel are shown to be unresponsive to nature – indeed, it is precisely this fact that serves as a sign of their depravity. Schedoni's inability to respond to the beauty of nature indicates that he lacks a capacity for genuine or spontaneous feeling, that he is too much the narrow rationalist:

> Their track now lay through a country less savage, though scarcely less wild than that they had passed in the morning. It emerged from the interior toward the border of the forest; they were no longer enclosed by impending mountains; the withdrawing shades were no longer impenetrable to the eye, but now and then opened to gleams of sunshine – landscape, and blue distances; and in the immediate scene, many a green glade spread its bosom to the sun. The grandeur of the trees, however, did not decline; the plane, the oak, and the chestnut still threw a pomp of foliage round these smiling spots, and seemed to consecrate the mountain streams, that descended beneath their solemn shade.
>
> To the harassed spirits of Ellena the changing scenery was refreshing, and she frequently yielded her cares to the influence of majestic nature. Over the gloom of Schedoni, no scenery had, at any moment, power; the shape and paint of external imagery gave neither impression or colour to his fancy. He contemned the sweet illusions, to which other spirits are liable, and which often confer a delight more exquisite, and not less innocent, than any which deliberative reason can bestow.[39]

Such a description is heavily coded. For Schedoni has raised the alarming prospect that Ellena may be his daughter, and consequently any sign that they are temperamentally different may offer some hope to the reader that Schedoni's conclusion is mistaken – as, indeed, it proves to be. The narrative itself implies that Ellena's tribulations may be drawing to an end, since the travellers are no longer enclosed by impenetrable mountains but are surrounded by scenery characterised by clarity, transparency and openness. The connection between man and nature in this scene is not hard to discover. Ellena responds to the landscape because it is in keeping with her own sunny and spontaneous disposition; but we should hardly expect Schedoni to warm to a 'green glade' that spreads its bosom to the sun, since his own character is gloomy and introverted. His dark past and his brooding, guilt-ridden nature cut him off from the world of authentic feeling. This distinction is so important to Mrs Radcliffe that she returns to it again only a little while later. As they approach Naples, Ellena weeps as they see the summit of Vesuvius and other well-known scenes: 'when every mountain of that magnificent horizon, which enclosed her native landscape, that country which she believed Vivaldi to inhabit, stood unfolded, how affecting, how overwhelming were her sensations!'[40] But Schedoni, who feels nothing, becomes prototypical of the consciousness that becomes alienated from the real world through an obsession with distinctions consti-tuted through language:

> Her expressive countenance disclosed to the Confessor the course of her thoughts and of her feelings, feelings which, while he contemned, he believed he perfectly com-prehended, but of which, having never in any degree experienced them, he really understood nothing. The callous Schedoni, by a mistake not uncommon, especially to a mind of his character, substituted words for truths; not only confounding the limits of neighbouring qualities, but mistaking their very principles.[41]

The only truthful responses are spontaneous and intuitive; an excess of ratiocination does not simply lead to error – it leads to a total disjuncture between the objective world and the mind that purportedly contemplates it. Schedoni's blindness to the beauty of nature is shared by his patroness, the Marquesa: the villa has a splendid view over the bay of Naples, but she is totally incapable of responding to it: 'her eyes were fixed upon the prospect without, but her attention was wholly occupied by the visions that evil passions painted to her imagination'.[42] The horror of the demonic is that it knows only itself. Subjectivity becomes a prison. Thus, in some sense, the crucial moral distinction in *The Italian* becomes the line of demarcation that separates good from bad subjectivity: one points towards freedom, the other towards oppression.

The phenomenology of *The Italian* is significantly constituted

through the imagery of the cloak and of the veil – tokens
of the way in which relations become obscured and mystified
and of the destructive nature of the intervention of the church
between man, the world and his own nature. The omnipresent and omnipotent figure of *The Italian* is that of a monk
muffled in cloak or cowl with no clue as to his identity, his
character or his intentions. If the world becomes nightmarish
and confused, if nothing is what it seems and if no outlines or
lineaments can be discerned, this is because the church has
made it so. The torments suffered by Ellena and Vivaldi are
above all the torments of uncertainty: they endure not so
much physical agonies as the mental anguish of having to live
in a world deprived of clarity, transparency and truth.
Although Ellena, like Antonia, is first presented to the reader
in a veil, its significance is progressively transvalued as it
becomes a marker of oppression and terror. When Ellena is
brought to the convent she refuses to accept the nun's veil. In
the veiling ceremony witnessed by Vivaldi the replacement of
a white veil by a black one signifies a kind of terrifying
oblivion, but Vivaldi, who recognises Ellena in her half-veil, is
able to come to her rescue. The veil initiates Ellena into a
world of treachery and false appearances. Although she is
able to make her escape by actually wearing a nun's veil – that
of Olivia – its wearing is laden with menace. She unveils to the
wrong person, while her disguise provides a basis for the
charge against Vivaldi that he has stolen it; as she is seized and
taken away the fainting Vivaldi revives to see her veil floating
away – the veil is associated not so much with innocence as
with its loss, with an initiation into a world of violence,
corruption and deception. Veil and cowl alike are the signs of
a world that has lost its transparency, where anything can be
anything and where nothing is but what is not.

The most alarming scenes in *The Italian* are connected with
this feeling of obscurity. There is Ellena's journey in the
carriage with the blinds drawn; her frustration at receiving a
letter from Vivaldi in circumstances where it is so dark that she
finds it impossible to read it; the fact that Vivaldi, before the
Inquisition, is unable to identify those who accuse him. Mrs
Radcliffe's stylistic method is well represented by the following description of the room in which the inquisitionary
proceedings are held:

Round the table were several unoccupied chairs, on the back of which appeared figurative signs, at the upper end of the apartment, a gigantic crucifix stretched nearly to the vaulted roof; at the lower end, suspended from an arch in the wall, was a dark curtain, but whether it veiled a window or shrouded some object or person, necessary to the designs of the Inquisitor, there was little means of judging. It was, however, suspended from an arch such as sometimes contains a casement, or leads to a deep recess.[43]

We are presented with intangibles, with gaps in the world waiting to be filled. The chairs are unoccupied, the signs are enigmatic, the purposes of the Inquisitor obscure. The description focuses on a 'dark curtain', but this itself only leads to vague speculation and the proliferation of imponderables. The torment of the Inquisition is seen not so much in terms of torture as in terms of epistemological uncertainty. The quintessential symbol of the whole work is the bloody garment of a monk, 'vest and scapulary rent and stained with blood',[44] which Vivaldi discovers in the vault. The explanation of how it came to be there is eventually provided, but the garment conveys its own indisputable message: the association of the church with intrigue and mysterious violence. Although a mystery, it simultaneously supplies its own solution to the riddle of the novel – suggesting as it does the guilt of Schedoni, though in reality the result of the wounding of Nicola di Zampari by Paulo, Vivaldi's servant.

The greatest mystery in the novel is connected with the character of Schedoni. Schedoni is an absent presence: he does not directly appear in large sections of the narrative, but he nevertheless figures as the point of imaginative focus for the reader. His gigantic stature, his apparent omnipresence and omniscience, his formidable memory, which permits him to memorise down to the last detail an official document of the Inquisition – all this suggests the Superman. But Schedoni is also imposing because he represents the complex, multifarious personality, as contrasted with the simple, unambiguous personality of Ellena and Vivaldi. Everything connected with Schedoni raises problems of identity. Is he identical with the cowled figure who warns Vivaldi not to go to the villa Altieri? Is he the same person whose agonising symptoms of guilt and remorse created a stir at the confessional of the Black Penitents? Is he Ellena's father? Is he Ferrando, Count di Bruno, and was Ferrando also the man who confessed? Schedoni has a multiplicity of doubles. His assumed identity as Schedoni makes him his own double, but there is also Spalatro, his evil minion, and Nicola di Zampari, who is many times confused with him. The difficulty of making all these connections, of ever really establishing anything for certain, is precisely what constitutes the nightmare of a world deprived of transparency. To nail Schedoni down is extremely difficult, since he can be proved guilty only if all the identities can be clarified. A multiplicity of evidence is required: from Nicola di Zampari, from Father Ansaldo, to whom he confessed, from Beatrice, Olivia, the old peasant who found a dead body in a sack and also from Spalatro. The mystery element in *The Italian* actually has far more substance than *The Mysteries of Udolpho*, since Udolpho simply confronts us with one or two puzzles and shocks, while *The Italian* is an intricately constructed detective story, whose denouement has great moral force: the labyrinths which Schedoni has constructed are symptomatic of his own tortuous and alienated subjectivity – evidence of the heavy price to be paid when man deserts the spontaneous and the natural.

Nevertheless, Schedoni is not altogether without redeeming features – for the Romantic mind the hypocrite must always be a figure of compassion, as well as an object of moral censure. Schedoni, though lost in the labyrinthine workings of his own mind, is not altogether bereft of the redeeming power of sympathy. And the reader himself must sympathise a little with Schedoni, if only because he may be under the illusion that Schedoni really is Ellena's father. Although he frequently teeters on the brink of evil, the Schedoni who is actually present in the novel is rarely able to bring himself to commit it: at the last moment he fails to murder Ellena and the knife falls from his hand; in response to Ellena's pleading he spares the life of Spalatro. But Schedoni must be condemned because for him there is no path leading back to humanity: his actions have cut him off irrevocably from the world of the human – for the Romantics the most terrible punishment of all. Schedoni may be superhuman, but he is also less than human. By implication Mrs Radcliffe is also making a statement about authenticity: the novel suggests that once you have lost it there can be no going back. This also reflects intriguingly on Schedoni's indecisiveness at critical moments: a man possessed by bad faith, he lacks any genuine basis for action.

The figure of Schedoni, when taken in conjunction with the thematic doubling of the theme of oppression, through the alternation of the narrative from Ellena to Vivaldi, creates a richer and more complex novel than *The Mysteries of Udolpho*. It is structurally polycentric and allows us to see events from a number of different points of view. Nevertheless, it may be objected that Mrs Radcliffe draws back from the more interesting implications of her subject, by first raising the possibility that Schedoni may be Ellena's father, only subsequently to discount it in a manner that appears anticlimactic. However, this is to ignore the obvious but important point that *The Italian* is a novel written by a woman. The mysterious omnipotence of Schedoni signifies the fact that woman lives in a world of masculine domination and her attempts to develop her identity and personality are thwarted at every turn. In Ellena's struggle towards self-realisation, it is Schedoni who stands there blocking the path and impeding her progress at every step of the way. It is therefore indispensable that Schedoni, like Montoni in *Udolpho*, be stripped of the appearance of grandeur. The full significance of the attempted murder of Ellena by Schedoni is that, symbolically, it is an attempted rape, a violation of the last vestige of her independence. But his inability to go through with it produces a reversal of roles: now it is Ellena who is dominant, Schedoni who is abject. But Schedoni's claim to the paternity of Ellena must be repudiated by Mrs Radcliffe not simply because he is the kind of man he is, but also because a validation of it would also be a symbolic validation of male dominance and omnipotence. Ellena has lost not only a father but also a mother, and Mrs Radcliffe quite consciously stresses the importance of this relationship in the closing pages of the narrative:

> Ellena no longer returned her caresses; surprise and doubt suspended every tender emotion; she gazed upon Olivia with an intensity that partook of wildness. At length she said slowly – 'It is my mother, then, whom I see! When will these discoveries end!'

'It is your mother!' replied Olivia solemnly, 'a mother's blessing rests with you!'

The nun endeavoured to soothe the agitated spirits of Ellena, though she was herself nearly overwhelmed by the various and acute feelings this disclosure occasioned. For a considerable time they were unable to speak but in short sentences of affectionate exclamation, but joy was evidently a more predominant feeling with the parent than with the child. When, however, Ellena could weep, she became more tranquil, and by degrees was sensible of a degree of happiness such as she had perhaps never experienced.[45]

The significance of the mother–daughter relationship in the novel is not that a daughter necessarily feels more affection for a mother than for a father, but primarily that a mother is supportive of the feminine role; she can provide a strong and clear sense of what it is to be a woman. We may remember that in *Udolpho* it is through a false mother-figure that Emily is delivered into the hands of Montoni. In *The Italian* the discovery of her mother makes her marriage to Vivaldi possible:

Then, irresolute, desolate, surrounded by strangers, and ensnared by enemies, she had believed she saw Vivaldi for the last time; now, supported by the presence of a beloved parent, and by the willing approbation of the person, who had so strenuously opposed her, they were met to part no more![46]

In a very real sense Ellena's task in *The Italian* is to lose a father and find a mother.

The other important reworking of the thematic materials of *The Monk*, E. T. A. Hoffmann's *Die Elixiere des Teufels*, appears in quite a different cultural context and considerably later: the Germany of 1816. This context is in all respects highly significant. The defeat of Napoleon and the re-establishment of 'order' in Germany indicates a reactionary political climate very far from the context of earlier Gothic. Hoffmann himself embodied the contradictions of bourgeois culture in an acute form. Though a *Kunstler* in multifarious guises, a writer, musician and theatrical producer, he had nevertheless, in

1814, abandoned these occupations as a means of financial support in order to become a deputy judge in Berlin. The preoccupation with a splitting of the ego in *Die Elixiere des Teufels* bears a clear relationship to his own personal experience as a man split between contradictory roles, even though there is an unmistakable provenance for such a concern in the literature of the Gothic itself. The elements of social criticism in Hoffmann are even more subterranean than they are in Lewis, though they are undoubtedly there. In *Die Elixiere des Teufels* Hoffmann makes an ironic focus of the novel the discrepancy between his occupation and his passion when he has Medardus, the monk, answer the question as to why he withheld certain information from the judge by saying, 'How could I expect him to attach any importance to a story which could only have sounded fantastic to him? Is an enlightened court of justice allowed to believe in the miraculous?'[47] – but this only has the force of implying that the individual and the social are incommensurable. Hoffmann deflects attention from the individual's conflict with society, yet even here the falsity of the social world is apparent.

Die Elixiere des Teufels not only self-consciously alludes to Lewis's *The Monk*, rendering transparent its own character as an over-determined fiction, but also picks up many of its motifs. Medardus's love for Aurelia repeats Ambrosio's love for Antonia, but it is intensified by the fact that Hoffmann transposes the motif of the picture to her, thus making his love for her more ideal. In *The Monk* it was Matilda who bore a resemblance to the Madonna and thus caused Ambrosio to fall away from the ascetic ideal. Antonia's attraction for him is primarily erotic. Hoffmann more deliberately restructures the fable in terms of a contradiction between sacred and profane love. Francesco, the painter who figures in one of the interpolated narratives, intends to transform a sacred representation of Saint Rosalia into a secular one, by portraying her in the nude, as Venus. However, in the process of composition he mysteriously finds himself reverting towards the original spiritual conception, but is unable to complete the face. Only under the influence of the devil's elixirs can he supply the face – that of a Venus whose glance is filled with voluptuous passion. This constant slippage between the erotic and the ideal becomes the novel's obsessive theme. It is, moreover, connected with the thematic of love and death. Hoffmann introduces the second part of the narrative by saying, 'the supreme rapture of love, the fulfilment of the miracle, is manifested in death'.[48] Medardus dies exactly one year after Aurelia/Rosalia, to the day and hour, symbolically indicating that they can be united in death as they never could be in life. *Die Elixiere des Teufels* postdates Goethe's *Faust* Part I (1808) and can be seen as reworking of *The Monk* in corresponding terms. Medardus, like Faust, is torn between a spiritual restlessness and a desire for peace, a man caught up in the dynamics of a quest that offers no finality no matter how much he may long for it. In Hoffmann the quest has its own peculiar tortuousness, since Aurelia is simultaneously an ideal he longs for and yet something he unconsciously desires to deface. Medardus's constant switching between the codes of sacred and profane love produce in him only agony and torment – guilt, frustration and resentment.

Die Elixiere is unquestionably the most intricate treatment of the problem of identity to be found in Romantic literature. In Lewis the hypocritical monk exemplified a contradiction between a false social appearance and an immoral but authentic deeper self. But for Hoffmann the notion of hypocrisy points to a situation of non-correspondence in which identity is always slipping away from and eluding the forms in which it manifests itself. For Hoffmann, unlike many of his contemporaries, the idea of sincerity is virtually an impossibility, for it predicates a correspondence between inner and outer that could never be validated, since the 'inner' is always escaping inspection, fixity or capture. Medardus fractures into a variety of identities: he is Franz(iscus), Medardus, his double Medardus, Victor, Herr Leonard Crczynski, and he is more than one of these at the same time. The ontological status of these identities of the visions and hallucinations they experience becomes confusingly blurred. Medardus destroys one part and replaces it with another – in the hands of Pietro Belcampo (himself split as Belcampo/Schönfeld) he abolishes his monkish persona – he has his hair cut differently, wears fashionable clothes and adopts new ways of walking and of holding his body and arms.

The discontinuities in the narrative and the articulation of the narrative structure through a series of complex paral-

lelisms rather than through a purely linear progression
reinforce this sense of fracturing. Even the distinction between internal and external disappears, since Medardus is
unable to recognise as 'his' certain actions that he performs,
yet at the same time is forced to acknowledge that his doubles
really are him. 'I recognised myself'[49] is his response to the
Medardus figure who torments him in prison; yet when he
runs away after the killing of Hermogenes he scarcely
recognises himself when he sees his own image reflected in the
stream. In playing two parts at the palace of the Baron – as
Victor, the lover of Euphemia, and Medardus, the lover of
Aurelia – he loses all sense of who he really is: 'I am what I
seem to be, yet do not seem to be what I am; even to myself I
am an insoluble riddle, for my personality has been torn
apart.'[50] The self paradoxically recognises itself only in the act
of cognition that there is no central or stable self to be
identified. In this way Medardus is truly a hallucination and
not even a person who has hallucinations: 'I was the disem-
bodied spirit of my personality, appearing as a red glow in the
sky.'[51] The alarming aspect of Medardus's situation is that the
very idea of an inner voice becomes problematic. There is
simply endless mental turmoil and conflict that has no focus or
resolution:

> Tossed to and fro in this cruel conflict, I could see no escape
> from the ruin that faced me on all sides. Gone was that
> mood of exaltation which made my whole life seem like a
> dream; I saw myself as a murderer and a common libertine.
> All that I had told the judge and the physician was nothing
> but foolish, clumsy lies: there had been no inner voice
> speaking to me, as I had tried to persuade myself.[52]

Medardus in so far as he can be defined is described by a series
of involuntary actions: either those ascribed to the Medardus
double or those which he carries out himself. He fails to stab
himself, to stab Aurelia – he saves his own life by instinctively
pouring a corrosive drink he has been given into his sleeve.
The stabbing of Hermogenes is just something that occurs in
their struggle without any attribution of intentionality. So
these actions do not 'belong' to Medardus in any obvious
sense; they are simply things which he does but which in no

way serve to characterise him as a person. Medardus himself is
an enigma – in fact, even to call him 'Medardus' seems
questionable, since this is to give ontological priority to what is
only one of his many roles. The only real basis of his identity is
the love of Aurelia: if he is anyone he is the person who loves
Aurelia. Yet even this can be threatened: 'A sense of apathy
crept over me; I became indifferent to everything, and even
the vision of Aurelia faded.'[53] But at crucial moments it is the
name and thought of Aurelia that sustain him. This love,
endlessly criss-crossing between the sacred and profane, is the
only thing that threads together a multiplicity of identities and
perceptions. Desire is the only and irreducible ground of
being.

The disintegration of personality implies that man is
necessarily subject to the inscrutable operations of fate – for,
as Peter Schönfeld ironically asks, with a question whose
implications resonate through the novel, ' "What is direction,
reverent Capuchin?" he said softly, still with that bitter-sweet
smile on his lips. "Direction presupposes a goal from which we
take our bearings." '[54] Medardus is marked at an early age by
the red wound which he receives on the neck from the abbess's
diamond crucifix. This mark designates his symmetry with his
own double: that is to say, it shows fate, not identity, as the
principle that constructs and organises. This wound, like
Medardus's loss of his arm through corrosive poison, seems
symbolically associated with the stigma of *eros*: the abbess is
Medardus's first love and she indicates the necessary connection between love and pain – 'I have hurt you, but we shall still
become good friends.'[55]

The narrative of *Die Elixiere des Teufels* demonstrates
through its connections, repetitions and parallels that the
miraculous is not dead in the world and that man's destiny is in
the power of strange, mysterious but ultimately beneficent
forces. Implicitly Hoffmann's providence is an artist, a
Kunstler like the writer himself. Medardus's destiny is watched
over by two artist figures, Belcampo/Schonfeld and the
mysterious painter from Linden with his red cloak – a figure
clearly derived from the self-portrait of Salvator Rosa,
another of Hoffmann's heroes. In a curious way, Medardus
believes that he is not responsible for what he does: 'More and
more I became convinced that an inscrutable destiny had knit

together my fate and hers, and that what had sometimes appeared to be as a sinful crime was only the fulfilment of an irrevocable decree.'⁵⁶ Every action includes within it the possibility of its own transcendence: the committing of a crime makes possible the process of spiritual redemption, a profane love for Aurelia can be transvalued into a love that is purer and more spiritual. Thus, despite discontinuity, Hoffmann does postulate a principle of internal dynamism whereby man is always capable of going beyond whatever he is, or may have been.

The intersection between the concerns of *Faust* and those of Gothic is equally strongly represented by Mary Shelley's *Frankenstein, or the Modern Prometheus*, published two years later, in 1818. The narrative articulation of Frankenstein is remarkably incisive: Frankenstein is simultaneously a scientist – artist figure who goes beyond what is either lawful or possible, a Gothic 'hypocrite' in the tradition of Mary Shelley's father, William Godwin, and at the same time a fable of the irrational, a demonstration of how reason itself produces the uncontrolled, unpredictable and involuntary.

Not the least interesting aspect of Frankenstein is that he appears to the reader as a somnambulist: a man who is mysteriously led in a particular direction by forces that seem to override his conscious control, despite the fact that he is, at the same time, a hero of reason, a man whose phenomenal lucidity and insight enable him to solve the mystery of life itself. The path that leads Frankenstein to create his monster is one delineated not so much by conscious intention as by chance circumstances, mysterious impulses, switches of mood and unforseen conjunctions. At one moment Frankenstein is prompted to give up the study of natural philosophy, which has exercised a deep fascination on him, for the study of mathematics: 'All that had so long engaged my attention suddenly grew despicable. By one of those caprices of the mind, which we are perhaps most subject to in early youth, I at once gave up my former occupations.'⁵⁷ This prompts the reflection, 'Thus strangely are our souls constructed, and by such slight ligaments are we bound to prosperity or ruin'⁵⁸ – which is confirmed by the fact that this change of heart is itself only temporary: 'It was a strong effort of the spirit of good; but it was ineffectual. Destiny was too potent, and her immutable laws had decreed my utter and terrible destruction.'[59]

Henceforward Frankenstein's progress is strongly marked by a spirit of perversity. As he listens to his chemistry professor at Ingoldstadt, Mr Waldman, drawing a sharp distinction between modern science, which in his view aims low but delivers a great deal, and ancient alchemists, who 'promised impossibilities and performed nothing',[60] he feels forming within himself a response of contradiction: 'As he went on, I felt as if my soul were grappling with a palpable enemy; one by one the various keys were touched which formed the mechanism of my being: chord after chord was sounded, and soon my mind was filled with one thought, one conception, one purpose.'[61] Frankenstein's project of unfolding to the world 'the deepest mysteries of creation'[62] in a way that will reflect the noble ambitions of the ancients is generated not in pure lucidity but out of an internal unrest that leaves him with an intention but with no real understanding as to how it was arrived at:

> I closed not my eyes that night. My internal being was in a state of insurrection and turmoil; I felt that order would thence arise, but I had no power to produce it. By degrees, after the morning's dawn, sleep came. I awoke, and my yesternight's thoughts were as a dream. There only remained a resolution to return to my ancient studies, and to devote myself to a science for which I believed myself to possess a natural talent.[63]

As Frankenstein becomes more and more deeply engrossed in his mysterious purpose he appears possessed, he begins to lose all consciousness of himself as a person:

> One secret which I alone possessed was the hope to which I dedicated myself; and the moon gazed on my midnight labours, through which, with unrelaxed and breathless eagerness, I pursued nature to her hiding-places. Who shall conceive the horrors of my secret toil, as I dabbled among the unhallowed damps of the grave, or tortured the living animal to animate the lifeless clay? My limbs now tremble and my eyes swim with the remembrance; but then a

resistless, and almost frantic impulse urged me forward; I seemed to have lost all soul or sensation but for this one pursuit.[64]

The notion of torturing the living in order to animate the dead has a particular pertinence to Frankenstein himself: he has become physically emaciated and emotionally numb from his researches; after creating the monster, he lives on shattered and overcome by such a deep sense of his own wretchedness, what is virtually a sickness unto death, that it is as if the life that has gone into the monster has passed out of Frankenstein. The monster embodies the truth of Frankenstein: a will to creation that is in reality destructive, a rationality deeply contaminated by the irrational, a secret spirit of negativity:

> I considered the being whom I had cast among mankind, and endowed with the will and power to effect purposes of horror, such as the deed which he had now done, nearly in the light of my own vampire, my own spirit let loose from the grave, and forced to destroy all that was dear to me.[65]

The monster is separated from Frankenstein by a double involuntariness: Frankenstein neither intended the monster to be like that *nor* to have the consequences which his being like that generates, but this brings us back to the paradox that Frankenstein himself did not intend anything – he produced his monster out of causes unknown to himself. The real meaning of the monster is that of a suicide, the destruction of Frankenstein as a human being. Frankenstein notes that Mr Waldman places before him the instruments 'which were to be afterwards used in putting me to a slow and cruel death'[66]: his death at the hands of the monster is a further multiplication of the involuntary – an act of self-destruction which he did not intend, but nevertheless produced. The popular confusion by which the appellation 'Frankenstein' can be applied as readily to the monster as to the creator embodies a significant truth: the monster is Frankenstein's double and is just as much entitled to the name; the inception and being of the monster are indissolubly linked.

The creation of the monster initiates a double severance

between Frankenstein and the world. Frankenstein's unlawful scientific researches place a barrier between him and ordinary humanity. At the same time, by his involvement in activities which cannot be revealed to any other person, Frankenstein places himself in the position of the Godwinian hypocrite – a man who because of a secret that he keeps buried within creates a discrepancy between inner and outer that becomes a source of torment to him and cuts him off from family, friends and the pleasures of human society. Mary Shelley emphasises that the separation between Frankenstein and his family occurs even before the birth of the monster. He fails to write to his father and forgets all about his friends and those close to him. His father writes that, if this study 'has a tendency to weaken your affections', it is 'certainly unlawful'.[67] Nevertheless, Frankenstein's situation after the death of his brother William and his return to the family is infinitely more painful, for his genuine concern is negated and rendered inauthentic by his recognition that he himself is the true murderer and by the fact that he cannot disclose the secret of his involvement: 'Anguish and despair had penetrated the core of my heart; I bore a hell within me that nothing could extinguish.'[68]

In this way, the death of Justine becomes Frankenstein's greatest crime: for from the other deaths he can be partially exonerated, but Justine, who is falsely accused, tried and condemned to death for a crime that she did not commit, pays the price wholly because of his bad faith. *Frankenstein* becomes an allegory of the origin of evil: an inquiry in the tradition of Shaftesbury and Godwin as to how destructive consequences can follow from benevolent intentions. Both Frankenstein and his creation are basically benevolent and filled with good intentions, but these become dislocated and diverted from their proper course. After the death of Justine, Frankenstein is unable to face the world and human society; he is consigned to the living death of solitude:

Nothing is more painful to the human mind, than, after the feelings have been worked up by a quick succession of events, the dead calmness of inaction and certainty which follows, and deprives the soul both of hope and fear. Justine died; she rested; and I was alive. The blood flowed freely in my veins, but a weight of despair and remorse pressed on my heart, which nothing could remove. Sleep fled from my eyes; I wandered like an evil spirit, for I had committed deeds of mischief beyond description horrible, and more, much more (I persuaded myself), was yet behind. Yet my heart overflowed with kindness, and the love of virtue. I had begun life with benevolent intentions, and thirsted for the moment when I should put them into practice and make myself useful to my fellow-human beings. Now all was blasted: instead of that of serenity of conscience, which allowed me to look back upon the past with self-satisfaction, and from thence to gather promise of new hopes, I was seized by remorse and the sense of guilt, which hurried me away to a hell of intense tortures, such as no language can describe. This state of mind preyed upon my health, which had perhaps never entirely recovered from the first shock it had sustained. I shunned the face of man; all sound of joy of complacency was torture to me; solitude was my only consolation – deep, dark, deathlike solitude.[69]

Frankenstein's torments are directly caused by his inability to confess, but at the same time the split Frankenstein/monster and the mysterious process by which the one generates the other becomes an obscure allegory of the way in which the benevolent can produce the perverse. Thus, in some sense Frankenstein becomes an 'explanation' of what cannot really be explained.

The monster duplicates the spiritual alienation of Frankenstein but in an inverted form. The inner–outer discrepancy with Frankenstein manifests itself as an awareness that he is not what he appears to be, that he is in fact the monster. Yet, though his ugly, physically revolting exterior cuts himself off from the possibility of any kind of relationship – even with Frankenstein himself, who has confided to his diary his feelings of repulsion – behind this carapace there lies a genuine sensitivity. The monster is shown to be more sensitive and more genuine in his responses than Frankenstein himself: we sympathise with his indignation when he exclaims in outrage, 'Unfeeling heartless creator! You had endowed me with perceptions and passions, and then cast me abroad an object for the scorn and horror of mankind.'[70] Even Frankenstein concedes that his creation is 'a creature of fine sensations'[71] – but these feelings, lacking any proper outlet, can only be discharged in anger, resentment and violence. In different ways both Frankenstein and the monster are instances of a ruined and wrecked humanity: excluded from full humanity both by the fact that they are cut off from normal intercourse and society and by the flaw that makes them both discrepant, the one internal, the other external. Frankenstein characterises himself as 'a blasted tree': 'The bolt has entered into my soul; and I felt then that I should survive to exhibit, what I shall soon cease to be – a miserable spectacle of wrecked humanity, pitiable to others, and intolerable to myself.'[72] Thus the relationship which Frankenstein bears to himself closely parallels the feelings of his creature, who is similarly alienated both from humanity and from his own self. What Frankenstein and the monster both have in common is 'sensibility'. Just prior to their fateful encounter in the sublime surroundings of Mount Blanc, Frankenstein asks,

> Alas! why does man boast of sensibilities superior to those apparent in the brute; it only renders them more necessary beings. If our impulses were confined to hunger, thirst, and desire, we might be nearly free; but now we are moved by every wind that blows, and a chance word or scene that that word may convey to us.[73]

This formulation comes closest to unravelling the enigma propounded by the novel. Frankenstein, in a milieu that should fill him with feelings of exhilaration and self-confidence, feels only melancholy and doubt: man's capacity for feeling, the more complex nature of his passions and desires render his freedom problematic and cut him off from the possibility of happiness. He lacks for his desires an adequate object: the monster is not adequate for Frankenstein, the monster himself feels a lack that Frankenstein cannot supply.

Perhaps the most interesting feature of the novel is that it ends not with Frankenstein contemplating the death of his monster, but with the monster's thoughts and feelings after he has murdered his creator. This focuses the reader's attention on the problem of transcendence. The monster has been created as a flawed and isolated thing, potentially capable of happiness, but objectively cut off from it by the circumstances of his creation. His noble impulses are distorted, he is punished for his good intentions. The self-consciousness of Frankenstein's monster must be insisted upon: he grasps more fully the conditions of his existence, of his freedom and unfreedom, than does Frankenstein, the spiritual somnambulist. In Frankenstein's monster the ghost of the superhuman that haunted the Gothic in Radcliffe, Lewis and Hoffmann becomes a palpable thematic presence. The monster takes on himself the knowledge of good and evil, the consciousness of a decadent and sinful world as well as of his own sin. He lies beyond the world of human justice and can only judge himself: his death thus has an existential grandeur and significance that was wholly lacking at the moment of his inception. The monster is thus the true hero of Frankenstein.

The preoccupation with the Superman, so evident in *Frankenstein*, is equally conspicuous in Charles Maturin's *Melmoth the Wanderer* (1820), a novel which is inheritor of the whole tradition of Gothic, and at the same time the definitive statement of later Romanticism. Apart from the notable advocacy of Baudelaire, Maturin is a writer who has never received the recognition that he deserves. His fiction violates so many of the canons, tacit, unacknowledged or overt, by which literature is so often judged. Maturin's great novel *Melmoth* lacks any simple or unified plot but appears rather as a spinning globe suddenly arrested by the malignant author to disclose scenes frightening, grotesque, phantasmagorical. The novel appears as totally and hopelessly fragmented as the many indistinct manuscripts invoked by Maturin to shed partial light on the exploits of his extraordinary hero. One fragment is cut into another. The young Melmoth on the death of his uncle is presented with the reminiscences of an English traveller named Stanton, filled with hiatuses in the most alarming places, a document which itself seems to represent the bafflement of man before the inconclusiveness of the world – 'The manuscript was discoloured, obliterated, and mutilated beyond any that had ever before exercised the patience of a reader'[74] – and its tendency is not to clarify but to frustrate: 'He could but just make out what tended rather to excite than assuage that feverish thirst of curiosity which was consuming his inmost soul.'[75] *Melmoth the Wanderer* is a vast game played by Maturin on the reader in which the reader's very desire for a conclusion, for a terminus that will seem to justify the whole enterprise of embarking on it in the first place, is parodied and mocked.

In experiencing a multiplicity of torments, disappointments and frustrations – the agonies of Stanton in the madhouse, the torments of Moncada at the hands of the Spanish church and the Inquisition, the education of the beautiful and innocent Immalee into the repressions and perversities of civilised life, the cruel sufferings and starvation of Walberg and his family, the betrayal of Elinor by her lover – the reader is paradoxically forced into the position of Melmoth himself, into taking up the stance of the cynical and world-weary observer, who can see in all this human misery no conceivable purpose. The lesson of the novel is that there is no such thing as an ending, let alone a happy ending – when Maturin supplies his readers with a positive conclusion, it is one from which no comfort can be derived. Walberg and his family, heirs of the wealthy Spaniard Guzman, find themselves disinherited through the machinations of the church. They are reduced to the utmost penury, in which Walberg actually contemplates the murder of his own family but is saved from the drastic consequences of his own intentions by his own delirious and near insane condition. At this point a priest arrives to tell them that the true will of Guzman has been found. But no reversal of fortune can expunge the memory of the horrors which they have experienced. In writing in this fashion, Maturin appears as a dishevelled and importunate intruder on the tranquillity of the reader, as uncouth and unwelcome as Coleridge's Ancient Mariner to the wedding guest. For the reader is unlikely to have forgotten Maturin's initial statement that the stories of Elinor and of Walberg are founded on fact, not his own concluding avowal:

> I cannot again appear before the public in so unseemly a character as that of a writer of romances, without regretting the necessity that compels me to it. Did my profession furnish me with the means of subsistence, I should hold myself culpable indeed in having recourse to any other, but – am I allowed the choice?[76]

The contract between author and reader is one sealed not in

the concord of the imagination but in blood, money, sweat and tears. Maturin is too close to his own work and the sentiments it expresses to be either a convincing embodiment of aesthetic transcendence or, indeed, of clerical sanctimoniousness. So with this confession he destroys two reputations at once.

With *Melmoth the Wanderer* we are forcibly reminded of the essential duplicity of the Gothic after Lewis. The genre permits the expression of subversive attitudes behind a more or less transparent veil of sententious moralising. Maturin's novel purports to be an exposé of the inquities of Catholicism, which indeed it is. But, since Catholicism appears also as symbolic of the generally destructive and demoralising role which religion plays in human affairs – strong stuff indeed from an Irish clergyman – no wonder Baudelaire respected 'la grande création satanique du reverend Maturin'.[77] Maturin's strongest criticism of the church appears in 'The Tale of the Spaniard', Monçada. Its role is to subvert, warp and distort every normal human feeling: it sets Moncada at odds both with his father and mother and also with his brother, distorting their relations for religious ends. Spontaneity and genuineness are destroyed and in their place are set hypocrisy, self-seeking and manipulation. 'The virtues of nature are always deemed vices in a convent',[78] writes Maturin on behalf of his protagonist Monçada, who is led to reflect 'with increasing horror on a system that forced hypocracy to a precocity unparalleled, and made the last vice of life the earliest of conventual youth'.[79] The monastic system, like all systems of 'civilised' behaviour, is one based on coercion, intimidation and fear. The statement of Monçada's brother that 'The basis of all ecclesiastical power rests upon fear'[80] brings out the fact that 'The Tale of the Spaniard' is intended by Maturin to be in careful contrast with 'The Tale of the Indians', since Immalee on her island in the Pacific 'could not be conscious of fear, for nothing of that world in which she lived had ever borne a hostile appearance to her'.[81] By contrast, Monçada is subject to the most unyielding and implacable compulsion:

> I returned to the convent – I felt my destiny was fixed – I had no wish to avert or arrest it – I was like one who sees an enormous engine (whose operation is to crush him to

atoms) put in motion, and, stupified with horror, gazes on it with a calmness that might be mistaken for that of one who was coolly analysing the complication of its machinery, and calculating the resistless crush of its blow.[82]

The consequence of his initiation into the church is catastrophic – it leads to a virtual extinction of the processes of consciousness:

Day followed day for many a month, of which I have no recollection, nor wish to have any. I must have experienced many emotions, but they all subsided like the waves of the sea under the darkness of a midnight sky – their fluctuation continues, but there is no light to mark their motion, or trace when they rise and fall. A deep stupor pervaded my senses and soul; and perhaps in this state, I was best fitted for the monotonous existence to which I was doomed. It is certain that I performed all the conventual functions with a regularity that left nothing to be blamed, and an apathy that left nothing for praise. My life was a sea without a tide. The bell did not toll for service with more mechanical punctuality than I obeyed the summons. No automaton, constructed on the most exquisite principles of mechanism, and obeying those principles with a punctuality almost miraculous, could leave the artist less room for complaint or disappointment, than I did the superior and community.[83]

In these descriptions we find Maturin invoking states of feeling that are simultaneously states of non-feeling, a disturbing absence of voluntary mental or emotional processes. The full nightmare of 'L'homme machine' is realised. These are characteristic moments in Maturin's work: his protagonists are so shocked, stunned and traumatised by the shocks which life gives them that they lack any capacity to respond adequately. Their emotional disorientation leads to insanity, derangement and madness. They lose touch with the normal world of human feeling. This once again feeds back into a critique of the Catholic Church and of religious institutions in general. Maturin refers to 'the sterility of human nature in a convent'[84], and Monçada's reflections, when he has escaped from the power of the Inquisition, are strongly impregnated with the atmosphere of *Caleb Williams* and with the Godwinian philosophy of human sympathy:

> Many days elapsed, indeed, before the Jew began to feel his immunity somewhat dearly purchased by the additional maintenance of a troublesome and, I fear, deranged inmate. He took the first opportunity that the recovery of my intellect offered, of hinting this to me, and inquired mildly what I purposed to do, and where I meant to go. This question for the first time opened to my view that range of hopeless and interminable desolation that lay before me – the Inquisition had laid waste the whole track of life, as with fire and sword. I had not a spot to stand on, a meal to earn, a hand to grasp, a voice to greet, a roof to crouch under, in the whole realm of Spain.
>
> You are not to learn, Sir, that the power of the Inquisition, like that of death, separates you, by its single touch, from all mortal relations. From the moment its grasp has seized you, all human hands unlock their hold of yours – you have no longer father, mother, sister, or child. . . . Absolute famine stared me in the face, and a sense of degradation accompanied by consciousness of my own utter and desolate helplessness, was the keenest shaft in the quiver, whose contents were lodged in my heart. My consequence was actually lessened in my own eyes, by ceasing to become the victim of persecution, by which I had suffered so long. *While people think it worth their while to torment us, we are never without some dignity, though painful and imaginary.* Even in the Inquisition I belonged to somebody, – I was watched and guarded; now, I was the outcast of the whole earth, and I wept with equal bitterness and depression at the hopeless vastness of the desert I had to traverse.[85]

It is society that provides the individual with his *raison d'etre*, and, when he is cut off from it, this is equivalent to ceasing to exist. It is far from irrelevant to observe that this is also the predicament of an artist such as Maturin: fated no longer to be feared or reviled – even by a Coleridge – but to be ignored.

With the 'Tale of the Indians' the philosophical base of *Melmoth the Wanderer* is expanded. It becomes clear that

Catholicism is merely the type of the misery which religion
inflicts on mankind and that, in turn, it is this form of
oppression which is normally known as 'civilisation'. The
telescope which Melmoth hands to Immalee shows humans
being sacrificed to the Juggernaut, and discloses to her
simultaneously human life as a world of religion and a world
of suffering. The whole episode can be seen as an ironic
parody of the vision of the future history of the world
disclosed to Adam in Milton's *Paradise Lost*, since what for
Milton was part of a providential design is seen by Maturin as a
process of destruction and futility inaugurated by religion
itself. Thus, Maturin's identification of Melmoth with Satan at
this point has a good deal of force – for to oppose such a
design tends to put both Melmoth and Satan in the right.
Melmoth observes,

> 'It is right,' he continued, not only to have thoughts of this
> Being, but to express them by some outward acts. The
> inhabitants of the world you are about to see, call this
> *worship* – and they have adopted (a Satanic smile curled his
> lip as he spoke) very different modes; so different, that in
> fact, there is but one point in which they all agree – that of
> making their religion a torment; the religion of some
> prompting them to torture themselves, and the religion of
> some prompting them to torture others. Though, as I
> observed, they all agree in this important point, yet unhap-
> pily they differ so much about the mode, that there has been
> much disturbance about it in the world that thinks.[86]

Maturin encourages the reader to associate himself with
Immalee's reaction of shock and horror; but the reader can
scarcely evade the fact that the place from which Immalee can
do this is, in fact, no place, a place that exists only hypothetically, like Romantic literature itself. The very island where
Immalee lives has been invaded by Indians, who are intent on
seeing her as a 'goddess'.[87] Immalee responds to the sight of
the destruction before the Juggernaut by invoking the
Romantic insistence on feeling: 'The world that thinks does
not feel. I never saw the rose kill the bud.'[88] For Maturin
religion is to be seen not as an alien deformation of the world
of civilisation but as the most characteristic manifestation of it,

a warping, wrenching, perverting and dislocating of human feeling. Madness in a very real sense embodies the truth of civilisation: it is scarcely accidental that in every episode of the narrative madness figures prominently, as the price that human nature has to pay for its location in a civilised world.

Melmoth himself is the principle vehicle for Maturin's social critique, but it is a motif constantly reiterated. The Jew Adonijah says to Monçada, 'thou art come from where the cruelty of man, permanent and persevering, unrelenting and unmitigated, hath never failed to leave the proofs of its power in abortive intellects, crippled frames, distorted creeds, and ossified hearts'.[89] Melmoth introduces 'civilisation' to Immalee by describing how man has invented 'by means of living in cities, a new and singular mode of aggravating human wretchedness'.[90] Civilisation is itself a form of social madness, since it involves a multiplication of misery in a way that is both unjustified and unnecessary: in addition to the natural hazards of famine, disease and sterility, human society heaps on top of this a multiplicity of artificial miseries. Civilisation is closely identified with coercion in the case of Immalee herself, when Melmoth refers to himself as 'the hunter of your form and your steps, even amid the complicated and artificial tracks in which you have been concealed by the false forms of existence you have embraced!'[91] Immalee expostulates, '"Embraced!" – Oh no! they seized on me – they dragged me here – they made me a Christian.'[92]

In Maturin's view the social contract is one that has only inimical consequences: man sacrifices his freedom in return for moral corruption. Since society places man out of key, the sounds that it produces must necessarily be parallel: 'The harmony of civilised society, of which she was at once weary and proud, was discord to his ear. He had examined all the strings that formed this curious but ill-constructed instrument and found them all false.'[93] Society frustrates man's noblest impulses and finest energies, as Immalee/Isidora discovers:

> All that day she thought how it was possible to liberate herself from her situation, while the feeling that liberation was impossible clung to the bottom of her heart; and this sensation of the energies of the soul in all their strength, being in vain opposed to imbecility and mediocrity, when

aided by circumstances, is one productive alike of melancholy and irritation. We feel, like prisoners in romance,
bound by threads to which the power of magic has given the
force of adamant.[94]

This philosophic view conditions the nature of Maturin's own
narrative, which seeks not to move forward or resolve, but to
envelope, entangle and bind both reader and protagonist in a
web of social forces from which there is no possible release.
Thus the *raison d'être* of Melmoth himself – the 'extraordinary
being'[95] whose offer of freedom with eternal damnation can
become meaningful only in a context where freedom is seen as
requiring so desperate a price.

The character of Melmoth himself, represented only in a
relatively brief section of the novel, is nevertheless remarkably
suggestive. The Gothic rhetoric of hypocrite/double persists
in that hypocrisy is a persistent focus of religious inquiry
(Moncada describes himself as 'the worst of all hypocrites'[96]),
while Melmoth himself is the malignant double who presents
himself to the various characters. The importance of Melmoth
as a device is that he transvalues the character of striving so
often assigned to Romantic literature: he is neither Don Juan
nor Faust, but Mephistopheles, Statue or Stone Guest.
Melmoth represents the exhaustion of the field Romantic
possibility – simultaneously the recognition of the emptiness
of social existence and the barrenness of postulated alternatives to it. The subject of *Melmoth the Wanderer* is not a
celebration of imaginary but unlawful fields of possibility but
an acceptance of repetition, *in*difference, the dearth of
possibility. For Maturin there is both pathos and irony in the
encounter of Immalee and Melmoth, alternate sides of the
Romantic coin – Immalee is the child of wonder, Melmoth the
man who has become incapable of it:

> His destiny forbid alike curiosity or surprise. The world
> could show him no greater marvel than his own existence;
> and the facility with which he himself passed from region to
> region, mingling with, yet distinct from his species, like a
> wearied and uninterested spectator rambling through the
> various seats of some vast theatre, where he knows none of
> the audience would have prevented his feeling astonish-

ment, had he encountered Isidora on the summit of the Andes.[97]

Melmoth can only corrupt Immalee, i.e. initiate her into the nature of the world, yet paradoxically he has much in common with her, since they both transcend it. Thus the novel constitutes a dual indictment of man and the world he has made from the position of impossibility.

In the closing sections of the narrative, the pretext of diabolical intervention becomes transparent, since Maturin has shown abundantly that the evils he depicts are of human contrivance. It is therefore only appropriate that Melmoth himself should demystify the idea of the devil:

> 'Enemy of mankind!' the speaker continued – 'Alas, how absurdly is that title bestowed on the great angelic chief, – the morning star fallen from its sphere! What enemy has man so deadly as himself? If he would ask on whom he should bestow that title aright, let him smite his bosom, and his heart will answer – Bestow it here!'[98]

The true meaning of Melmoth's alienation from the world, the fact that '*I have traversed the world in the search, and no one, to gain that world, would lose his own soul!*'[99] is that he has seen the vacuity and malignancy of the world that man has constructed for himself – a recognition that no one else is willing to share. For, as Maturin points out, in a striking anticipation of Nietzsche – and what is Melmoth after all if not Zarathustra born early? –

> In a morbid state of heart, we cannot bear truth – the falsehood that intoxicates us for a moment, is worth more than the truth that would disenchant us for life – *I hate him because he tells me the truth*, is the language natural to the human mind, from the slave of power to the slave of passion.[100]

Yet perhaps even here we might detect a tinge of qualified optimism, for Maturin does not present man's repugnance for truth as completely endemic – or, at least, there is a shift of emphasis from one sentence to the next! – in that his suggestion that it is natural to the human mind is prefaced by the ascription of such a condition to a morbid state of heart. For no matter how pessimistic the Romantic writer may be, he is always capable, at least in theory, of postulating a better or nobler state, of invoking the possibility of a man or world that is not warped, perverted or perverse.

Admittedly signs of such optimism are still harder to find in James Hogg's *The Private Memoirs and Confessions of a Justified Sinner*, the very title of which is redolent with irony, since his protagonist indeed regards himself as a justified person, and justified precisely in the fact that he sins. Hogg's novel is one which in its ingenuity and subtlety always goes beyond its overt and ostensible intentions. The novel, the hero of which, as a staunch Calvinist convinced of his own righteousness, is persuaded by the Devil that his mandate therefore extends to the destruction of whomsoever might be deemed wicked, might be thought to have a certain surface plausibleness and to function moderately well as a malicious cautionary tale. But its true power stems from its penetration and insight as a portrait of a disturbed and paranoid consciousness, of what Mrs Radcliffe would have styled a 'vitiated mind'.[101] But, of course, to speak of such a 'vitiated mind' immediately raises a problem that is seldom absent in the Gothic: which is that the notion of a vitiated mind erodes all sense of moral integrity on the part of the individual. The mind is always deemed to have some capacity for self-rectification; if the individual sins or goes astray then conscience or a sense of guilt will work powerfully to restore the individual to the path of righteousness and to redress the balance. But with a vitiated mind there can be no such guarantee. The mind, as vitiated, has no power to stabilise or reorient itself, and, having once gone askew, finds its attempts to get itself back on course warped by the very fact that the course to which it is trying to return is the wrong one. Such is the case with Robert Wringhim Colwan. It is not that he possesses no moral sense, no conviction of the difference between good and evil: it is rather that his pride and self-certainty as a 'justified' person make possible his temptation by the Devil, who may be Maturin's devil within, so that his tragedy or catastrophe is not simply that he sins by killing with calculation and brutality individuals who are essentially blameless, but that he himself is completely incapable of recognising the fact. His own self-consistent rationality becomes more dangerous than the most chaotic madness: it is an irrationalism that does not know its own nature, a closed consciousness that cannot escape from its own terms and constructions.

Yet, although Hogg criticises the excesses and dangers of the belief in justification, he does so from a standpoint that is characteristically Protestant, that insists on the value of private judgement. For his sinner is not simply proud, he is also unduly deferential: he succumbs almost completely to the admonitions of his diabolic second self, regarding him as 'one who knew right and wrong much better than I did',[102] referring to his ascendancy over him as being 'as complete as that of a huntsman over his dogs'[103] and describing him as 'my tyrant'.[104] Moreover, lack of openness and sincerity can also be seen as a cause of his downfall, since Wringhim/Colwan is a solitary, incommunicative person and by failing to discuss his new acquaintance with others, thereby places himself more completely in the hands of a nightmarish solipsism. By regarding himself as simply the instrument of a divine purpose and nothing more, he devalues his own spiritual identity and his own freedom as an individual. He becomes a cypher in the cause of a good that it is in reality evil, and Hogg thereby implies that such an evil is generated by the denegation of his own authenticity as a free and responsible person. For Wringhim/Colwan's assumption of his tremendous might as a justified person produces a cognate sense of his own nullity. In presenting his memoirs to the reader he insists that it is only his great purpose and not he that will render them of interest, a suggestion that could not be more deeply ironic:

> I depended entirely on the bounty of free grace, holding all the righteousness of man as filthy rags, and believing in the momentous and magnificent truth, that the more heavily loaden with transgressions, the more welcome was the believer at the throne of grace. And I have reason to believe that it was this dependence and this belief that at last ensured my acceptance there.
> I come now to the most important period of my existence, – the period that has modelled my character, and influenced every action of my life, – without which, this

detail of my actions would have been as a tale that hath been told – a monotonous *farrago* – an uninteresting harangue – in short, a thing of nothing. Whereas, lo! it must now be a relation of great and terrible actions, done in the might, and by the commission of heaven. *Amen*.[105]

Self-assertion and self-liquidation are mysteriously combined.

Wringhim/Colwan's actions appear almost entirely involuntary and to be produced by processes over which he can scarcely be deemed to have control, but there is a problem as to how this involuntariness is itself produced. Undoubtedly Hogg sees Calvinism itself as responsible in part for this state of affairs, since election itself is a problematic question and notions of predestination make the individual's own part in his actions seem obscure. At an early age Hogg's protagonist sins freely but regards his sins as accidents and his inability to repent of them as something for which he cannot be blamed: 'the grace of repentance being withheld from me, I regarded myself as in no degree accountable for the failure'.[106] In Hogg's presentation of it Calvinism is capable of being a religion in which energy takes the place of conscience and reason, in which the believer transforms himself into a moral automaton and unquestioningly hurls himself into the murk of the predestined – in the words of Gil-Martin, his diabolic confidante,

> Depend on it, the advice of the great preacher is genuine:
> "What thine hand findeth to do, do it with all thy might, for none of us knows what a day may bring forth? That is, none of us knows what is pre-ordained, but whatever is pre-ordained we *must* do, and none of these things will be laid to our charge."[107]

In some sense the second self of Wringhim/Colwan is therefore liberated by Calvinism; however, even here the question of moral responsibility is obscure, for, since he has been brainwashed by his mother and father, since he has simply followed their guidance, since he is the product of their ideological conditioning, in what real sense can he be held to blame? Like other religious hypocrites, Wringhim/Colwan's fate is to lose touch with himself and with the sources of inner spontaneity. The forcing of his conscience has the effect of distorting his behaviour, of creating inward monitions that are not truly his own but those of his second self, which both is and is not him. The double reinforces and rewards the inauthentic within him. He becomes a sleepwalker who performs actions without truly knowing why he does them. He is possessed in the fullest sense of the word. Even before his killing of the saintly minister Mr Blanchard he dreams of it: 'Thus, by dreaming of the event by night, and discoursing of it by day, it soon became so familiar to my mind, that I almost conceived it as done.'[108] Yet even the commission of it has an involuntary character. Just as Jim in Conrad's *Lord Jim* jumps before he even realises that he has done so, so Wringhim/Colwan's killing is one that he simply reports on without intending: 'and that moment my piece was discharged'.[109] His subsequent murders become still more distorted: he takes Gil-Martin's word for it that he has slain his brother in combat instead of killing him deceitfully from behind; he has no consciousness at all of murdering his mother and his late father's mistress. If his invasion by a second self represents the triumph of the involuntary, the presence of a second self is a paralysis and suspension of reason: 'over the singular delusion that I was two persons, my reasoning faculties had no power'.[110] In effect the existence of a double represents a hiatus in the personality, an inability to correlate aspects of identity, where contradictory aspects separately and unco-ordinately pursue distinct purposes:

I had heart-burnings, longings, and yearnings, that would not be satisfied; and I seemed hardly to be an accountable creature; being thus in the habit of executing transactions of the utmost moment, without being sensible that I did them. I was a being incomprehensible to myself. Either I had a second self, who transacted business in my likeness, or else my body was at times possessed by a spirit over which it had no controul, and of whose actions my own soul was wholly unconscious. This was an anomaly not to be accounted for by any philosophy of mine, and I was many times, in contemplating it, excited to terrors and mental torments hardly describable. To be in a state of consciousness and unconsciousness, at the same time, in the same body and the same spirit, was impossible.[111]

What he feels is not the traditional guilt or remorse but *powerlessness* and impotence; if not responsible, the self that does not know becomes derealised. For identity is traditionally associated with volition, and, although the volitions that he is not consciously in control of may indeed be his volitions, they nevertheless become menacing, because in the multiplications of selves he ceases to know whether there is an authoritative standpoint from which his actions can be viewed. He, Wringhim/Colwan, is caught between the other that advises him and the other that acts. He is a voyeur of himself in which the self he sees may be truer than the self that inspects, so that all theories of the examined self become falsified:

> I was become a terror to myself; or rather, my body and soul were become terrors to each other; and, had it been possible, I felt as if they would have gone to war. I dared not look at my face in the glass, for I shuddered at my own image and likeness. I dreaded the dawning, and trembled at the approach of night, nor was there one thing in nature that afforded me the least delight.[112]

Night signifies the fear of a still further deconstruction of the personality; morning an awakening to the loss of self that might have seemed initially only a bad dream. In the last stages of the novel the double takes over completely. Colwan dons Gil-Martin's garb of green frock-coat and turban as a disguise, which thus becomes the symbol of his alienation from mankind. He is truly an outcast, since he has lost his humanity. The episodes that occur are of a symbolic nature: he is caught in the threads of the weaver's loom, representing his capture in the tortuous threads of a distorted reason, his enclosure in the stables with wild and maddened horses a sign of derangement in reason and in the world. If he is damned it is because he is no longer accountable.

The last vestiges of Wringhim/Colwan's identity are associated with doubting. His fall is associated with the demise of inner spontaneity; he refers to Gil-Martin as 'my great companion and counsellor, who tyrannised over every spontaneous movement of my heart'.[113] Yet, though incapable of acting, he continues to doubt. He questions that the elect are infallible, he is overwhelmed by doubts that hold him back from killing his brother, he fears that fratricide is a mortal sin, and so on. His killing of his brother is also the murder of himself, because in that moment the last vestiges of independence and autonomy are violated. There is nothing now that can hold him back.

Hogg's Justified Sinner becomes a Superman. He is led beyond the normal paths of human action and the ordinary constraints of human morality to a transcendental position in which he believes he is capable of judging all other men. As a justified person 'An exaltation of spirit lifted me, as it were, far above the earth, and the sinful creatures crawling on its surface; and I deemed myself as an eagle among the children of men, soaring on high, and looking down with pity and contempt on the grovelling creatures below.'[114] As judge of others, he consequently lacks any capacity to judge himself. Good and evil are merely functions of his own actions – values that flow from what he does and not criteria distinct from them. Yet as a supremely self-validating law he is also the most powerless and abject of men, faced with a self, behaviour and actions that have become indecipherable. That it is his will and identity that are imperilled Hogg makes abundantly clear in the closing pages, when the sinner is tormented by hideous fiends: 'Horrible as my assailants were in appearance, (and they had all monstrous shapes,) I felt that I would rather have fallen into their hands, than be thus held captive by my defender at his will and pleasure, without having the right or power to say my life, or any part of my will, was my own.'[115] Of all his victims his fate is the worst. The loss of a soul could not be more vividly demonstrated.

Following the publication of *The Monk* the discourse of the Gothic is significantly transposed. From good and noble heroines and heroes whose autonomy, freedom and happiness are thwarted by an oppressive, unjust and hypocritical society the emphasis shifts to the hypocrite and the oppressor. Yet, paradoxically, the criminal hypocrite is accorded a great deal more sympathy than might be expected. The Gothic heroes are perhaps the first fictional protagonists to be thoroughly saturated with negativity, though Milton's Satan and Richardson's Lovelace are their obvious precursors. Psychology becomes a more crucial concern than social criticism, though this presentation of pyschological processes itself embodies a social critique, since, if the characters' minds are vitiated, their upbringing and social and ideological conditioning have importantly contributed to that state of affairs. It is perhaps one of the great contradictions of Romantic literature, as a literature that posits an autonomous self at war with society, that it should simultaneously indicate how problematic that category of the individual is. The Gothic hero is a spiritual cripple, a man in whom the springs of action have dried up, whose attempts to define himself liberate violence, cruelty and madness. But this presence only manifests itself as the truth of the initial absence.

Lewis's reformulation proved influential not simply because of *The Monk*'s great success, but also because the path he indicated was politically expedient. Fiction in the preceding decade had had a radical cast in which major institutions of British society were questioned and criticised and where democratic values came to the fore. But after *The Monk* the critical side of Gothic goes underground. In practice many of the targets are the same; for the Church is a major institution in any society of the time and plays a crucial role in maintaining the dominant ideology and in reinforcing reactionary politics. Holcroft had attacked the Church in *Hugh Trevor*. But, in making religious hypocrisy, especially as manifested in the Catholic Church, a principle target, the Gothic novelists could dissociate themselves from any imputation of supporting radical or revolutionary politics and suggest that their work implied nothing more than the superiority of British culture and British religion to the perverse, alien and corrupted ways of foreigners. That the Gothic always walks a tightrope is attributable not purely and simply to the nature of the genre itself but also to its character as a radical and political discourse that persists in a social context that is hostile and alien to it.

A major problem in the Gothic centres on the notion of involuntary action. The Gothic protagonist typically finds himself performing actions that he did not necessarily intend or envisage. He becomes tied in knots of his own devising and bound by previous involvements and commitments; the very nature of his actions and the reasons for them acquire such an obscurity that he does things while scarcely knowing why, and he scarcely seems to be 'an accountable creature', in Hogg's phrase. Yet on the face of it there seems to be no obvious reason why religious hypocrisy should have such catastrophic consequences or why it should generate a second self over which the individual has no control. One might equally well argue that the hypocrite, as an actor playing a part, would know better than most at what point feigning ends. But, according to Godwin, whose political philosophy and psychology cast such a spell over the Gothic, this is not the case. And, of course, Godwin's political thought is importantly grounded in his analysis of human dispositions. Not the least ground of his criticism of an oppressive and authoritarian society is that it is harmful to all, including the oppressors. It is to this axiom that the Gothic holds fast. For Godwin, an established church has the most severe consequences for its members, since it is a machine for spiritual coercion and the production of hypocrisy, in which individuals are compelled to assent to and espouse doctrines in which they do not truly believe. Similarly, Maturin refers to the 'fatal lesson of monastic institutions', 'the necessity of imposition'.[116] For Godwin, religion cannot represent the dictates of conscience; otherwise it would not be necessary. Therefore it can only represent the deformation of conscience, the perversion of all true thought and feeling:

> The sublimest worship becomes transformed into a source of depravity when it is not consecrated by the testimony of a pure conscience. Truth is the second object in this respect, integrity of heart is the first: or rather, a proposition that, in its abstract nature, is truth itself converts into rank falsehood and mortal poison, if it be professed with the lips only, and abjured by the understanding. It is then the foul garb of hypocrisy. .Instead of elevating the mind above sordid temptations, it perpetually reminds the worshipper of the degrading subjection to which he has yielded. Instead of filling him with sacred confidence, it overwhelms him with confusion and remorse.[117]

So that hypocrisy represents a rent in and disruption of consciousness, an intrusion from without that generates contradiction and instability in the mind.

Godwin objects to codes of religious conformity, such as the

Thirty Nine Articles, which were regularly signed by individuals who did not subscribe to all of them, because their
tendency is 'to make men hypocrites'.[118] He bitterly attacks the
arguments, casuistical in intent and consequence, that have
been used to justify such acts of subscription. For Godwin
truth and untruth cannot exist side by side and he attacks such
duplicity in terms that seem curiously prophetic of the
direction taken by the Gothic novel:

> Can we believe that men shall enter upon their profession
> with so notorious a perversion of reason and truth, and that
> no consequences will flow from it, to infect their general
> character? Rather, can we fail to compare their unnatural
> and unfortunate state with the wisdom and virtue which the
> same industry and virtue might unquestionably have pro-
> duced, if they had been left to their genuine operation?
> They are like the victims of Circe, to whom human
> understanding was preserved entire, that they might more
> exquisitely feel their degraded condition.[119]

The Gothic protagonist is such a figure: a man of signal
capacities warped and distorted by society and by his upbringing who is led astray from his true path. In becoming other
than he is he becomes yet other than he is, yet always the
conscious and unavailing witness of his own degradation and
destruction.

According to Godwin, the price paid by the hypocrite, or
the man who lacks sincerity, is very extensive. In his attempts
to manipulate others he becomes less than a man. Discussing
the virtues of sincerity, the core of Godwin's political thought,
Godwin writes,

> Reserve, deceitfulness, and an artful exhibition of ourselves
> take from the human form its soul, and leave us the
> unanimated semblance of what man might have been; of
> what he would have been, were not every impulse of the
> mind thus stunted and destroyed. If our emotions were not
> checked, we should be truly friends with each other. Our
> character would expand: the luxury of indulging our
> feelings, would raise us to the stature of men.[120]

For Godwin the integrity of the individual is grounded in the
spontaneity of his thoughts and impulses. Once they are

subject to constraint and once a man acts as though he thinks and feels other than really is the case, not only does he lose the core of his identity, but, in addition, his own deceits become a veil through which he becomes unable to perceive or analyse his own behaviour. The cardinal doctrine of the examined self is put in question, both because the individual has no authentic self and because he has no power to examine it. If, as a sincere person, 'I should not harbour bad passions and unsocial propensities, because the habit of expressing my thoughts would enable me to detect and dismiss them in the outset',[121] then, conversely, as a hypocrite I should have no control over my behaviour and be at the mercy of destructive and anti-social passions. In hypocrisy the self becomes occluded. A barrier is raised in the mind between a hypocritical and socially generated false consciousness and the impulses that lie beneath it. If integrity is a function of a transparency and clarity in the mind and conscience in which everything can be clearly viewed, the hypocrite finds his mind transformed into an impenetrable gloom, in which the second self that he dimly espies can be nothing other than himself, yet is a self whom he neither knows nor recognises. The hypocrite can act with impunity, since there is nothing to hold him back. His dark actions are not truly his, since there is no one there who can possess them or know them or assume responsibility for them. Perverse drives are the product of a perverse reason that thwarts and represses everything that is natural and spontaneous. Moreover, this hypocrisy involves an oppressive and manipulative relation to others rather than a relation based on cordiality, sincerity and mutual respect, so that its emotional truth can only be displayed as domination and violence. In going against every natural human feeling, by making others mere objects and victims of an uncontrollable destructiveness, he shows what happens when such natural feelings are destroyed in the first place. Yet the Gothic protagonist is himself finally not to blame. His crimes are society's crimes, his victims theirs. It is civilisation that produces hypocrisy and bad faith. The misdirected struggles of the Gothic are both a symptom of that and an involuntary and perverse rebellion. Yet who can truly witness this madness? Not society, not the hapless individual – only the reader who can ponder the implications of their fate.

PART II

Historical Drama and Historical Novel

3 Historical Drama

'Historical' is a word which we commonly use, but to confront the historical dramas of Goethe and Schiller, the historical novels of Scott, some of the most complex and representative works of a whole phase of European culture, is to recognise how problematic the term is, how nuanced and inflected by usage and tradition. For we are apt to overlook the fact that before the phase of Enlightenment and Romanticism the writing of history was an unusual form of activity; so that the whole sum of history from Herodotus to Gibbon forms a relatively slight and compact body of knowledge when weighed in the balance with theology and works of a doctrinal nature. It was the Enlightenment of Gibbon and Voltaire that freed history from its subordination to religious concerns, but it was the historical drama of Goethe and Schiller and the historical novel of Scott that served to define what the historical was: they presented it not simply as some generalised concern with the past, but as a complex and concrete thematicising of certain problems in human history. We should never see the historical drama or historical novel as simply fiction plus history: we must acknowledge that in this case literature was the forerunner, articulating forms of awareness that only very much later entered the domain of historiography itself. The case of the historical novel presents fewer difficulties: it is a form so definitively tied to the nineteenth century that any discussion of it cannot fail to acknowledge that it is in some way connected with new modes of awareness. But the drama of Goethe and Schiller undoubt-edly presents a puzzle; for are not many of these works tragedies, concerned with fate and human destiny, and therefore does it not involve some kind of programmatic distortion to insist on their *historical* nature rather than on their universality? Moreover, even if this point is to be conceded, what justification have we for attempting to distinguish these plays from the history plays of Shakespeare: are not they all linked by a common concern with prior events that will exhibit them in a dynamic relationship with the present? But to pose the problem in this way is immediately to become aware of a fallacy: which is that there is no uniform and unchanging 'history' with which art engages, and therefore that we should not regard history as a 'field' of concern, but rather see 'the historical' as the name for a whole complex of concerns which the past can help to articulate. Passing by the illusion that the historical genres are some kind of dangerous engagement between fiction and truth, we should be prepared to see them precisely as thematicised and try to decode the messages which they attempt to communicate. We must see them not as sculptured monoliths as impressive and impenetrable as the Sphinx, but as attempts to present a new form of awareness through structured thematic relations. The task of analysis is not to postulate some historical beyond which drama and novel gesture more or less imperfectly towards, but to show how the genre itself articulates this awareness. The historical genre is historical in a specific way: it invariably focuses on the processes of social change, on the transition from one form of society to another in which each type of society is seen as having its own characteristic value system and where the transition itself is seen as irreversible. In this light, society appears not as fixed, normative and invariable but becomes something that can itself be *questioned*. It embodies the notion not that man is made for society, but that society is made for man: the test of any given society becomes its capacity for releasing and developing the highest and noblest propensities of man. It is only from this standpoint that the programme of Schiller's *On the Aesthetic Education of Man* can be understood. For Schiller, the goal of political activity is identifiable with the purposes of aesthetic education: both aim or should aim at the fullest development of human potentiality. Communities should not promote knowledge, memory, mechanical skill or mere tabularising intelligence at the expense of other potentialities. For Schiller, humanity is to be opposed to savagery; it is the creation of culture and will only be completely fulfilled as an ideal when man has achieved a completely harmonious relationship with society. If earlier forms of social organisation – the Greece of

Pericles, feudal France or Germany, tribal Scotland – offer images of a moral and spiritual integrity that seem to surpass the present, the act of presenting these cultures in the light of change serves to constitute a perennial source of hope; for the very pathos of the moment when a particular form of society passes away is transfigured by the nobility of the hero who continues to embody its highest virtues even when its hour is past – like the last triumphant chord of a piano composition that is held by the sustaining pedal. Man is shown as being simultaneously the product of his own time and having the capacity to transcend it. The motto of the historical drama and historical novel could well be taken from Schiller's *Aesthetic Education*: 'Live with your century; but do not be its creature.'[1]

The remote instigator of the complex body of ideas deployed through the medium of the historical genre is undoubtedly Montesquieu, whose *L'Esprit des lois* created an intersection of historical, political and sociological awareness that made it the most influential work of its day. And yet these ideas are not fully present in the work of Montesquieu, who appears rather as a man who sets off various trains of inquiry and speculation, a beater, who drove a covey of pheasants before the attentive, assembled guns. In *L'Esprit des lois* there are four ideas that Montesquieu insists on that would seem to be particularly significant: Honour, Corruption, Empire and Despotism. The paradox of Montesquieu's approach is that it is simultaneously objective and partisan. On the one hand Montesquieu simply appears to be analysing what type of laws are most appropriate, whether of monarchy, democracy or despotism; on the other the book is undoubtedly a warning against despotism in all its forms and especially against the danger of freer society relapsing or sliding into a state of despotism. Despotism is the ultimate corruption of political institutions. Corruption is an extremely alarming concept: it serves to direct the reader's attention to problems of social change and to analyse the reasons for a transition from one state of society to another. 'The danger', Montesquieu warns, 'is not when the state passes from one moderate government to another moderate government, as from a republic to a monarchy, or from a monarchy to a republic; but when it is precipitated from a moderate to a despotic government.'[2] A warning against despotism was, at the same time, a warning against large empires, which in Montesquieu's view necessitated despotic authority:

> It is necessary that the quickness of the prince's resolutions should supply the distance of the places they are sent to; that fear should prevent the remissness of the distant governor or magistrate; that the law should be derived from a single person, and should shift continually, according to the accidents which incessantly multiply in a state in proportion to its extent.[3]

In Montesquieu's analysis one of the main characteristics that distinguishes a monarchy from despotism is that it is more restricted in size. Montesquieu warns that a monarchy ought not to 'aim at conquests beyond the natural limits of its government'[4], and 'When a monarchy has extended its limits by the conquest of neighbouring provinces, it should treat those provinces with great lenity.'[5] In the Germany of Goethe and Schiller, these animadversions had a particular significance: they suggested that the role of the Austrian Empire was harmful, potentially despotic, even unnatural. Most of the historical drama of Goethe and Schiller is directly concerned with the corrupting effects of a centralising and powerful empire and seeks to show that the tendency towards empire is directly connected with the erosion of personal liberty.

In *L'Esprit des lois*, Montesquieu made direct connections between forms of political organisation and types of moral behaviour in a way that was both original and influential. He pointed out in the most trenchant fashion that virtue was incompatible with monarchy, honour with despotism. He ventured to affirm that 'in a monarchy it is extremely difficult for the people to be virtuous'[6] and referred to the 'wretched character' of courtiers as follows:

> Ambition in idleness; meanness mixed with pride; a desire of riches without industry; aversion to truth; flattery, perfidy, violation of engagements, contempt of civil duties, fear of the prince's virtue, hope from his weakness, but, above all, a perpetual ridicule cast upon virtue, are, I think, the characteristics by which most courtiers in all ages and countries have been constantly distinguished.[7]

Virtue at court is impossible because of the dependent position of the courtier, while the code of honour of the nobleman will not be found in a despotism, because the relative autonomy which the nobleman enjoys will have been abolished: 'as honour has its laws and rules; as it knows not how to submit; as it depends in great measure on a man's own caprice, and not on that of another person: it can be found only in countries in which the constitution is fixed, and where they are governed by settled laws'.[8]

Obviously, Montesquieu's work embodies many diverse tendencies; its contribution to the development of Western thought is based on Montesquieu's many pregnant passing allusions rather than on its pretensions to systematic analysis. Moreover, in reading Montesquieu it is important to attend to the tone, to try to catch the general drift of a man who was, after all, writing at a time when expression had to be guarded. A superficial reading of *L'Esprit des lois* will yield a theory of climatological determinism, but the real bias that informs the work is that of a determined and self-confident provincialism. The Baron was raised in Bordeaux, where the country estate of his family was located. It was there that he spent most of his life, being actively involved both in local politics and in the Academy of Science at Bordeaux. His periods of residence in Paris were usually brief and were associated with many personal rebuffs and disappointments. It seems symbolic that Montesquieu's first attempt to obtain election to the Académie Française should have been rejected on the ground that he was a resident of Bordeaux. Montesquieu's response seems to have been not an attempt to purge himself of the guilt of provincialism but rather a determination to validate it. *L'Esprit des lois* is saturated with a distrust of centralised power – of precisely the tendencies exemplified by the reign of Louis XIV. His great contemporary Voltaire, on the other hand, in his history of the period, viewed with notable complacency the fact that 'the state acquired a sort of geometrical unity, with each line leading to the centre'.[9]

Indeed, it would be difficult to think of two works published within three years of one another that are more dissimilar in character than *L'Esprit des lois* (1748) and *Le Siecle de Louis XIV* (1751). Voltaire is perhaps the first philosopher of modernisation, and, if anything characterises his portrait of the age, it is his readiness to characterise absolutist France as the very type of the modern: in the development of industry and commerce, in the establishment of a powerful standing army, in the diffusion of culture and the spread of more civilised manners, in the suppression of ancient and outdated feudal laws – 'the rubbish from a ruined Gothic building'[10] – and the decline of religious controversy. Voltaire had scant sympathy for French Protestants, whom he viewed as benighted religious fanatics. With reference to Louis XIV's persecution of religious dissent, Voltaire could only observe, 'It was a strange contrast to see such harsh and pitiless orders emanating from a pleasure-loving court famous for its gentle manners, its graces and its social charm'[11] – a remark which escapes bathos only through the terrifying weighting of values in which the lives of fanatics scarcely tip the scales against so much charm. More generally, Voltaire's sense of the progressive tendency of Louis XIV's reign is well represented by the following passage:

> the glory which for fifty years surrounded Louis XIV, together with his power and the firm and vigorous nature of his government, deprived the reformed party, as it did all other orders of state, of any idea of resistance. The magnificent entertainments of a pleasure-loving court even made the pedantry of the Huguenots look ridiculous. With the development of good taste, the psalms of Marot and Besa gradually came to evoke nothing but distaste. These psalms, which had charmed the court of Francis II, appealed only to the populace under Louis XIV. Sound philosophy, which began to make its way in the world toward the middle of the century, was bound to contribute even further in the long run to making decent people disgusted with controversial disputes.[12]

For Voltaire the establishment of unchecked centralised power, the establishment of uniformity in matters of religion, politics, the legal system, taste and behaviour, is tangible evidence of the coming of a better world. To his mind, difference, above all, is the *infame* that must be crushed.

Montesquieu did not share Voltaire's complacency about absolutism. If the law as a social institution particularly concerns him, it is because he believes that laws are an important safeguard against the abuse of power and a method of restricting it. Laws are a safety net that can prevent a fall into despotism. Far from being intoxicated with the civilising potential of the court, Montesquieu sees in it only a source of corruption and moral decay. He distrusted centralised power partly because of this moral corruption (and Acton's famous correlation of corruption and power is very much in the spirit of Montesquieu), partly because it could lead to a totalitarian monopolisation of power in which distinctive levels are eliminated, and partly because he felt that only the inhabitants of a particular locality could be truly responsive to its particular interests and needs. Montesquieu's work sets up a pattern of oppositions that can be displayed as follows:

Despotism	Moderation
Unification of powers	Separation of powers
Court	Provinces
Corruption	Virtue
Erosion of or absence of traditional rights	Retention of traditional rights

By contrast with Voltaire, Montesquieu was remarkably responsive to feudalism; for feudalism might well seem to typify everything the Enlightenment defined itself as against. His suggestion that the British system of government, which he so much admired, was borrowed from early German culture – 'This beautiful system was invented first in the woods'[13] – fathered a whole tradition of Anglo-German historiography. But more interesting still is his poetic description of the feudal laws themselves: 'The feudal laws form a very beautiful prospect. A venerable old oak raises its lofty head to the skies, the eye sees from afar its spreading leaves; upon drawing nearer, it perceives the trunk but does not discern the root; the ground must be dug up to discover it.'[14] This passage seems to encapsulate not simply feudalism but the Romantic perception of the world: the belief that institutions are organic and all of a piece; the sense of nostalgia and loss for a world which has passed away; the recognition that to understand this other culture is a complex matter that demands deep study, reflection and inquiry, an analysis of origins.

Montesquieu's writings were widely influential, but they struck a particular chord in Scotland and Germany, both provincial centres of culture that were acutely conscious of their own identity and resentful of cultural and political imperialism. In particular, Montesquieu made a deep impression on Adam Ferguson – who in 1767 wrote, perhaps with excessive modesty, 'when I recollect what the President Montesquieu has written I am at a loss to tell why I should treat of human affairs'[15] – and on the young Herder in his Riga period (1764–9). Ferguson presented diachronically what Montesquieu had presented through a synchronic method. Ferguson dealt with determinate stages in 'the history of civil society' and with the transitions from one to another. But Ferguson, writing out of a different cultural milieu, also stressed the importance of the division of labour, the harmful consequences of bourgeois individualism, and the virtues of a simpler and more heroic form of society, in which the leader and his followers live on the same level and follow the same honour code. By this Ferguson certainly had in mind the traditional Scottish clan. Ferguson's implication that this was a more organic form of society certainly had great consequences: Carlyle's powerful critique of the alienation of industrial society in *Past and Present*, his insistence on the need for leaders to be closely attached to their own people and to be deeply responsive to their needs and wishes, his nostalgia for a form of society where people were closely tied together by bonds of loyalty, is worked out along thoroughly Fergusonian lines. But what is most characteristic and important in Ferguson in his determination to demythologise the notion of historical development, to sidestep Rousseau's suggestion that man has lost his innocence in the development of civilisation, just as much as the Hobbesian notion that he has escaped a brutal and vicious state of nature. For Ferguson every form of society will have its pros and cons. He writes,

> We are generally at a loss to conceive how mankind can subsist under customs and manners extremely different from our own; and we are apt to exaggerate the misery of barbarous times, by an imagination of what we ourselves should suffer in a situation to which we are not accustomed. But every age hath its consolations, as well as its sufferings.

In the interval of occasional outrages, the friendly intercourse of men, even in their rudest condition, is affectionate
and happy. In rude ages, the persons and properties of
individuals are secure; because each has a friend, as well as
an enemy; and if one is disposed to molest; the other is
ready to protect; and the very admiration of valour which in
some instances tends to sanctify violence, inspires likewise
certain maxims of generosity and honour, that tend to
prevent the commission of wrongs.[16]

Ferguson's readiness to acknowledge the perspective of an
alien culture is particularly striking because it remains no
abstract formulation, but is supported by a footnote that cites
the case of a man who happily adopted Scythian customs
because he found the Scythian way of life more congenial than
the domination of Rome. Within the classical tradition such an
equivalence is unthinkable, since it means placing 'civilisation'
and 'barbarism' on the same footing. This transvaluation
became explicit in Delacroix's marvellous painting *Ovid among
the Scythians*, where the conventional image of an Ovid
suffering under the ultimate sanction of banishment from the
metropolitan centre is supplanted by a scene of lyricism,
beauty and innocence from which Ovid, because of his
cultural conditioning, must remain apart. Amid the scantily
clad Scythians Ovid's robes bind him like a chain. But to
acknowledge how different life may be under circumstances
other than those with which we are familiar demands a great
imaginative leap: it is therefore not altogether surprising that
the vehicle for this new awareness should have been imaginative literature.

The belief in the distinctiveness of particular cultures was
asserted even more forcefully by Herder. He recognises the
cultural differences described by Montesquieu but instead
feels that Montesquieu in attempting to subsume all these
variations under general laws is fighting the sea. Having
mentioned a number of different types of government in
different countries Herder continues, 'Who can go through
all the smaller republics and state constitutions – in all lands,
in all their changes? Even Rome alone – how much it contained! When was it consistent with itself? Never!'[17] Herder's
notion of the incommensurability of cultures is generated by

the concept of individual genius. If, as Young had insisted, every individual has his own particular genius, if each person is unique, the same is true, perhaps even more true, of a whole nation. Herder in *Yet Another Philosophy of History* (1774) argues quite explicitly along these lines:

> Have you noticed how inexpressible is the individuality of one man, how difficult it is to know distinctly what distinguishes him, how he feels and lives, how differently his eyes see, his soul measures, his heart experiences everything? What depth there is in the character of a single nation which, even after repeated and probing observation manages to evade the word that would capture it and render it recognisable enough for general comprehension and empathy. If this is so, how can one survey an ocean of entire peoples, times and countries, comprehend them in one glance, one sentiment or one word, a weak incomplete silhouette of a word? A whole *tableau vivant* of manners, customs, necessities, particularities of earth and heaven must be added to it; you enter the spirit of a nation before you can share even one of its thoughts or deeds.[18]

Here is a characteristic paradox. Every nation is so complex and many-sided that it resists every attempt to define it and circumscribe it; language is inadequate to the task. The project of sociology, the attempt to seek out uniformities and laws, is inherently flawed. Yet what Herder takes away with one hand he gives back with the other: the notion of 'spirit' provides a unifying principle under which the manifold assemblage of institutions, practices, customs and traits can be grasped. It is in terms of 'spirit', not laws, that reality becomes tangible.

At this point it is necessary more precisely to delineate the nature of the intellectual configuration that shaped the historical drama and historical novel. It must be distinguished from the historical accounts of Adam Smith and Rousseau. Adam Smith's sense of history developing through four cultural stages – hunting, pastoral, agricultural and commercial – is primarily analytical and does not necessitate a particular emotional stance, although such a tendency is seen as broadly progressive. Rousseau takes a more pessimistic view of the development of civilisation. Since man's natural inclinations are transformed by the inequalities of civilisation, it is such a state of affairs that is responsible for our discontents. Rousseau's thinking pivots around notions of loss and recapture: if the possibility of recapture is problematic, the loss itself is certain. Moreover, in his *Discourse on the Origin of Inequality*, he placed the moment of the fall very far back in history, in the prehistorical stage when men first adopted the practice of agriculture. But for Goethe, Schiller and Scott the critical moment of transition occurs very much later in history. It is connected with the decline of feudal society, which had provided a basis for individual and regional autonomy, and with the development of centralising, modernising powers that tend to absolutism and despotism. For Ferguson, who provides the closest analogue to their thinking and who deploys concepts drawn from Montesquieu and Adam Smith, though in a manner that is at the same time innovatory and distinctive, the trend away from individual autonomy towards a more centralised type of society is also bound up with the development of the commercial type of society. This linkage is particularly clear in the case of Louis XIV. Additionally, the problematic of historical literature is neither progressive or regressive, but dialectical. The value systems of different cultures are relativised; there is a recognition that modes of behaviour found in one type of society will not manifest themselves in another that is differently organised, and that after a determinate transition there can never be any going back. But at the same time the lost values are not forgotten: they stand as a continual reminder of the many-faceted nature of human potentiality and gesture beyond the artwork in such a way as to imply that they can be recapitulated and incorporated in the transition to a new and higher level. The significance of the historical genre, its refusal to take up a posture of either nostalgia at or acquiescence in the course of historical development is sharply in evidence in Schiller's critique of the idyll, which is also a critique of Rousseau:

> Set before the beginnings of civilisation, they exclude together with its disadvantages all its advantages, and by their very nature they find themselves necessarily in conflict with it. *Theoretically*, then, they lead us backwards, whilst

practically they lead us forwards and ennoble us. Unhappily
they place this purpose *behind* us, *toward* which they should,
however, lead us, and hence they imbue us only with a sad
feeling of loss, not with joyous feelings of hope.[19]

Our involvement with history cannot be either a matter of
abstract and arbitrary preferences or of striking grandiose
moral postures, but must involve a confrontation with the
complex and recalcitrant processes of history in which the
problem of value is worked out. The choices and the options,
whether in the past or in the present, are themselves historically determined. This profound insight is at the core of the
new historical genre.

   At the same time, it would be wrong to assume that the
historical drama of Goethe and Schiller represents an engagement with historical materials pure and simple. It is also
significantly enmeshed with aesthetic theory and aesthetic
debate. Lessing is the significant figure, for in Germany no
one did more than Lessing to destroy the influence of
neo-classicism. In his *Hamburg Dramaturgy* (1767–8) Lessing
insists, in the spirit of Young, on the superiority of creativity to
mere unimaginative copying: 'To act with a purpose is what
raises man above the brutes, to invent with a purpose, to
imitate with a purpose, is that which distinguishes genius from
the petty artists who only invent to invent, imitate to imitate.'[20]
But, of course, he also questions the general terms in which
the debate has been couched, highlighting the fact that the
issue is also a moral one: purposive activity is free activity and
intelligent activity. In the task of dislodging French neo-
classicism from its position of influence Lessing calls to his aid
the practice of the English stage and the theory of Aristotle: he
shows the French drama to be inferior to the former and to
have perverted the latter. Not the least noteworthy feature of
the historical drama of Goethe and Schiller is that it deliberately flouts the unities of time, place and action and defies
neo-classicism in other ways: by failing to be decorous and by
not maintaining a unity of tone; by ignoring Voltaire's
insistence on total clarity and transparency of motive and on a
complete historical fidelity. Goethe's utter indifference to the
requirements of neo-classicism could not be more obvious in
Götz von Berlichingen. It is virtually a primer in how not to write

a neo-classical play. *Götz* is described by Goethe as a tragedy. Voltaire had criticised Corneille's *Le Cid* on the grounds that a box on the ear should not be permitted in a tragedy – so Goethe includes one in the very first scene! In the second scene he has Götz wander off stage for no very pressing reason, leaving a notable hiatus in the dialogue until he returns. Lessing's writing tended to encourage, if it did not altogether sponsor, such infringements; it also tended to promote a national bias in the German drama by emphasising the advantage for the dramatist of drawing his material from native customs and events.

Lessing's other major critical work, *Laocoon*, bears an altogether more complex relationship to the historical genre. *Laocoon* is often seen primarily as a repudiation of *ut pictura poesis*, but to present the argument in this way is to over-simplify it; for Lessing's disagreement with Winckelmann is as notable as his refutation of Horace. In its day Winckelmann's *History of Ancient Art* represented something of an intellectual counter-revolution. Eighteenth-century aesthetic theory in England had been concerned to assert the superiority of the sublime to the beautiful. Winckelmann reasserted the authority of the beautiful by recasting the controversy in historical terms, a manoeuvre that represents one of the very first manifestations of historicism. Winckelmann distinguishes three main styles: the grand, the beautiful and the decadent. He argues that these stages follow one another with the inevitability of the stages in the life-cycle of an organism: the grand style is simpler and less sophisticated, the beautiful represents the ideal of harmoniousness and maturity, while the decadent is the final phase where deterioration has both become necessary (since what can be better than perfection?) and inevitable. Winckelmann's style of typologising has become so widely copied in Western culture that the arbitrariness of such models and the tenuous assumptions that underpin them go all too often unrecognised. It is highly praiseworthy that Lessing recognised the dangers inherent in such a 'methodology' long before such practices had become an intellectual scandal. Lessing objects both to Winckelmann's hierarchisation of values and to his determination to structure works of art into schematic and inflexible historical sequences – so that works that are beautiful and harmonious can occur only at the point of maturity, with all others assigned to either an earlier or a later date. Winckelmann, of course, established the mode of working of the art historian, which need not necessarily be as suspect as his own practice, since general assumptions about stylistic consistency may well be justified; but Lessing recognised how it could lead to a forcing of evidence, that the movement from artwork to cultural phase to criterion of value could lead to a nightmarish circularity. Lessing shatters Winckelmann's entire structure of assumptions. He shows that noble simplicity and quiet grandeur need not be the highest or only set of values; he suggests that in literature other values may be more important and implies that works of high aesthetic merit may occur in a later cultural phase. In this way *Laocoon* is a subtle blow struck on behalf of the moderns against the ancients: there can be no single set of criteria applicable to works of art nor a single moment when greatness can flourish. Moreover, Lessing's distinction between painting, which is concerned to fix a single, transitory moment, and the poetic, which, as his example of Homer's description of the shield of Achilles shows, is always concerned with duration – since Homer shows not just the shield but the whole process of making it – serves to define and orient literature towards the historical. Literature does not just show things as they are but shows how they come to be so; its power to exhibit the interconnectedness of events in time and to weigh their relative significance and meaning is of incalculable importance. Lessing does not hesitate to designate Homer as 'sublime' or to speak disparaging of the tendency of the artist to assemble beautiful bodies in beautiful attitudes – an aesthetic commonplace that is punningly reflected in Keats's 'O Attic shape! Fair attitude!'. By contrast, the great virtue of imaginative literature, to which the example of Homer testifies, is that it possesses the power to *analyse*; to endow men, objects and historical events with a reality and density by presenting them historically; to liberate men by showing them that their destiny is open, not closed. In Lessing's conception of literature we find both a rationale for the historical drama and a striking adumbration of principles subsequently associated with Brecht's epic theatre. Lessing's *Laocoon* is the orchestral prelude to a whole new phase in German culture.

The historical drama is relativist in that it consciously

juxtaposes different sets of values, but it is not unequivocally determinist. Rather, the very procedure of juxtaposition, the strategy of focusing on a historical period of transition, when a feudal type of society characterised by freedom and personal autonomy is being displaced by centralised power, serves to open up an area of freedom for the spectator, by reminding him of a nexus of possibilities which once had a historical reality and which become revivified at the moment of their disappearance. Its posture, initially at least, is of challenging the *status quo*, of throwing down the gauntlet, not passively acquiescing. The mythic core of the historical genre is the anachronistic hero, the noble, honest, independent and courageous man, who stands as a vivid reminder of the highest human qualities in a dark time, when compliance, obseqiousness and deceit appear the order of the day. In his *Aesthetics* Hegel aptly discusses Goethe's *Götz von Berlichingen* and Schiller's *Die Räuber* under the heading 'The Reconstitution of Individual Independence', for the plays are dramatic gestures that seek to recover the notion of individual autonomy and to show that this is to be regarded not as a congenial fiction but as an existential necessity. Of Goethe's play Hegel writes,

> The time of Götz and Franz von Sickingen is the interesting period in which chivalry with the independence of noble individuals was passing away before a newly arising objective order and legal system. Goethe's great insight is revealed by his choosing as his first subject this contact and collision between the medieval heroic age and the legality of modern life. For Gotz and Sickingen are still heroes who, with their personality, their courage, and their upright, straightforward good sense, propose to regulate the states of affairs in their narrower or wider scope by their own independent efforts; but the new order of things brings Gotz himself into the wrong and destroys him. For chivalry and the feudal system in the Middle Ages are the only proper ground for this sort of independence.[21]

Here Hegel fastens on to an essential feature of the historical genre: a particular form of society is seen as defining the field of individual potential. A society is implicitly judged by the scope that it offers the individual: this is the essential criterion. Moreover, if Götz is placed in the wrong this does not at all mean that he is in the wrong; on the contrary, we recognise that Götz himself has not diverged one iota from his traditional code and that a society that seeks to pass judgement upon him commits a double crime, by wronging a noble individual and by falling away from its own former values. In the historical genre we find the strongest and most unequivocal validation of the role of the individual; for the historical perspective makes true what would otherwise only be a conundrum: that Götz is the only man in step!

In Goethe's play Götz's iron hand becomes symbolic of his unswerving integrity; the handshake he offers is an unalterable as his oath. Goethe sets up a pattern of oppositions that is strikingly reminiscent of the Gothic novel: on the one hand, openness, truth, honesty; on the other, concealment, treachery and deceit. Goethe shows that the German bishops seek to evade moral obligations under a casuistical form of words. He presents Adela von Walldorf as typifying the new spirit of the age. She seduces Weislingen from his loyalty to Götz and persuades him that his oaths are of no consequence, yet later poisons him when he will no longer serve her ambitious purposes. Weislingen is the shifter, the wavering hero, who haunts the historical genre in so many different guises; a man torn between two competing value systems, uncertain as to which he should commit his allegiance. His death by poison, a surreptitious method, is representative of the encroaching moral decadence: fittingly Adela is herself condemned by a secret tribunal. Götz's commitment to truth is conveyed by his blunt and forceful manner of speaking. When his wife, Elizabeth, describes the Imperial Commissioners who are to judge him – 'Their awful presence, the splendour of their dress, and the golden chains which mark their dignity...' – Götz completes her sentence with the words, 'Becomes them like a necklace on a sow.'[22] The garments themselves appear as a form of symbolic deceit, casting splendour and lustre on an ignoble purpose. Götz's sense of freedom and independence has no place in the new order of things. He is imprisoned and dies in the garden attached to the prison, with a last glimpse of the sky. Götz's final words serve to mark the moment of transition. He cries, 'Lock your hearts carefully as your doors. The age of frankness and freedom is past – that of treachery begins.'[23] Yet he dies with the words 'Freedom! freedom!' on his lips. The final utterance of the play, Lerse's 'woe to the future, that cannot know thee',[24] involves a complex referencing out of the dramatic context, since the audience is thus forcibly reminded of what, supposedly, it cannot know. Yet the radiance of Götz and what he represents is all the more intense for being glimpsed at the moment of its passing and serves as an exemplary reminder that a man can transcend and resist the spirit of his time. Weislingen senses what Götz most deeply signifies: 'He alone is great and happy who fills his own station of independence, and has neither to command nor to obey',[25] but he cannot put it into practice. The example of Götz acquires meaning only in action.

Goethe's dilemma in *Götz von Berlichingen* is that the very values he invokes as positive must simultaneously be shown as problematic: society can be criticised only from a perspective that has already disappeared. His subsequent dramatic ventures represent an attempt to overcome this. They hinge on the paradox that ancient = modern; the going back to an earlier system of values is seen not simply as a return but as a progressive movement beyond the present. Knowledge of the past is no passive mirroring but represents a conscious and dynamic moral decision, through which human activity can be revalorised and endowed with an independent significance. Such a procedure cannot be seen as anything other than dialectical; for both Goethe and Hegel posit as a goal the recovery of a lost totality of being that would, at the same time, represent a transition to a higher level.

Egmont is an anachronistic figure, since he represents the ideal of the complete, harmonious personality in an age of discord and division. For Goethe, Egmont is a conscious going beyond those earlier avatars Werther and Götz, since Egmont is pointedly contrasted with the Werther-like figure of Brackenburg in his nobility and heroism, while, unlike Götz, his actions do not seal him off from the future but contribute to the shaping of it. The many virtues attributed to Egmont (almost, indeed, to the point of stultification) – his frankness, openness, naturalness and spontaneity; his tolerance, courage and stoical acceptance of destiny – all these are insisted on by Goethe because they represent the value-system of the heroic age and because the very fact that they are now anachronistic endows them with a greater luminosity. To be uncontaminated in a world characterised by deceit and intrigue is a profound spiritual achievement. In *Egmont* a struggle to define the modern is at the centre of the action. For Margaret the Regent, the development of Protestantism in the Netherlands is viewed as an innovation and therefore suspect. For Egmont, on the other hand, such a tendency toward freedom in religious belief is closely bound up with the attempt to preserve and recover traditional freedoms of the individual. It is the Dutch people, with their strong sense of their own past and of their time-honoured rights, who are the traditionalists. Modernisation is identified with the drive toward centralisation – the despatching from Spain of the Duke of Alba, in order to bring the Netherlands even more closely under Spanish supervision and control. The case of Holland exhibits to perfection Montesquieu's thesis that small states tend to the preservation of personal liberty, empires toward despotism. The secret diplomacy, intrigue, deception and treachery that characterise Alba's approach to problems are symptomatic of a deep-seated moral decadence. Moreover, even Orange, the other leader of the Dutch people, is not free from this: his action in avoiding the meeting with Alba, which for Egmont leads to death, may well be politic but it lacks nobility and involves concessions to the very evil against which they are fighting. In 'choosing' his own death by remaining the free, spontaneous and honest man that he has always been, Egmont refuses even the slightest compromise with the tendencies of his age. His acquiescence in his own fate, the bracketing of character and destiny, is the sign of the authentic, autonomous personality. Yet this cannot truly die. His sacrifice paradoxically preserves the value it represents as a legacy to his people. Indeed, only this gesture can express both the personality of Egmont and the noble, yet uncompromising spirit of the Revolution. In this moment past, present and future are one. Significantly, the last word in the play is 'example' (*Beispiel*). Egmont furnishes the pattern for a better world.

Iphigenie auf Tauris establishes itself as the culminating work in this Goethe trilogy and, equally, as the resolution of the problem posed by the anachronistic hero. *Götz von Berlichingen* gestured beyond the play to a dilemma which it could only formulate; *Egmont* pointed within the play to a historical resolution that lay outside it; but *Iphigenie* poses and resolves within its own compass the conflict between past and present. *Iphigenie auf Tauris* is the definitive articulation of the values of the Enlightenment; its 'classicism' has little to do with the Greece of Aeschylus and Sophocles and everything to do with the primacy assigned to the individual and with the concern with truth, purity, spontaneity and openness that is so characteristic of late eighteenth-century Europe. Although this is not made thematically explicit, it is significant that the action of *Iphigenie auf Tauris* centres on a cultural relativism, the contrast between Greek and Scythian culture: and that the Scythians, as in Ferguson, should be assigned a more positive significance, though Goethe may not have actually been acquainted with Ferguson's work. Goethe's wise ignorance kept him in touch with much contemporary thinking without ever leaving irrefutable traces. The Scythians are direct and honest, but their culture is flawed by the barbarous practice of executing strangers. The Greeks, on the other hand, are part of a culture where treachery and deceit are regarded as perfectly normal – so that such behaviour requires no justification – but which has a deeply entrenched tradition of hospitality toward strangers. It is the role of Iphigeneia, who has long served as a priestess at the temple of Diana in Tauris and who has persuaded the Scythians to moderate the severity of their treatment of foreigners, to mediate between the two cultures. The arrival in Tauris of her brother Orestes seeking sanctuary creates within her a severe conflict of loyalties: shall she support her long-lost brother or King Thoas, who has behaved with such understanding towards her? The obvious solution to her dilemma is deceit, and this, in fact, is the course which Orestes and Pylades urge upon her. But Iphigeneia rejects it: not simply because deceit and deception are deeply abhorrent to her, but also because to dissimulate would constitute a refusal to act as transmitter and mediator between Greek and Scythian culture, enabling each to transcend its cultural limitations. The Greeks must learn the value of openness; the Scythians the virtue of hospitality and compassion. Iphigeneia's purity of heart is the conductor which permits the transmission of positive values but which negates negativity. Though Iphigeneia herself symbolises the transcendence of limitation in each of the cultural codes, this is in itself not enough: what she herself has realised must be realised in others. The revelation of the truth is given a paramount moral and dramatic significance within the structure of the play. The traditional Greek device of narrative disclosure is here a categorical imperative. The play is a succession of disclosures. Iphigeneia tells Thoas that she is descended from the doomed race of Tantalus. Orestes is forced to reveal his true identity to his sister Iphigeneia, who in turn tells him who she is, and, finally, Iphigeneia identifies the strangers to Thoas. This last step is fraught with danger, since Thoas has the power and the right to execute Orestes, Pylades and Iphigeneia herself. But Iphigeneia does not hesitate, since she believes that her own openness will be answered by a similar frankness and spontaneity in others. Against Thoas's appeal to ancient custom she invokes the still more ancient custom of charity and hospitality toward strangers. She asks Thoas to act as his *feelings* prompt, to give an instantaneous response to their request for a free passage back to Greece. Thoas tells them to go – proof that the heart has its reasons that reason knows not of, that spontaneity can never lead man astray. But the play has, at the same time, an intellectual movement: Thoas realises the moral value of charity. Orestes recognises that there can be no opportunistic solution to the curse on the house of Atreus; release can only come, if at all, through repentance and purity of heart. Both Orestes and Iphigeneia invoke the image of the lost innocence of childhood. But the unity of being that seemed vanished for ever at the end of the play is restored. In this way the theme of the anachronistic hero is psychologised: the 'lost values' represent a world that *can* be recovered through a transition to a higher level. The ennoblement of the conclusion represents a cancellation of all that is negative in the past, a preservation of all that is positive; a liberating gesture that is both determined in so far as it represents the pressure of culture to go beyond itself, and free because it is the spontaneous action of the individual. *Iphigenie auf Tauris* represents the dialectical transcendence of past and present, Scythian and Greek, the possibility of a progressive movement in history. In this way the pessimistic implications of *Götz von Berlichingen* are nullified.

For Schiller the idea of anachronism was as crucial as it was for Goethe, but it manifests itself in a much more problematic fashion. The exhortation 'Live with your century; but do not be its creature' represented for Schiller not an obvious maxim but the most arduous intellectual and moral programme imaginable. Only in his late works did Schiller present the possibility of transcendence that Goethe had postulated from the outset.

Initially, the notion of 'anachronistic hero' assumes the form of a contradiction in terms. Schiller's early heroic rebel, Karl Moor, traumatised by his father's brutal and final rejection of him, turns his back on society and becomes the leader of a band of outlaws. He sees this as the opportunity to wreak summary justice on the wealthy, greedy and extortionate, who shelter behind the law. Karl is made into a sympathetic figure, partly because the spectator is shown the cruel machinations employed by his brother, Franz, against him, and partly because Karl is seen as a potentially heroic figure who can transcend the pettiness of the age. When Karl exclaims,

> Never yet has law formed a great man; 'tis liberty that breeds giants and heroes. Oh! that the spirit of Herman still glowed in his ashes! Set me at the head of an army of fellows like myself, and out of Germany shall spring a republic compared to which Rome and Sparta will be but as nunneries[26]

he is explicitly shown as establishing connections with noble examples from the past that offer hope for renewal in the present. Moreover, his love for Amelia and hers for him are symbolically dignified through the song Amelia sings of the parting of Hector and Andromache. So Karl is always potentially more than a Werther. But, since Karl is explicitly presented as a criminal and as a man whose actions have terrible, if unintended, consequences, it is rather difficult to determine precisely what it is that Schiller sees in his creation or why he feels he has a particular claim on our attention. Schiller argues that he has given Karl many redeeming features, since an utterly depraved character is not a suitable subject for art, and yet Karl's crimes, if we respond to them with the horror that Schiller evidently envisaged, have the effect of cancelling his heroism altogether. From the later standpoint of Schiller's *Naive and Sentimental Poetry* it is not hard to see where Karl has gone wrong: he has failed to see that

> you must subject yourself to all the *ills* of civilization, respect them as the natural conditions of the only good.... Be not afraid of the confusion around you, only of the confusion within you; strive after unity, but do not seek conformity; strive after calm, but through harmony, not through the cessation of your activity.[27]

But there are obvious dangers in reading back into the work of a twenty-two year old poet the sober reflections of a man of thirty-six. In this same passage Schiller insists that one should not overreact to the injustices of modern society, but his younger incarnation hardly felt that we should respond with such equanimity either to the fate of Karl or to that of Kosinsky, who owes his life to the willingness of his intended bride to become the mistress of a prince. Schiller's earlier and later discussions of this question are somewhat disingenuous, since for the play to work we *must* feel that Karl's revolt and alienation are both necessary and inescapable. Once we allow discussion to centre, Jane Austen fashion, around whether or not Karl has acted sensibly, let alone harmoniously, the play can only collapse into intense bathos. It is Hegel rather than Schiller himself who points to the real significance of Karl:

> In this connection we can marvel at the youthful poetic genius of Schiller and Goethe, at their attempt to win back again within the circumstances existing in modern times the lost independence of the heroic figures. But how do we see Schiller carrying out this attempt in his earliest works? Only by a revolt against the whole of civil society itself. Karl Moor, injured by the existing order and by those who misused their authority in it, leaves the sphere of legality, and, having the audacity to burst the bonds that restrain him, and so creating for and by himself a new heroic situation, he

makes himself the restorer of right and the independent avenger of wrong, injury and oppression.[28]

Karl – and Schiller – attempt to recover the ideal of the heroic in a context in which the individual appears as both restricted and unrepresentative. His actions break these restrictions but they do not thereby become socially representative; his revenge still has a 'private' character. As Hegel sees clearly, the field of possibility for Karl is limited: his response to his situation lacks the characteristic of 'adequacy' or 'appropriateness' not simply because of himself but because of the nature of the world. Schiller characteristically masks and deflects our recognition of this by stressing the chaos that Karl releases within himself, the 'mistake' of attempting to promote the harmony of the world through discord. Yet, from another point of view, Karl's adoption of the role of outlaw is already implicit in his being outcast. The outcast–outlaw shift represents an existential choice for Karl in which, like Genet, he becomes the truth of what society says he is and releases criminality together with freedom. Freedom and criminality are one and the same since both represent an opposition between the individual and a general moral order. Despite Schiller's own careful condemnation of his hero, who could in any event, given the temper of the times, hardly have been held up for unqualified admiration, it is difficult to resist the conclusion that the 'fault' lies not in Karl but in the world; in a situation where freedom can only assume the form of criminality. His fate is at once dictated and chosen.

Schiller's most illuminating comment on the meaning of the play occurs in the original Preface, where he remarks, 'To these enthusiastic dreams of greatness and efficiency it needs but a sarcastic bitterness against the unpoetic spirit of the age to complete the strange Don Quixote whom, in the robber Moor, we at once detest and love, admire and pity.'[29] Karl is anachronistic not in the mode of Götz but in the mode of the Knight of la Mancha – a man endeavouring to repeat a nobility which in a degraded age can only have the character of incongruity, since there is nothing in the world against which he can worthily set himself. Implicitly the fate of Karl is also a comment on the predicament of the youthful poet Schiller: his dream of greatness set against the anti-poetic spirit of the age can only have the character of a 'mistake'. Thus, although on the face of it *Die Räuber* appears very different from Goethe's *Götz von Berlichingen*, primarily because Goethe's very positive view of his hero is at variance with Schiller's more negative assessment of his, they are both structured around an anachronistic hero and posit a similar problem: how can a world that excludes contradiction be contradicted; how can value and dignity be given back to the notion of the individual in bourgeois society?

If *Die Räuber* appears as a relatively broad formulation of these questions, *Die Verschwörung des Fiesko zu Genua* is a much more specific and historical treatment, based on the work of the respected historians of the day, Robertson and Cardinal de Retz. *Die Räuber* was assigned to a Germany of indeterminate date. *Fiesko*, by contrast, is located in the city of Genoa during the year 1547. But *Fiesko* is also an elaborately coded inquiry into political morality, the first work of Schiller in which the influence of Adam Ferguson becomes apparent. Schiller criticism has long recognised that the poet was familiar with Ferguson's writing from an early date, but it has tended to see Ferguson primarily as a channel through which Schiller became acquainted with the ideas of Montesquieu before he actually read Montesquieu for himself.[30] But *Fiesko* and such later works as the *Aesthetic Education* strongly suggest that it was the distinctively Fergusonian interpretation that Schiller appropriated and found intellectually most congenial. Like Schiller, Ferguson in his *Essay on the History of Civil Society* stressed the importance of play. He pointed out that the gambler turns his amusement into an intensely serious matter and argued that there was no good reason why the converse should not equally apply:

> If men can thus turn their amusement into a scene more serious and interesting than that of business itself, it will be difficult to assign a reason why business, and many of the occupations of human life, independent of any distant consequences or future events, may not be chosen as an amusement, and adopted on account of the pastime they bring[31]

and he continues, even more emphatically,

Whoever has the force of mind steadily to view human life under this aspect, has only to chuse well his occupations, in order to command that state of enjoyment, and freedom of soul, which probably constitute the peculiar felicity to which his active nature is destined.[32]

This triad enjoyment/freedom/activity is as characteristic of Ferguson as it is of Schiller. It springs from a common concern that man should bring all his faculties and all his activities into relation with one another. The loss and recovery of unity is crucial in both. Nevertheless, there is an important difference. For Ferguson this loss is primarily a social problem, historically determined; for Schiller it is primarily a problem for the individual. But the stress on the one-sided nature of modern man as the result of the division of labour in Schiller's *Aesthetic Education* owes much to Ferguson's presentation in his *History of Civil Society*. Ferguson noted that the enlargement of the capacities of a privileged few as the result of this division has the effect of impoverishing the many:

Even in manufacture, the genius of the master, perhaps, is cultivated, while that of the inferior workman lies waste. The statesman may have a wide comprehension of human affairs, while the tools he employs are ignorant of the system in which they themselves are combined. The general officer may be proficient in the knowledge of war, while the skill of the soldier is confined to a few motions of the hand and foot.[33]

Moreover, despite Ferguson's great admiration for Greek culture and for that of Sparta in particular, he pointed out that the most negative feature of that culture, the position of slaves and women, could be ascribed to such a division:

Freemen would be understood to have no object beside those of politics and war. In this manner, the honours of one half of the species were sacrificed to those of the other; as stones from the same quarry are buried in the foundation, to sustain the blocks which happen to be hewn for the superior parts of the pile.[34]

Such an analysis, interestingly enough, also implies the Marxian distinction between base and superstructure. In whole sections of Schiller's *Aesthetic Education* the imprint of Fergusonian categories is clearly discernible. For example, in the sixth letter Schiller protests,

> When the community makes his office the measure of the man; when in one of its citizens it prizes nothing but memory, in another a mere tabularizing intelligence, in a third only mechanical skill; when, in the one case, indifferent to character, it insists exclusively on knowledge, yet it, in another, is ready to condone any amount of obscurantist thinking as long as it is accompanied by a spirit of order and law-abiding behaviour; when, moreover, it insists in special skills being developed with a degree of intensity which is only commensurate with its readiness to absolve the individual from developing himself in extensity – can we wonder that the remaining aptitudes of the psyche are neglected in order to give undivided attention to the one which will bring honour and profit?[35]

It was Ferguson who prompted Schiller to view modern societies not purely in the light of their technical progress or even political freedom, narrowly construed, but in terms of their blocking the potential of every individual. And from this perspective political solutions may appear superficial, since the political might be as much part of the problem as part of the solution.

For Ferguson the separation of the political from the social world was itself a sign of cultural decadence and there can be little doubt but that Schiller shared this belief. Schiller's early drama in particular is preoccupied with the notion of a 'fall into the political': the sense that the political constitutes a corrupted world in which human nature becomes warped and in which man is never able to draw upon his full human capacities. Schiller makes this conviction quite explicit in the Preface to *Fiesko*, where he observes, 'If it is true that sensibility alone awakens sensibility, we may conclude that the political hero is the less calculated for dramatic representation, in proportion as it becomes necessary to lay aside the feelings of a man in order to become a political hero.'[36]

At first sight Fiesko himself might seem to represent the personal focus for Schiller's play, but it is clear that Schiller is concerned to raise a larger and much more daunting problem: the possibility of social and moral regeneration within a decadent cultural milieu. It appears as critical because of the interweaving of the individual with his environment. How, indeed, can the hero raise himself above his own age, by his own bootstraps as it were. This issue is broached in the opening phase of *Fiesko* in a conversation between Sacco and Calcagno, where Sacco reveals that an overthrow of the government of Genoa has become indispensable to him in order to liquidate his debts. At which Calcagno remarks ironically, 'By heaven, Sacco, I admire the wise design of Providence, that in us would heal the corruption in the heart of the state by the vile ulcers on its limbs.'[37] How can symptoms of a social malaise simultaneously form part of a cure? – this is the question that hangs ominously over the action of *Fiesko* and which has a special relevance to Fiesko himself, the putative deliverer. Schiller comprehensively documents the decadence of Genoa. There is the prevalence to the point of normality of secrecy, deception and intrigue; the use of bribes and the employment of hired assassins. The nobility have become so preoccupied with commerce and the pursuit of private affluence that they neglect their political responsibilities. The employment of foreign (in fact, German) mercenaries is a sign both of the decline of a sense of social responsibility on the part of the citizens and at the same time an index of the encroachment of despotic power. The principle of subordination, so repugnant to Ferguson, is accepted without question in Genoa, urged as vehemently by Fiesko as by Doria, the Duke. Schiller implies that the people have become unfitted for liberty; for, when, through a mocking fable, Fiesko derides the principle of democratic or representative government and advocates dictatorship, not a single voice is raised against him. Fiesko's own personal irresponsibility is made only too manifest in the early part of the play, since he has given up politics for amorous intrigue.

Yet Fiesko is shown to have positive qualities and some of the most striking lines in the play are his. Fiesko alone seems to have the will and capacity to effect a transformation of Genoan society; yet Fiesko's own personal flaws, as links that bind him to the world, suggest his inability to transcend it. The play is haunted by the image of an ideal past – the antique republican virtue recreated by the painter Giulio Romano in his final masterwork, the story of Virginia and Appius Claudius. As Schiller perceives it, the problem is not to invoke that image but how it translate it into a living, contemporaneous reality. In a dramatic gesture Fiesko overturns the picture: 'Let the semblance give place to reality! I have done what thou – hast only painted.'³⁸ Moreover, it is Fiesko who, in an impassioned speech to the crowd, correctly lays his finger on the central issue: the indissoluble connection between various freedoms and the need to fight in order to maintain not merely the rights themselves but also the type of society that is able to sustain them: 'No one can surrender a hair's breadth of his rights without betraying the soul of the whole state.'³⁹ If Fiesko threatens to replace one form of tyranny with another, Schiller understands this not in personal terms but presents it as culturally over-determined. The manipulative talents that Fiesko displays both in his personal relations and in his political intrigues render victory suspect and his insistence on the title of duke shows how shallow are his republican sympathies. Yet this only alerts us to a paradox: how can republican virtues be created in a state and society that do not possess them and where they have never been naturalised?

Schiller has no answer to this question, which it is in the nature of the play to propound rather than to resolve, but he does seek to relativise the world of Fiesko with the anachronistic figure of Verrina, whose attachment to republican principles is inflexible and unyielding. Unlike Fiesko, Verrina, though determined to overthrow the Dorias, does not believe in deceit. When the method of bringing about the insurrection is discussed, Verrina insists that they should be open in their methods, since subterfuge would reduce them to banditti. They must urge the people to open revolt. Verrina, significantly, is the very last survivor of a noble family who for generations have dedicated themselves to the maintenance of their virtue and their honour; he is the only conspirator identified with a positive set of values. When, at the end of the play, he pushes Fiesko into the sea and drowns him, because he will no longer adhere to the republican cause, Verrina appears to have stepped out of the classical frame onto the stage of contemporary life. Verrina is symbolically linked with the painting of Giulio Romano, and even at his most positive we feel that a question-mark hangs over him and his actions, because they possess an indeterminate relationship with the world in which they figure. At best, his deeds mark an absence; they serve as a rather ineffectual proclamation of values that no longer exist and, it would appear, can no longer exist. The idea of potentiality, of a recovery of the past that would at the same time represent a going beyond it, an idea so dear to Schiller, in this play is blocked, thwarted and cancelled in the figure of Fiesko. Fiesko cannot but be a creature of his own particular circumstances of time and place.

When Schiller with *Wallenstein* returned to playwriting after an interval of ten years, he proved quite surprisingly faithful to his original dramatic concerns. The treatment is deeper, the working out more thoroughly saturated with historical source materials – Schiller had, after all, in the meantime written a history of the Thirty Years War – but the frame of reference is still that created by Montesquieu and Ferguson: the development of despotism and subordination, the decline of individual autonomy, the erosion of regional cultural centres by a centralised power. In reading or responding to *Wallenstein* we must not make the mistake of concentrating too exclusively on the figure of Wallenstein himself – not simply because of Schiller's determination and ability to present a whole gallery of characters – Max and Octavio Piccolomini, Wallenstein's wife, the Duchess, and daughter, Thekla, Butler and Illo – but also because Schiller intends a portrait of the age, a sketch of the field of human possibility in a determinate historical period. In the play absolutely everything is significant, and especially time and place – as the old astrologer Battister Seni actually says. In *Wallenstein* Schiller depicts the transition away from a feudal type of society, based on a balance between loyalty and personal autonomy, towards a centralised despotic empire, that of Austria under the Emperor. This transition is marked by the deterioration of traditional values. Not the least significant of these is the fact that Wallenstein commands a mercenary army for which the Emperor is reluctant to pay, although it has been employed in his service. The very existence of mercenaries, pointedly contrasted with the idealistic citizen army of the Swedes, represents a breakdown in society, a disposition of power that will be immoral, whether commanded by the Emperor or by Wallenstein himself. We should bear in mind that for Ferguson the most fatal of *all* the consequences of the social division of labour was the separation of the soldier from the citizen:

> The subdivision of arts and professions, in certain examples, tends to improve the practice of them, and to promote their ends. By having separated the arts of the clothier and the tanner, we are the better supplied with shoes and with cloth. But to separate the arts which form the citizen and the statesman, the arts of policy and war, is an attempt to dismember the human character, and to destroy those very arts we mean to improve. By this separation, we in effect deprive a free people of what is necessary to their safety; or we prepare a defence against invasions from abroad, which gives a prospect of usurpation, and threatens the establishment of military government at home.[40]

The choice that faces Germany is empire and centralised despotism or military government under Wallenstein. The court is seen by Schiller as central to the moral corruption of Wallenstein's world. At court, influence, favour and intrigue, as Montesquieu saw, count for far more than action or integrity of character. In his resentment of the manipulations and the stratagems that have been brought against him, Wallenstein is seen as fully justified. For having achieved great victories in the imperial cause, with an army that he himself raised, Wallenstein now finds himself on the point of being discarded like an outworn instrument. As he recognises, it is a matter either of using or of being used; manipulation is simply the mode of the times. Rank is the second great source of decadence and becomes significantly linked with the manipulative through Octavio Piccolomini's disclosure to Butler – a revelation that strikes him with all the violence of a blow – that Wallenstein never intended Butler to achieve the rank of count, but instead deliberately discouraged it in order to undermine Butler's loyalty to the court and turn him into a man totally dependent on Wallenstein's own favour. But the

moral force of Piccolomini's truth-telling is undermined with
the very last words of the play, as a messenger approaches with
a letter addressed to 'the Prince Piccolomini' – the corruption
of rank has invaded almost every character that figures in it.
At every moment the leading figures are tested by the
dilemma of how to be of their age without being a creature of
it.

In *Wallenstein* Wallenstein appears as an anachronistic hero,
whose anachronism consists in the fact that he belongs not to
the past but to the future. Wallenstein's objectives are such
that at a later date they could appear noble and far-sighted: he
seeks to resist the development of Austrian empire and
despotism, to bring peace and tranquillity to the people, to
reassert the territorial independence and autonomy of the
German lands. Moreover, Wallenstein himself represents the
progressive principle of individual autonomy, one which
postulates the self as a value in its own right and which rejects
dependence on extraneous sources. But Wallenstein's tragedy
is grounded not, like Götz's, in the fact that he is at odds with
his own time, but rather in his inability fully to transcend it.
Urging on Max Piccolomini the importance of independence,
Wallenstein immediately makes nonsense of the principle by
demanding that Max make Wallenstein his 'emperor'. Thus,
Wallenstein denies to others the right he demands for himself
and the values he apparently asserts become problematic.
Wallenstein is extremely self-conscious; he recognises that the
steps which he is taking place him at odds with his century.
Against him are arrayed the forces of custom, tradition and
power, which are no less formidable for the fact that they are
being hypocritically deployed. Wallenstein cannot be other
than misconstrued. As Schiller recognises, more profoundly
than Goethe, the problem of an age of transition is the
coexistence of different value-systems, so that it is always
possible to justify one's actions by switching to an alternative
frame of reference. Both Octavio Piccolomini and Butler can
justify themselves by invoking an imperial mandate, although
Butler acts from motives of personal revenge, while Octavio
maintains an 'integrity' the value of which it has been precisely
the function of the play to question. Octavio uses his friendship with Wallenstein to obtain information vital to the court;
he puts his signature to a document in a manner that is

tainted, even though the document itself involves misrepresentation; he acts from the best of motives, i.e. loyalty to the Emperor, but he never considers that there is anything else to which he might be loyal. This signing of the document – where Terzky sees to it that, in a second copy that is circulated of a declaration by which the generals pledge unswerving loyalty to Wallenstein, a proviso excepting from this their obligations to the Emperor is omitted – is of crucial importance. Wallenstein himself never signs anything and he clearly intends to use the document to bind the generals to him. But, as Max Piccolomini points out and as Wallenstein himself later admits, why is a document necessary? In effect we return to the paradox propounded by Ferguson about the nature of law: the society that needs the word lacks the thing. So the very need for written statements and deceit surrounding the form of words is a sign of a culture where loyalty cannot be taken for granted. Only Max Piccolomini recognises that there are two kinds of loyalty involved, the personal as well as the public; torn between them he does not resort to politic rationalisation but virtually commits suicide in a brave but doomed assault on the Swedish army. Max proves the truth of which Wallenstein only furnished the words: that man himself can be a source of value and that he need not be the puppet or instrument of others.

Wallenstein's world is ridden with ambiguity: this problem and that of all the other characters is to decipher a deceptive universe of signs – a task that borders on the impossible. The presence of Seni, the astrologer, is itself indicative of the deep obscurity in which Wallenstein moves. For every move that Wallenstein makes is open to construction, interpretation and misconstruction; the path from loyalty to rebellion is no obvious one, but involves a complex series of moves, a propounding of hypothetical courses of action that must necessarily become actualised through the dynamic processes of human interaction. The play is an enormous chess game in which Wallenstein puts himself into *Zugszwang* – so that he cannot make a move without losing. Yet, although Wallenstein is a plotter, he retains a curious innocence. He is prone to trust people in an age when mistrust is virtually universal. There is no more moving moment in the drama than that in *Wallensteins Tod* when Wallenstein leans on the 'faithful'

Butler's shoulder and buries his head in his breast. For we recognise that the warping in the relationship between these ancient comrades at arms is not anything that can be attributed to the two men individually, but is the product of circumstances in a particular time and place: between the bonds that should unite the two men have interposed the corruptions of court, rank and privilege. In *Wallenstein* tragedy means the impossibility of transcendence.

After the labyrinthine complexities of *Wallenstein*, the freshness, directness, clarity and simplicity of Schiller's later work comes almost as a surprise. How is it, we may ask, that such later protagonists as Mary Stuart, Joan of Arc and William Tell are able to find within themselves the capacity to negate the tendencies of their age – a capacity which, for Schiller the Sentimental poet, had always appeared as a temptation or a lure, something to be resisted and not indulged in. A partial answer may be found in the idea of the modern. *Fiesko, Don Carlos* and *Wallenstein* are all specifically set in the modern period; but *Maria Stuart* shows the historical transition to modernity and all of Schiller's other plays are set in a pre-modern world. However, such a solution is not entirely satisfactory, since Schiller more than anyone would have been aware of the inauthenticity of presenting values which, by definition, were excluded from the contemporary phase. Rather, Schiller's optimism seems to have been the product of his long period of aesthetic and philosophical reflection, with *Wallenstein* the play that at once encapsulated and exorcised the demons of the past. Schiller found grounds for hope in the notion of the moral autonomy of the individual, which had, of course, been deepened and intensified by his reading of Kantian philosophy. If Kant had the answer to Hume, he also had the answer to the dilemmas propounded by the Scottish students of society. Man's relation to himself has an absolute priority over his relation to his age; in adherence to the laws of his inner being, man can find the basis for opposition to the prevailing tendencies of the time. If Schiller presents us with Mary, Joan and William Tell as anachronistic and out of phase with the culture, he does indeed provide examples from the past, but he does so in the belief that what they represent is not and can never be lost; it is rather a capacity, a latency, that is available in any period in history. Historicism is overcome through a return to the original spirit of Protestantism: the belief in the inner light, the deep and uncontaminated sources of the self.

To refer to *Maria Stuart, Die Jungfrau von Orleans* and *Wilhelm Tell* is to become acutely conscious of the degree to which Schiller's plays, understandably in the light of the historical situation of Germany at the time, are concerned with problems of imperialism and colonialism. Schiller focuses on the English dominations of France and Scotland, on Austrian power in Germany and Switzerland, on Spanish rule in Holland. In *Don Carlos* and *Wallenstein* his concern with presenting the pervasive moral corruption of the court creates a situation fraught with determinist overtones, in which it is hard to present, let alone make convincing, an alternative source of moral values. But in his later work Schiller turns to the periphery: it is the very distance of Mary, Joan and the Swiss from the centres of metropolitan power and corruption that enables them to tap the sources of strength within themselves. Switzerland, in particular, has an exemplary significance for Schiller, for Switzerland shows how ancient traditions of freedom can be preserved and maintained despite the imposition of enormous external pressure. The symbolic hat to which William Tell refuses to bow is also a sign of the ultimate emptiness of imperialism in the face of a free and independent people determined to stand up for their rights – it will always be a 'paper tiger'. Indeed, Tell's refusal to acknowledge the hat brings together all the implications of Romantic symbolism: the hat is the irrationality of arbitrary power, the denial of the autonomy of the individual, the fetishised nature of domination. The message it carries is radical – for the whole point of the hat, as arbitrary power, is that it is not necessary, it is wholly redundant. And in this final image Schiller's obsession with the fall into the political is liquidated: the political can be abolished and with it the perversion of humanity that it has brought about. So that, in reality, Schiller's last play is more radical than his first!

4 Scott and the Historical Novel

With the historical novel of Scott, the intellectual tradition of Montesquieu and Adam Ferguson passed into the hands of its most faithful follower and perhaps its most eloquent exponent. Scott, as translator of Goethe's *Götz von Berlichingen*, and, intimate of Adam Ferguson's household, was uniquely well placed to continue the development of the genre and to translate it onto a higher philosophical level. Scott did not necessarily surpass his predecessors, since no simple comparison can be made when his intentions differed considerably from theirs. Indeed, Scott himself was significantly a critical innovator in recognising the relevance of intention to evaluation; and, in the Preface to *Waverley*, in acknowledging the importance of the signals a writer throws out for indicating to the reader what kind of response is appropriate. His subtitle "Tis Sixty Years Since' was specifically chosen to exclude the possibility of reading the novel either as an essay in the Gothic, or as a study of fashionable manners, the two principal fictional modes of the day. For Goethe and Schiller the historical was the ground to set off a tragic figure; if they focused on different sets of cultural values they did so with a great sense of urgency, commitment and partisanship. Their subject-matter embraces relativism, but their own standpoint is not relativistic. But Scott, in his Preface to his translation of *Götz*, sounded a distinctly Fergusonian note:

> Amid the obvious mischiefs attending such a state of society, it must be allowed that it was frequently the means of calling into exercise the highest heroic virtues. Men daily exposed to danger, and living by the constant exercise of their courage acquired the virtues as well as the vices of a savage state; and among many instances of cruelty and rapine,

occur not a few of the most exalted valour and generosity.[1]

Here we find not only the characteristically Fergusonian balancing of advantages and disadvantages, but also that small phrase 'state of society' which does so much to alter our perspective on Götz. For Goethe, the chivalrousness, courage and fidelity of Götz are personal characteristics – part, no doubt, of a vanishing world in which such characteristics were highly regarded – but personal nevertheless. The effect of Scott's approach is to bracket and qualify this emphasis on the individual and to see these values simply as a particular code that is liable to prevail in a particular type of society. Values pertain to groups, not to individuals pure and simple.

It is this emphasis on the group that is the most significant innovation in the historical novel of Scott. When Shakespeare portrays a Hotspur or an Owen Glendower, they stand for sections of the country that are dissatisfied, they are fully representative, yet powerful figures in their own right. Lukács, in his perceptive suggestion that Scott's characters 'always represent social trends and historical forces',[2] almost understates the case for Scott's originality, for Scott goes beyond this kind of representative symbolisation to show how the fate of individuals is always bound up with the fate of particular groups and sections of society and, in fact, always blocks off any possibility of transcendence, either symbolic or actual. Even the notion of 'world-historical individual' is misleading in relation to Scott, for he very seldom portrayed such a character; and, when he did so, as in the case of Louis XI of France, he deliberately chose a man placed in a situation of the greatest difficulty and danger, who voluntarily places himself in the power of his greatest enemy, in order to shed light on the customs and traditions of the time, and to show that even such an adroit king as Louis might nevertheless be extremely credulous and superstitutious. So that even here a notable figure is not allowed, as it were, to stand outside the frame of his age, but is pointedly thrust back within it. All play with the same counters and think and act in the light of common assumptions.

This dominating concern with the group is founded on the precept of Adam Ferguson, who, in his *History of Civil Society*, trenchantly affirms,

Mankind are to be taken in groups, as they have always subsisted. The history of the individual is but a detail of the sentiments and the thoughts he has entertained in the view of his species: and every experiment relative to this subject should be made with entire societies not with single men.[3]

Ferguson does not simply argue for the priority of the group as the analytical basis for any inquiry into values (the position of Nietzsche also), but insists that apart from the group and human society his existence has no meaning:

From this source are derived, not only the force, but the very existence of his happiest emotions; not only the better part, but almost the whole of his rational character. Send him to the desert alone, he is a plant torn from his roots: the form indeed may remain, but every faculty droops and withers; the human personage and human character cease to exist.[4]

In Scott the bonding between individual and group, whether already established or in the process of formation, is a matter of the utmost importance. If Scott's work acquires tragic overtones it is not through the presentation of a single heroic individual but through our sense that it is a whole community or section of society that is doomed in a disaster that brings down not one but many. Loyalty is a recurring thematic concern not simply because this is seen as the central value of a passing heroic age, but because it is through loyalty that the individual avows his solidarity with a particular social group, his choice to be what he is, for good or ill. For Scott, as for Ferguson, groups have an ontological status that the individual lacks: they generate customs, folk-ways and values and they are the most significant structuring principle of the world of human action – structuring it, though, not statically but dynamically, in the determinate conflicts, oppositions and tensions that arise from the fact that different sections of society have divergent ambitions and goals. These groups also perceive the world differently and express this perception in a linguistically and mythically coded fashion which is essentially idiosyncratic; it cannot be 'translated', for the 'truth' of a particular perspective is not universal but comes from the very fact that these groups exist and commit themselves in distinctive ways. The rejection of bourgeois legality by the followers of Rob Roy or Donald Bean Lean, the biblical analogies of the Covenanters make perfectly good sense as far as they themselves are concerned; it is only to the outsider committed to different values that they appear baffling.

Similarly, the term 'honest party' acquires a complex coded significance in the ranks of the loyalists, who use it to define their own identity and self-consciousness as a political movement. Honesty, in this sense, ceases to be an absolute but becomes very much a matter of where you are standing and what you mean or imply when you use the term. An amusing example of such a conflict of viewpoints occurs in the scene in *Old Mortality* where Lady Margaret Bellenden visits the humble cottage of the Covenant-supporting Mause Headrigg and demands to know why her son, Cuddie, has not made himself available for a military parade, or 'wappenschaw'.[5] This confrontation is articulated in terms of distinct linguistic codes in which each of the participants refuses to acknowledge the validity of the other's language. Lady Margaret's terminology is technical and legal. She uses such words as 'abulyiements', 'delegate', 'hosting', 'watching', 'warding', 'barony', 'indwellers', 'liege vassals'. Mause Headrigg uses figures and analogies drawn from the Bible. The word 'warrant' brings their disagreement into focus. Lady Margaret refers to 'the warrant of the sheriff'; Mause, denying the validity of the 'wappenschawings', as she pejoratively calls them, says that she can find 'nae warrant for them whatsoever' – meaning, of course, in the Bible. Each is appealing to a different form of authority, the one legal, the other biblical. In answer to Lady Bellenden's demand for an explanation, Mause launches into the story of Nebuchadnezzar, who sets up a golden image in the plain of Dura, and the following exchange occurs:

> 'And what o' a' this, ye fule wife? Or what had Nebuchadnezzar to do with the wappenschaw of the Upper Ward of Clydesdale?'
> 'Only just thus far, my leddy,' continued Mause, firmly, 'that prelacy is like the great golden image in the plain of Dura, and that Shadrach, Meshach and Abednego were

borne out in refusing to bow down and worship, so neither shall Cuddie Headrigg, your leddyship's poor ploughman, at least wi' his auld mither's consent, make murgeons or Jennyflections, as they ca' them, in the house of the prelates and curates, not gird him wi' armour to fight in their cause, either at the sound of kettle-drums, organs, bagpipes, or any other kind of music whatever.'[6]

Although, in *Old Mortality*, Scott showed himself distinctly unsympathetic to the Covenanting cause as a whole – a lack of empathy which he attempted to rectify in *The Heart of Midlothian* – it says much for his breadth of vision and imaginative insight that he could nevertheless show, as here, how the Bible could create a sense of dignity and independence in the common people, so that they could confront their social superiors with confidence and implicitly deny their status as 'liege vassals'. This confidence comes from membership of a group.

This scene also serves to dramatise how much of Scott's fiction is built around strong and dramatic contrasts, especially contrasts of culture. There is the moment of Waverley's entry into the cave of Donald Bean Lean, the confrontation of Godfrey Bertram with Meg Merrilies after he has driven out the gypsies, Edie Ochiltree's attempt to persuade Lovel and Captain McIntyre not to fight, the meeting between Richard and Saladin in *The Talisman*, the clash between Sir Geoffrey Peveril and Bridgenorth in *Peveril of the Peak*, the appearance of the gaunt and dishevelled Edgar Ravenswood in the genteel surroundings of Ravenswood Castle, at the very moment when Lucy Ashton is to sign her marriage contract, in *The Bride of Lammermoor*. These juxtapositions are conceived by Scott in strongly visual and scenic terms. The case for such a fictional method is argued by Dick Tinto, the painter, in the Preamble to *The Bride of Lammermoor*, where Dick severely criticises those novels that are composed of 'mere chat and dialogue'[7] and contrasts them with 'that instant and vivid flash of conviction', which is instilled in the mind of the spectator through the complex imagery of a pictorial composition,

which darts on the mind from seeing the happy and expressive combinations of a single scene, and which gathers from the position, attitude, and countenance of the moment, not only the history of the past lives of the personages represented, and the nature of the business on which they are immediately engaged, but lifts even the veil of futurity, and affords a shrewd guess at their future fortunes.[8]

Scott deliberately draws a frame around these moments in his novels and asks the reader to stand back and savour them; to consider not only what they mean but what they will lead to. Their pictorialism is underlined by his own introductions of them: the departing gypsies would have made 'an excellent subject for the pen of Calotte',[9] while, if Donald Bean Lean is not at all how Salvator Rosa would have conceived the outlaw, the reference to Salvator nevertheless signals a composition in the picturesque manner. Such cultural juxtapositions were Scott's most important legacy to the romantic opera. Donizetti's influential *Lucia di Lammermoor* was of course directly based on Scott's novel, but his legacy can be traced in many other places: in the contrast between the Romans and Druids in Bellini's *Norma*, in Verdi's *Don Carlos*, where the thoughts of Carlos are alternately framed by choruses of huntsmen and monks, or Berlioz's *Les Troyens*, which develops a dual opposition Greece/Troy, Rome/Carthage. In this way ideas of culture and of cultural relativism become dramatic and tangible.

The idea of the picturesque is also connected with the central theme of the historical genre: that of a transition from one type of society to another. The moment of transition makes it possible to present different sets of values simultaneously in a manner that is aesthetically appealing and intellectually illuminating. Scott himself makes this connection, in the most unlikely of places, the Introduction to *The Fortunes of Nigel*:

Lady Mary Wortley Montague has said, with equal truth and taste, that the most romantic region of every country is that where the mountains unite themselves with the plains or lowlands. For similar reasons, it may be in like manner said, that the most picturesque period of history is that when the ancient rough and wild manners of a barbarous

age are just becoming innovated upon and contrasted by
the illumination of increased or revived learning, and the
instructions of renewed or reformed religion. The strong
contrast produced by the opposition of ancient manners to
those which are gradually subduing them, affords the lights
and shadows necessary to give effect to a fictitious narrative;
and while such a period entitles the author to introduce
incidents of a marvellous and improbable character, as
arising out of the turbulent independence and ferocity,
belonging to old habits of violence, still influencing the
manners of a people who had been so lately in a barbarous
state; yet, on the other hand, the characters and sentiments
of many of the actors may, with the utmost probability, be
described with great variety of shading and delineation,
which belongs to the newer and more improved period, of
which the world has but lately received the light.[10]

In this passage, Scott articulates the notion of the picturesque
in terms of a cultural relativism: the opposition and contrast
between different sets of manners corresponds to the pain-
terly use of 'lights and shadows'. Scott's terminology here
parallels that of Uvedale Price in his essays on the picturesque;
where comparing the 'picturesque' Rubens with Claude, Price
observes,

His landscapes are full of the peculiarities, and picturesque
accidents in nature – of striking contrasts in form, colour,
and light and shadow: sunbeams bursting through a small
opening in a dark wood – a rainbow against a stormy
sky – effects of thunder and lightning, torrents rolling
down, trees torn up by the roots, and the dead bodies of
men and animals – are among the sublime and picturesque
circumstances exhibited by his daring pencil. These sudden
gleams, these cataracts of light, these bold oppositions of
clouds and darkness which he has so nobly introduced,
would destroy all the beauty and elegance of Claude.[11]

Indeed, it is significant that the use of the term 'picturesque' is
linked with a movement towards relativism in the application
of aesthetic criteria. Price juggles with three different
terms – the beautiful, the sublime and the picturesque –

which are constantly shading into one another and overlapping and which are yet intended to demarcate separate areas within which these criteria can most appropriately operate. Moreover, since Price's main enemy is the regular style of landscape gardening, promulgated by 'Capability' Brown, his notion of the picturesque is always on the point of becoming an aesthetics of irregularity, a system of the non-systematic. Richard Payne Knight, in his acute comments on Price's thinking, brought out more clearly the general drift of this kind of thinking: that the criterion of the picturesque was not an immanent quality of the art object or prospect to which it was applied, but lay very much in the eye of the beholder. Knight insists,

> Show either picturesque, classical, romantic or pastoral scenery to a person, whose mind, how well soever organised, is wholly unprovided with correspondent ideas, and it will no otherwise affect him than as beautiful tints, forms, or varieties of light and shadow would, if seen in objects, which had nothing of either of these characters.[12]

but, he continues, 'Novelty will, indeed, make mountainous scenery peculiary pleasing to the inhabitant of a plain; and richly cultivated scenery to the inhabitant of a forest; and *vice versa*.'[13] In effect, Knight is acknowledging that the criteria Price is employing are codified: it is necessary to have a background in the way in which these terms are employed in order to understand them. This is particularly obvious in the case of the picturesque, where it is necessary to have some background in the type of scenery and manner of composition favoured by painters in a given period in order to designate or mark out such scenery appropriately. But for Knight the picturesque is a purely positional concept and depends on the cultural relation that the spectator bears to an object. A Tyrolean village, for example, would appear picturesque to the tourist, but would not have that quality for its native Austrian resident. But both Price and Knight draw back from fully acknowledging the relativism they are edging towards. It is in Scott that an awareness of relativism is erected into a clear-cut and consistently applied aesthetic principle.

For Scott, however, the contrast between mountains and

lowlands, between ancient and modern manners, was not simply an aesthetic contrast but a cultural and social fact. On the one hand, in Scotland, there were the Highlands with a more archaic form of society, organised into clans, primarily based on hunting and pastoral activities but supplemented with the spoils of war, plunder and the proceeds of cattle-stealing; on the other, the peaceful prosperous commercial Lowlands, a society essentially bourgeois–legal in character. For Scott, as for Ferguson, whose work is dominated by the same contrast, these two different ways of life present a complex problem of relative evaluation, since each possesses virtues that the other lacks. The way of life in the Lowlands is mercifully free from the violence to which the Highlander is inured, or in which, rather, he rejoices; but it lacks the complex and unwritten code of honour which gives dignity to the life of the Highlander and it does not offer the same degree of personal freedom and autonomy. In polarising this contrast the idea of law assumes great importance for Ferguson and Scott. Ferguson differs from his mentor, Montesquieu, in attaching far less importance to laws; he does not believe that laws in themselves provide any safeguard against despotism – indeed, his comments on the law are consistently disparaging. The very most that he will concede is that laws, though no guarantee of individual liberty, may be useful as a kind of *aide-memoire*, serving to spell out for and remind people what their rights are or should be. But Ferguson in general sees the prevalence of law as symptomatic of a kind of social failure and decadence, where law is vainly thrown into the balance to make up for deficiencies in society as a whole. Ferguson contrasts ancient Sparta, which 'prospered for ages, by the integrity of its manners, and by the character of its citizens'[14] with modern societies, where

> men must be rich, in order to be great; pleasure itself is often pursued from vanity; where the desire of a supposed happiness serves to inflame the worst of passions, and is itself the foundation of misery; where public justice, like fetters applied to the body, may without inspiring the sentiments of candour and equity, prevent the actual commission of crimes.[15]

In general, for Ferguson the law is a deceptive veil which

serves to obscure men's real situation by implying a pretension to 'equal influence and consideration'[16] for all men, even though vast differences in economic wealth and power undoubtedly exist and are actually reinforced by the existence of laws which are then partially applied. Moreover, the existence of laws may encourage men to relax their vigilance and make them believe that, because a right exists on paper, it therefore necessarily exists in reality. Ferguson is crushingly dismissive of the exaltation of law that has permeated so much of modern culture:

> If forms of proceeding, written statutes, or other con-
> stituents of law, cease to be enforced by the very spirit from
> which they arose; they serve only to cover, not to restrain
> the iniquities of power: they are possibly respected even by
> the corrupt magistrate, when it favours his purpose; but
> they are condemned or evaded, when they stand in his way:
> and the influence of laws, where they have any real effect in
> the preservation of liberty, is not any magic power descend-
> ing from shelves that are loaded with books, but is, in reality,
> the influence of men determined to be free; of men who,
> having adjusted in writing the terms on which they are to
> live with the state, and with their fellow-subjects, are
> determined by their vigilance and spirit, to make these
> terms be fulfilled.[17]

While in Scott there is a greater respect for the idea of legality and a greater commitment to the modern commercial type of society than can be found in Ferguson, Scott nevertheless sees this type of society from a perspective that is strongly influenced by Ferguson: if the commercial–bourgeois–legal type of society represents the 'newer and more improved period', it is nevertheless seen as morally inferior to the earlier state of society that it is replacing. For if, according to Ferguson, 'the last is always the most knowing'[18] it is not therefore the best.

The notion of a period of transition from one type of society to another and of the conflict of values generated by such a transition is worked out with particular thoroughness in Scott's *Legend of Montrose*. This novel is set in the period of the Civil War and deals with the successful campaign of the Duke

of Montrose – fought on behalf of the King with the Highland
soldiers against the supporters of the Covenant under the
Duke of Argyle. This historical material is mythically reinforced by a sub-plot (in effect the 'legend' of Montrose) which
depicts the bitter feud between the Highland Children of the
Mist, on the one hand, and Allan McAulay and the family of
Sir Duncan Campbell, on the other. Annot Lyle, a beautiful
young girl who is spared by McAulay after revenging himself
on the Children of the Mist and who becomes his protégée, is
revealed to be the long-lost daughter of the Campbell
family – a fact which clears the way for her marriage to the
noble Earl of Menteith. To bring this Highland culture into
focus and to bring out its distinctive character, Scott uses the
character of Captain Dugald Dalgetty, a Scottish mercenary
soldier who has fought all over Europe in military campaigns,
selling his services to the highest bidder.

Although Scott presents Dalgetty with considerable sympathy and humour, there can equally be little doubt that he
serves as the epitome of a degraded set of values. For
Ferguson, as for Machiavelli, the use of mercenaries was in
any event characteristic of moral decline. But Scott stresses
equally the difference between men who fight out of loyalty,
honour and commitment to a tradition and a cause, and those
who *contract* themselves only for a limited campaign, on
specific terms and for a specific rate of remuneration.
Dalgetty, of course, is by no means shown as inferior in all
respects: his care for his horse, Adolphus, is favourably
contrasted with the lordly indifference of the Highland
nobility – but it also indicates that he looks after his horse
because it is a primary tool of his trade. Dalgetty is indeed, as
everyone agrees, 'a man of the times'[19] but he represents a
movement away from an older and higher set of values. Scott
makes the point clearly in an implicit comparison between
Dalgetty and the Earl of Menteith:

> Montrose dearly loved his noble kinsman, in whom there
> was conspicuous a flash of the generous, romantic, disin-
> terested chivalry of the old heroic times, entirely different
> from the sordid, calculating and selfish character, which the
> practice of entertaining mercenary troops had introduced
> into most parts of Europe, and of which degeneracy

Scotland, which furnished soldiers of fortune for the service of almost every nation, had been contaminated with a more than usual share.[20]

This contrast gives Menteith's own criticism of Dalgetty, uttered in the moment of Dalgetty's greatest triumph after the award of a knighthood, particular force: 'nay, his very benevolence is selfish'.[21] Dalgetty is the modern individual, self-sufficient and self-regarding, announcing himself with the cry that he is for no particular party but only 'for God and my standard',[22] cut off from the complex web of group loyalties that motivate and animate the others.

The presence of Dalgetty in the narrative serves to point up the theme of decadence as it affects Scotland herself. Here Scott shows that Montrose and his Highland supporters have a higher and more consistent set of values than do the Covenanters of Argyle. This issue is presented not primarily in religious terms but through the Montesquieu/Ferguson tradition of speculation about the origins of despotism and subordination. Argyle in *A Legend of Montrose* is seen as representing the tendency towards centralising, dominant authority. Argyle seeks to break down the local strongholds of power and balances of influence among the clans in order to aggrandise his own position. Religion is only a pretext. His power, 'already exorbitant', has been 'still further increased by concessions extorted from the king at the last pacification'.[23] Scott draws a pointed contrast between Argyle's massive, imposing castle, 'another terrible spectacle of feudal power'[24] and his quasi-royal *levées* and the more unpretentious surroundings and democratic ways of the supporters of Montrose. At the house, or castle, as it was called, of Allan McAulay, Allan wins a bet that his candlesticks are of greater value than those of his English guests by producing a body of gigantic Highlanders carrying flaming torches. In the Highlands, at least, a man is still worth more than silver!

Argyle's unchecked exercise of power is contrasted with the complex checks and balances on the other side:

> Each chief, however small his comparative importance, showed the full disposition to exact from the rest the deference due to a separate and independent prince; while

the stronger and more powerful, divided among themselves by recent contentions or ancient feuds, were constrained in policy to use great deference to the feelings of their less powerful brethren, in order, in case of need, to attach as many well-wishers as might be to their own interest and standard.[25]

Montrose's right to lead them is conceded, but this is not automatic. And, on the opposite side, Sir Duncan Campbell stands as the single honourable figure and man who is likewise concerned at the possible erosion of Scottish freedom. But Argyle himself is shown as morally degenerate – he violates the safe-conduct given Dalgetty by Sir Duncan and throws him in prison; while, at the end of the novel, he ignominiously flees from his supporters at the prospect of defeat. Argyle's example demonstrates how Highland and Scottish independence can be undermined from within.

For, left to themselves, the Highlanders could never have allowed despotism or subordination to develop. Scott points out that the Highlanders never thought in terms even of a long campaign, let alone of permanent conquest. They would take part in a battle and then return home, if victorious, with the booty, to carry on the tasks of tending the cattle or reaping the harvest. War was never allowed to get out of proportion but was always subordinated to other concerns. Thus, Montrose's inability to leave a more permanent mark on the destiny of Scotland is, in reality, proof of the authenticity of a culture that shows no disposition to dominate or conquer, to use military strength to deprive others of their freedom and independence. The freedom which the Highlander seeks for himself guarantees it to others also.

The strongest commitment to individual freedom is to be found among the Children of the Mist, who live in remote mountain fastnesses. Although they are cruel and violent, they nevertheless show remarkable courage, resourcefulness, intelligence and dignity. The idea of the subordination of one man to another is foreign to them – Ranald refuses to kneel and kiss Montrose's hand, as he is prompted to do by Dalgetty. Dalgetty is astonished at the hospitality shown by the Children of the Mist: 'They actually refused my coined money when freely offered – a tale seldom to be told in a Christian land.'[26]

Scott's formulation makes this observation even more perci-
pient: the Children are not simply generous and friendly, they
do not live in a money-based, bourgeois type of society;
consequently as a sign it has no significance for them. Ranald's
eloquent dying speech strongly emphasises his clan's commitment to freedom and stresses how deeply it is connected
with the refusal of property and possessions:

> Remember the fate of our race, and quit not the ancient
> manners of the Children of the Mist. We are now a
> straggling handful, driven from every vale by the sword of
> every clan, who rule in the possessions where their
> forefathers hewed the wood, and drew the water for ours.
> Put in the thicket of the wilderness, and in the mist of the
> mountain, Kenneth, son of Eracht, keep thou unsoiled the
> freedom which I leave thee as a birthright. Barter it not,
> neither for the rich garment, nor for the stone-roof, nor for
> the covered board, nor for the couch of down – on the rock
> or in the valley, in abundance or famine – in the leafy
> summer, and in the days of the iron winter – Son of the
> Mist! be as free as thy forefathers. Own no lord – receive no
> law – take no hire – given no stipend – build no hut –
> enclose no pasture – sow no grain – let the deer of the
> mountain be thy flocks and herds – if these fail thee, prey
> upon the goods of our oppressors – of the Saxons, and of
> such Gaels as are Saxons in their souls, valuing herds and
> flocks more than honour and freedom.[27]

Ranald's words serve to bring out how complexly the notion
of transition is worked out in *A Legend of Montrose*. The
Children of the Mist represent the primal state of society – the
hunting phase. Montrose's followers are to be placed in the
pastoral and agricultural stages. The possible transition to
despotism is signalled by Argyle; the decline of a code of
honour and its replacement by bourgeois–legal, individualis-
tic values is marked by the figure of Dalgetty. The message of
A Legend of Montrose could not be more clear: in the modern
world the values of honour and freedom, the sense of group
loyalty, are all seriously threatened.

Scott's early fiction is greatly concerned with the passing of
traditional folk-ways and practices. He sees cultural differ-

ences based on mutual tolerance being eliminated through the rigorous application of the principles of bourgeois legality and equally through the diffusion of what he called, in the Preface to *The Antiquary*, 'that general polish which assimilates to each other the manners of different nations'.[28] The implications of such a transition are pessimistically spelt out in Scott's second novel, *Guy Mannering*. The decline of the house of Ellangowan is initiated by the over-zealousness of Godfrey Bertram in applying the law, when he is first appointed magistrate. His purge on a whole variety of individuals and groups who are notionally acting contrary to the law is shown by Scott to be little short of catastrophic, not simply for the individuals themselves but also for the community in relation to which they perform virtually indispensable social functions:

> These things did not pass without notice or censure. We are not made of wood or stone, and the things which connect themselves with our hearts and habits cannot, like bark or lichen, be rent away without our missing them. The farmer's dame lacked her usual share of intelligence, perhaps also the self-applause which she had felt while distributing the 'awmous' (alms), in shape of a 'gowpen' (handful) of oatmeal, to the mendicant who brought the news. The cottage felt inconvenience from the interruption of the petty trade carried on by the itinerant dealers. The children lacked their supply of sugar-plums and toys; the young women wanted pins, ribbons, combs and ballads; and the old could no longer barter their eggs for salt, snuff and tobacco.[29]

Godfrey Bertram's persecution of vagrants, whose activities only appear illegitimate on the bourgeois assumption that private property takes precedence over everything – even the livelihood and survival of human beings – has the character of a brutal enforced modernisation carried out through the instrument of the law. His policy culminates in the driving out of a band of gypsies who have long been permitted to live on his property. Bertram is somewhat reluctant to do this since he recognises that there is a considerable element of bad faith involved, in suddenly refusing to tolerate people who have been tolerated for so long. Doubtless in their case he might prefer to make an exception, but the whole point of the law is that it does not permit exceptions. Although they have long been regarded as 'privileged retainers'[30] on the estate of Ellangowan, they are now ejected from their ancient 'city of refuge'[31] and their primitive dwelling places are smashed to pieces by officers of the law. But Godfrey Bertram and his family are themselves to suffer at the hands of the very law he has invoked. The young heir, Harry Bertram, mysteriously disappears and the absence of any successor on the death of Godfrey makes it possible for the cunning lawyer Glossin to take over the property himself. Thus, in *Guy Mannering* legitimacy is directly opposed to the law, not identified with it: the true basis for the rights of the house of Ellangowan, as with the rights of the gypsies, is that of custom and tradition. Glossin, himself a magistrate, consistently misuses his powers in the novel in order to eliminate the threat posed by Vanbeest Brown (Harry Bertram, the lost heir). If justice is eventually brought about in the novel, it is primarily through the agency of Meg Merrilies, the gypsy who curses Godfrey Bertram for driving her people away. Symbolically speaking, Meg Merrilies represents the traditional culture, Glossin the modern bourgeois–legal society, while the Bertram family, oscillating between the two as Godfrey Bertram had so obviously done, are eventually reclaimed for the former. These warnings against the law are reinforced in the sub-plot concerned with the farmer and sportsman Dandy Dinmont. Dinmont is contemplating a legal action against his neighbour in a boundary dispute, but the wise old lawyer Pleydell advises him against it: ' "So ye winna take on wi' me, I'm doubting?" "Me? Not I, – go home, go home, take a pint and agree." '[32] This advice, delivered as Pleydell is in his cups, suggests that men should regulate their affairs without recourse to the law – that, indeed, there is an element of perversity in the whole business of going to court. The law does not guarantee justice and is simply symptomatic of a cultural breakdown in which people are no longer willing to communicate with one another, to live and let live.

In a number of his early novels, Scott shows innocent people in conflict with the law: the result of this conflict is such as to make us question the law itself and the way in which it is operated. In *The Antiquary*, Edie Ochiltree, the venerable old bedesman, the very soul of integrity, is brought before a court of law to answer charges preferred by the swindler and charlatan, Dousterswivel. The essence of the matter is that Edie declines to answer questions, because, as Bailie Littlejohn puts it, he 'knew the danger of a judicial declaration on the part of an accused person – which, to say the truth, has hanged many an honester man than he is'.[33] But, for the reader, Edie's forthright and uncompromising manner has a far greater force than this: it implies that Edie himself embodies a certain principle of legitimacy and that he feels able to question the legitimacy of the proceedings in which he is forced to take part:

> 'Bailie Littlejohn,' said the mendicant, 'if it be your honour's pleasure, we'll cut a lang tale short, and I . . . just tell ye I am no minded to answer ony o' thae questions; I'm ower auld a traveller to let my tongue bring me into trouble.'
>
> 'Write down,' said the magistrate, 'that he declines to answer all interrogatories, in respect that by telling the truth he might be brought to trouble.'
>
> 'Na, na,' said Ochiltree, 'I'll no hae that set down as part o' my answer; but I just meant to say that in a' my memory and practice, I never saw ony gude come o' answering idle questions.'[34]

We should not overlook the fact that Edie himself forms a kind of tribunal as far as ordinary people are concerned: he is frequently called upon to settle arguments and disputes between various parties – a role which he performs very successfully. Thus Edie is connected with ways of solving problems without resorting to the law and performs precisely this function in the narrative of *The Antiquary*. By implication the legal proceedings are nothing more than 'idle questions' – they demonstrate the arbitrariness, unfairness and even downright injustice that can be involved when the law is brought in to resolve issues. Edie Ochiltree's appearance before a court signals the supersession of traditional forms of authority and arbitration by an abstract judicial system which is less responsive to the real needs of people and less capable of grasping the nature of problems it has to deal with, because of its distance from them.

Edie's trial is symbolically important, but it is without serious consequences. In *Old Mortality*, however, Scott presents us with a tribunal that is infinitely more morally repugnant in its cruelty and injustice: the proceedings of the Privy Council at Edinburgh. This scene, in which MacBriar the Covenanting divine is viciously tortured and then executed, serves more than any other to validate the claims of the Covenanters, because it brings out strongly the partisan nature of the 'justice' being administered and suggests how empty it is to apply principles of legitimacy to which whole sections of the Scottish people are fervently opposed. If whole masses of people find themselves on the wrong side of the law, for Scott this means not that there is something wrong with the people but that there is something wrong with the law. This is abundantly clear in *The Heart of Midlothian*. Again we find over-zealousness on the part of law-enforcement officers: first in the drive against smuggling and contraband, which leads to the arrest of one of the most notorious smugglers, Andrew Wilson, and then in the action of Captain Porteous in firing on the crowd after Wilson's hanging. Scott notes, 'Smuggling was almost universal in the reigns of George I and II; for the people, unaccustomed to imposts, and regarding them as an unjust aggression upon their ancient liberties, made no scruple to elude them whenever it was possible to do so.'[35] For Scott, both the campaign against smuggling and the action against the Edinburgh crowd are to be seen not in the light of the 'administration of the law' but as acts of oppression. Further criticism of the law can be found in the proceedings against Effie Deans for child-murder, a charge that has no foundation in fact. The law in this case is shown to be inflexible, inhuman in its application and blind. Moreover, by the very way in which he has constructed his narrative Scott brings out the class nature of justice. Robertson, the smuggler, is an enemy to society, but as Lord George Staughton he gets off scot-free. Effie Deans, the daughter of a humble Scottish farmer, is barely reprieved, thanks to the action of her sister, Jeanie, who walks to London to plead for her; but in another social situation such desperate and uncertain remedies would scarcely be required. Scott was no Godwinian, but in this novel at least he showed himself influenced by the ideas that had animated *Caleb Williams*.

Both *Rob Roy* and *The Bride of Lammermoor* have as their
theme the passing of traditional society and its supersession by
a commercial–legal type of society – in terms of Scottish
intellectual history the choice is between the values of Adam
Ferguson and those of Adam Smith. In *Rob Roy* Frank
Osbaldistone, who is reluctant to go into the family business,
brings forward the traditional Adam Smith argument for the
development of commerce, despite this: 'It connects nation
with nation, relieves the wants and contributes to the wealth of
all, and is to the general commonwealth of the civilised world
what the daily intercourse of ordinary life is to private society,
or rather, what air and food are to our bodies.'[36] The lack of
conviction that Frank brings to this particular argument
despite his recognition of its validity strikes a note that is to
recur throughout the book. The book centres on a contrast
between the progressive commercial Lowlands of Scotland,
represented by Bailie Jarvie, and the quasi-feudal society of the
Highlands, centred on the outlaw Rob Roy. The Lowlanders
are pious, industrious and hard-working but ultimately rather
prosaic; appropriately it is the Highlanders who have all the
best tunes. The distinction between the two worlds is well
formulated by Bailie Jarvie: 'But I maun hear naething about
honour – we ken naething here but about credit. Honour is a
homicide and a bloodspiller, that gangs about making frays in
the street; but Credit is a decent, honest man that sits at hame
and makes the pat play.'[37] On the one hand, honour and
violence; on the other, commerce and peace. But in the novel
the implicit superiority of commerce to the honour-based
society that Bailie Jarvie suggests is by no means enforced. For
Frank's own father's business is brought down by lack of
honour and trust – on the part both of Rashleigh, who abuses
the confidence placed in him, and of the Scottish firms who
will no longer extend credit. It is through the intervention of
Rob Roy that the family fortunes are restored. Scott is
eloquent about the Highlanders: their gravity and pride, their
friendliness and loyalty to one another, their bravery and
intrepidity, their romantic and poetic feeling, their simple
and unaffected manners. The impersonality, lack of trust and
cupidity of bourgeois society are dramatised in the scene in
which Rob Roy repays Jarvie the thousand marks he owes
him: the Bailie carefully weighs every single piece, but Rob

Roy deals with the problem of the bond, which requires two witnesses to validate it, by throwing it on the fire with the words, 'That's a Hieland settlement of accounts.'[38] Rob Roy completely rejects the system of legality, which he sees primarily as oppressing the Scottish people:

> I gie God's malison and mine to a' sort o' magistrates, justices, bailies, sheriffs, sheriff-officers, constables, and sic-like black cattle, that hae been the plague o' puir auld Scotland this hunder year – it was a merry warld when every man held his ain gear wi' his ain grip, and when the countryside wasna fashed wi' warrants and poindings and apprisings, and a' that cheatry craft.[39]

This is, of course, the speech of an outlaw, and Scott makes it clear that an acceptance of this freedom also means an acceptance of violence: the Highland idyll is overcast by the moment when the unfortunate Morris is hurled into the loch at the instigation of Helen MacGregor. Thus, again there is a dilemma that it is not possible to have a certain set of values without paying a price in some other way. But it would be wrong to suggest that, since Frank Osbaldistone returns to his counting-house this represents some sort of endorsement of the commercial state of society for Scott: rather he simply accepts that this is the modern state of society with which we must come to terms – but in so doing we should never lose sight of the virtues and example of such men as Rob Roy.

In the *Bride of Lammermoor*, the supplanting of an honour-based society by a commercial–legal one has the character of tragedy. Faults in the administration of justice are made by Scott the principle cause of the dispossession of Edgar of Ravenswood and his supersession by the cunning lawyer Sir William Ashton:

> The administration of justice, in particular, was infected by the most gross partiality. A case of importance scarcely occurred, in which their was not some ground for bias or partiality on the part of the judges, who were so little able to withstand the temptation, that the adage, 'Show me the

man, and I will show you the law' became as prevalent as it was scandalous.[40]

The Keeper's defence of himself – 'what has been between us has been the work of the law, not my doing; and to the law they must look, if they would impugn my proceedings'[41] – is both true and not true: is indeed the work of the law, – but not justice; moreover, the separation between 'my doing' and the idea of the objectivity of the law is quite mythical. Edgar is a tragic anachronism, a man of honour living on in a degraded world of opportunism and deceit, blocked off from any conceivable recourse or source of justice. Even his love for Lucy Ashton is warped into meaninglessness through the careerist ambitions of Lady Ashton, who forces her into a marriage with the opportunist Bucklaw. It is significant that the climactic moment in the novel centres around a legal document. The melancholy, dishevelled Edgar bursts into the room just as Lucy has given her blurred and blotted signature to the marriage contract, which, as Scott notes, had already been signed by Sir William Ashton 'with legal solemnity and precision'.[42] This emotional encounter is simultaneously the confrontation of two completely different worlds: one founded on the principle of honour, the other on the supremacy of law. The forcing of the contract on Lucy symbolically articulates what has been implicit in so much else: the forcing of the law on human nature and human institutions and traditions is fraught with disruptive and catastrophic consequences. As Scott had already written, 'we are not made of wood or stone'.[43] To adapt the phrase that Evan Dhu uses of Donald Bean Lean in Waverley, Lucy dies *'for the law'* – 'Ay, that is, with the law, or by the law'[44] – but unlike him she is not a conscious outlaw but a victim. In *The Bride of Lammermoor* the very possibility of standing outside the law is something that is itself passing away.

The historical novel of Scott is not simply concerned with history but deals with it specifically in terms of change, process, conflict; it shows the supersession of one set of values and customs by another, the perpetual shrinking and enlarging of the field of possibility both for particular individuals and for cultures as a whole. For Scott, as for Marx, men do not make history as they choose but act within the context of historically determined and determinate conditions. The passing of certain types of social formations – the licensed beggars or gypsies – often had for Scott a folkloristic interest. In the Preface to *The Antiquary* he linked his purpose with that of Wordsworth and described how he had looked for his 'principle personages in the class of society who are the last to feel the influence of that general polish which assimilates to each other the manners of different nations'.[45] Scott's use of the phrase 'principle personages' is of distinct interest, since it brings out quite forcibly the extent to which the narratives of *Guy Mannering* and *The Antiquary* were structured around the figures of Meg Merrilies and Edie Ochiltree, despite the fact that neither is technically the hero. It is through such anachronistic figures that Scott dramatises the passing of time, the changes in manners, the incursion of the modern. They serve as a kind of benchmark; for, as Scott wrote in the Postscript to *Waverley*, 'like those who drift down the stream of deep and smooth river, we are not aware of the progress we have made until we fix our eye on the now distant point from which we have been drifted'.[46] For all the apparent innocence with which the word 'progress' makes its appearance in this sentence, the repetition of 'drift' and 'drifting' suggests the real urgency in Scott's perception of the situation: the complacency with which people immerse themselves in the present can lead to an enormous blindness and render invisible the most far-reaching and catastrophic changes. Indeed, the moral value of the historical novel is that it is one of the few artistic forms which can lead us to interrogate and question the immediacy of the given. Scott is often presented as a sanguine apostle of progress, commerce and the middle way, and in his own critical utterances he indeed provides sufficient evidence to give substance to this view. But a Scott who could be summed up in this way would not have given us the novels, the great novels, that he has. Scott's vision of history was more profound than this: he could not believe in 'progress' pure and simple; the notion of an age of transition implied something more catastrophic: the destruction of a whole complex of cultural forms. If *Waverley* rightfully enjoys a position of prominence in the Scott canon, it is because Scott knows that what occurred in Scotland was nothing short of a catastrophe: not because 'Bonnie Prince Charlie' was defeated, but because of everything else that was brought down with him in that comprehensive collapse. Scott writes,

> There is no European nation which, within the course of half a century or little more, has undergone so complete a change as this kingdom of Scotland. The effects of the insurrection of 1745 – the destruction of the patriarchal power of the Highland chiefs, the abolition of the heritable jurisdiction of the Lowland nobility and barons, the total eradication of the Jacobite party, which averse to inter-mingle with the English or adopt their customs, long continued to pride themselves upon maintaining ancient Scottish manners and customs – commenced this inno-vation.[47]

Scott goes on to refer to the 'gradual influx of wealth and extension of commerce'[48] – progressive phenomena in-deed – but he knows that for this a price has been paid.

Waverley, like all of Scott's novels, is not a novel about an individual: it shows rather how intricate and manifold are the consequences of the defeat of the Jacobite rebellion and how it affects the lives of many different people – not simply Fergus MacIvor, who is sent to a 'lingering and cruel death',[49] or his sister Flora, who flees to a convent in Paris, but the old Baron Bradwardine, who hides himself in a hole in the ground, the half-wit David Gellatley, and Waverley himself, whose for-tunes become bound up with the losing side. The theme of the destruction of a culture is expressed by Scott through the destruction of Tully-Veolan – presented to the reader, rep-resentatively, as 'A Scottish Manor-House Sixty Years Since'. In the earlier part of *Waverley* Scott gives a leisurely and lingeringly picturesque description of his hero's arrival there: the venerable archway leading into a long avenue of chestnut trees and sycamores, the house itself with its multiplicity of towers and turrets, the fountain adorned with a stone bear, the raised terrace and old-world garden, filled with fruit-trees and ornate shrubs. Towards the end of the novel Waverley returns to Tully-Veolan and finds the gateway damaged, trees in the avenue cut down, the house burnt and blackened by fire, the fountain smashed, the balustrade on the terrace broken. It is this image more than any other that presents us with the passing of a world – the reality of '45. But sensing that this is too powerful, Scott will only allow it to remain as *an image* and concludes the novel with a transformation scene in which the obliteration is itself obliterated.

Seen in this light, as a concern with the way in which a whole culture can be shattered, broken up and made obsolete in a relatively short span of time, it becomes evident that Scott has enormously broadened the scope of the historical genre, for it takes as its subject-matter not so much the individual in history as the very processes of history itself. If it is no longer altogether appropriate to speak of an anachronistic 'hero', this is, in part, because the notion of anachronism, of cultures in the process of being superseded, has been greatly extended.

At the same time, however, it must be recognised that Scott is not simply the inheritor of the historical drama. His work owes just as much to his predecessors of the 1780s and 1790s, the practitioners of the Gothic and social novel. It would be easy to argue that such borrowings as there are to be found in Scott are quite superficial – a matter of taking up one or two threads here and there and weaving them into a larger and more comprehensive design. It certainly would be hard to deny that the Gothic legacy was not extensively and substantively transformed. But the influence of Gothic goes deep and affects the whole way in which Scott's fiction is formulated: motifs taken from the Gothic have no accidental quality but recur over and over again. The most obvious instance is Scott's use of madness and the supernatural. Scott's work embraces a multitude of mad and half-crazed figures, from David Gellatley to Madge Wildfire, Habbakkuk Mucklewrath and Peter Peebles in *Redgauntlet*. There is scarcely a single novel that does not make some use of superstition and magical practices. Moreover, their use is by no means trivial. Scott tries to make the reader enter into the spirit of another age and recognise that it is characterised by a greater precariousness and uncertainty. Superstition is seen by Scott as a cultural and not an individual phenomenon; so that even the sensible and down-to-earth Jeanie Deans is filled with apprehension, anxiety and foreboding when she goes to her noctural assignation at Muschat's Cairn. Scott notes,

Witchcraft and demonology, as we have had already

occasion to remark, were at this period believed in by almost all ranks, but more especially among the stricter classes of presbyterians, whose government, when their party was at the head of the state, had been much sullied by their eagerness to enquire into, and persecute these imaginary crimes.[50]

But superstition and the irrational also have a structural role to play: they serve to break down assumptions about continuity and orderliness and become symptomatic of an instability in the world and in men's conceptions of it. Scott's characters are faced with complex historical changes which they must necessarily attempt to 'read': superstition offers itself as a way of reading which has a distinct appeal, even though its conclusions are frequently wrong. The use of the magical serves to emphasise the arbitrary nature of Scott's narrative and forces the reader to understand that the 'riddle' to be solved is present both fictionally and in the real world of historical forces. Indeed, the historical novel carries a heavy burden: it is required of it that it have a certain 'rightness', which is not a purely aesthetic quality but is connected with the reader's sense of the adequacy with which the novel 'reads' the historical past.

Another important Gothic theme employed by Scott is that of imprisonment. *The Heart of Midlothian* is actually named after the famous Tolbooth prison in the centre of Edinburgh. Scott's imagination seems to have been particularly drawn to historical episodes in which imprisonment figures prominently. *The Abbot* centres on the confinement of Mary, Queen of Scots, at the castle of Lochleven; *Kenilworth* describes Leicester's shutting away of his bride at Cumnor Place so that Elizabeth would not know of his marriage. Peveril is forced to endure a prolonged stay in the ancient fortress of Newgate; while much of Nigel's visit to London is spent at odds with the law – first in hiding in the sanctuary of Whitechapel, whence he emerges only to be incarcerated in the Tower of London. In *Ivanhoe* most of the principal characters are held captive at his castle by Front-de-Boeuf; in *Quentin Durward* Louis XI is imprisoned by his rival the Duke of Burgundy; in *The Fair Maid of Perth* the Duke of Rothsay is cruelly murdered in the dungeon of Falkland Castle. The influence of the Gothic tradition is most apparent in *Redgauntlet*, where Darsie Latimer finds himself mysteriously confined in a strange house. The epistolary form of the novel and the use of a journal by Darsie to describe what happens to him while he is a prisoner places it in the tradition of Holcroft's *Anna St Ives* and Richardson's *Pamela*. For the Gothic novelist, prison provided a focus for radical ideas: it showed the unjust and unwarranted power of one individual over another, the bias and injustice of the law, a naked use of coercion that unmasked society's pretensions to fairness and reason. Prison was the definitive institution of the autocratic and anti-democratic state. Scott would not have expressed his own opinions in precisely this form, but it does seem significant that prisons should be such a recurrent feature of his novels and that they should so invariably be associated with unjust and arbitrary authority. In the fictional universe of Scott, imprisonment is a sign that something is amiss: that power is in the wrong hands or is being seriously abused. But this is also because of the absence of absolutes in Scott's novels: power, force, coercion will be used by one side against another, but the legitimating principles that are invoked to justify their use are often of questionable authority. The prison for Scott is a sign of the instability of justice.

The most important of Scott's borrowings from his novel-istic predecessors is the figure of the lost heir/heiress, which had been used by Mrs Smith in *Emmeline* and by Robert Bage in *Hermsprong*. In Scott this character is not always a lost heir but he is invariably 'lost' – in some way cut off, rejected by his family, lacking moral support from others or a place in which he belongs and is accepted. Scott's heroes, like Hawthorne's Wakefield, have lost their place in the world and their principal efforts are directed towards regaining it. In Scott's fiction this lost hero is ubiquitous: from Waverley, Harry Bertram, Lovel, Frank Osbaldistone and Edgar of Ravenswood to such later protagonists as Roland Graeme in *The Abbot*, Mordaunt Mertoun and Cleveland in *The Pirate*, Tyrrell in *St Ronan's Well* and Nigel in *The Fortunes of Nigel*. This lost hero displaces the anachronistic hero at the centre of the narrative, although this does not necessarily mean that his role is more important. Rather, the relation between the lost hero and the anachronistic figure becomes a structuring principle of the narrative. From a certain standpoint the progressive movement of the Scott novel can be seen in terms of psychological development: the hero seeks for a surrogate or substitute father as a source of values that are lacking in his own life and as a basis for his own identity, but he is invariably brought to a point where he must stand upon his own feet. This relationship also has the character of a rebellion, since it often means an involvement with dangerous, unpopular or seditious causes and contact with people outside the ranks of polite society. The opening up of the world for the protagonist is simultaneously an opening up of the world for the reader; it brings him into contact with values and cultures that are alien, disturbing, but also 'romantic' – as Scott himself put it in the opening pages of *Waverley*:

> Those who are contented to remain with me will be occasionally exposed to the dullness inseparable from heavy roads, steep hills, sloughs, and other terrestrial retardations; but with tolerable horses and a civil driver (as the advertisements have it), I engage to get as soon as possible into more picturesque and romantic country, if my passengers incline to have some patience with me during the first stages.[51]

The relationship between the lost hero and the anachronistic figure or outcast is often such that this character appears as the hero's double. In *Old Mortality*, for instance, Bothwell of Burley appears as a kind of malignant other to Henry Morton, a man as fanatical as Henry is moderate, who ceaselessly draws Henry into his own plans by invoking the name of Henry's father (so that Burley seems like his demonic spirit) and by the obligation imposed on him by the fact that Burley saved his father, an obligation which he is obliged to return. Similarly, in *Redgauntlet* Darsie Latimer is coerced by his uncle, Redgauntlet, who appears almost as some other self whom Darsie must come to terms with. Redgauntlet embodies the past of Darsie's family, a past which his mother has vainly tried to suppress. Redgauntlet's character as double become manifest in a striking scene when Darsie, in the same room as his uncle, catches a glimpse of himself in the mirror.

> As he glanced round, with a look which he had

endeavoured to compose to haughty indifference, his eye encountered mine, and, I thought, at the first glance sank beneath it. But it instantly rallied his natural spirit, and returned me one of those extraordinary looks, by which he could contort so strangely the wrinkles on his forehead. I started; but, angry at myself for my pusillanimity, I answered him by a look of the same kind, and, catching the reflection of my countenance in a large antique mirror which stood before me, I started again at the real or imaginary resemblance which my countenance, at that moment, bore to that of Herries. Surely my fate is somehow interwoven with that of this mysterious individual.[52]

This remarkably complex episode articulates the salient features of the relationship of the hero to the other. The attempt to insist upon difference only brings out similarity, the refusal of recognition only serves to precipitate it. The reflection in a mirror, significantly antique, represents the dimension of the past that has been suppressed. The mysteriousness that surrounds the other is also the mystery that surrounds himself. The secret can no longer be kept in obscurity, but must be brought into the open and worked through in a manner that is characterised by similarity difference. Redgauntlet both is and isn't Darsie. Symptomatically, Redgauntlet in his final words does not repudiate Darsie but gives him his approval – 'though to breed you up in my own political opinions has been for many years my anxious wish, I am now glad that it could not be accomplished'[53] – his benediction and blessing. Redgauntlet lays his hand on the sword of Darsie's father, saying to Darsie,

> You will, from henceforth, be uncontrolled master of all the property of which forfeiture could not deprive your father – of all that belonged to him excepting this his good sword ... which shall never fight for the House of Hanover; and as my hand will never draw weapon more, I shall sink it forty fathoms deep in the wide ocean. Bless you young man![54]

In this speech, Redgauntlet 'gives' Darsie his freedom. In taking away the sword he removes the curse of rebellion that has lingered over the family, while, by speaking in the name of and in the context of Darsie's father, Redgauntlet himself assumes the parental role and gives Darsie his approval. This is necessary because it removes the guilt attached to Darsie, who in some sense has been disloyal, both to the Jacobite cause and to the Hanoverian. This guilt is dispersed by approving the Hanoverian succession from a Jacobite point of view. At this point Redgauntlet speaks not simply for himself but for history; his words transcend all opposites, whether inter-subjective or historical.

The use of doubles in Scott, however, is not simply psychological but also analogous to the thematic doubling of the Gothic novel, where a motif is generalised and given wider significance by the use of repetition. The set Emmeline/Mrs Stafford/Lady Adelina is characteristic; but, of course, the original prototype of all this is *King Lear*. The most intricate example in Scott's work of this thematic doubling is *The Heart of Midlothian*. Wilson, the smuggler who saves Robertson's life and whom Robertson in turn tries to rescue from the gallows, can be seen as Robertson's double – for in Scott the idea of the double is often linked with a mutual exchange of obligations. But Robertson's real identity is Sir George Staughton. Sir George also doubles with another character, Madge Wildfire, whose identity he assumes in the siege of the Tolbooth gaol. But Madge Wildfire is also the double of Effie Deans, since both have an illegitimate child by Sir George. And Effie, in her role as Lady Staunton, is also her own double – since no one connects her with the person accused of child-murder, just as no one connects Sir George with 'Robertson'. Moreover, Sir George has one more double in his son 'the Whistler', who is brought up in the Highlands and whose life proves to be as wild as that of his father has been. These relationships can be shown diagrammatically as follows:

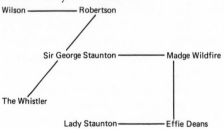

It is not difficult to perceive these structured parallelisms in
The Heart of Midlothian; but to decipher them is rather more
difficult. Clearly, the fact that both Effie and Sir George
Staunton have strict and repressive parents with strongly held
religious views serves to generalise the theme of generational
conflict and to suggest that the fathers, David Deans and the
Rev. Staunton, have an important role in precipitating the
emotional and psychological catastrophe. The use of madness
in the novel is also important. Sir George Staunton's impersonation of Madge Wildfire in the raid on the Tolbooth gaol is a
symbolic link between his own situation and that of Effie,
whom he is to marry, but it also serves to suggest the *innocence* of
madness – to imply that madness is always a symptom and a
consequence, never a cause. The case of Madge Wildfire, the
facts surrounding which are buried in the deepest obscurity, is
that of a woman deeply wronged; that she can be so wronged,
like Effie, is symptomatic of the way in which 'justice' is
distributed in a class society. Madge is punished for being a
victim, while Sir George, the man who casually harms her,
escapes the punishment of the law. Effie Deans is the shifter
who brings out the class nature of justice, since while she
belongs to the humble classes she is punished for a crime she
did not commit, but when married to Sir George she escapes
the consequences. It can now be seen that this motif is doubled
in the relationship between 'Robertson' and Wilson. For
Robertson is enabled by Wilson to escape, and Wilson takes
the whole punishment on himself. In effect the novel draws a
sharp distinction between human justice, which is unfair,
unjust and irrational in its application, and divine justice.
Although Effie and Sir George escape justice they are
nevertheless punished, and this punishment is the work both
of divine providence and of the internal monitions of the
heart. Sir George is killed in the attempt to recover his own
son, while Effie 'betrayed the inward wound'[55] by withdraw-
ing to a convent abroad. There is a symbolic appropriateness
in this, since she thereby resubmits herself to the punishment
of banishment which her social status had enabled her to
evade. The 'damnation' of Sir George is also inward, since his
crimes cut him off from his fellow human beings and leave
him in a terrible psychological isolation. As he announces to
the startled young clergyman, Butler, at St Leonard's,

I am the devil!—

   Yes! call me Apollyon, Abaddon, whatever name you shall choose, as a clergyman acquainted with the upper and lower circles of spiritual denomination, to call me by, you shall not find an appellation more odious to him that bears it, than is mine own.[56]

In these linked preoccupations – the class nature of justice, the emphasis on the terrible consequences for the individual of isolating himself from the rest of mankind, and Scott's final insistence that 'guilt, though it may attain temporal splendour, can never confer real happiness'[57] – the Godwinian sources of the novel become evident. If *The Heart of Midlothian* is closest to the structure of Gothic, it is also closest in terms of the message which it communicates, consciously or unconsciously, to the reader.

   Sir George Staunton is, of course, a representative instance of a third type of figure that recurs throughout Scott's work: that of the outcast. These outcast figures are, in part, the product of reciprocal influences between Byron and Scott, with Byron picking up clues from the figure of Marmion and amplifying them in a series of poems and Scott reincorporating these influences in his own work. A particularly significant conjuncture can be identified following the publication of *Manfred* in 1817, for Scott published in 1818 *The Heart of Midlothian* and in *The Bride of Lammermoor*, which featured two characters, Sir George Staunton and Edgar of Ravenswood, very close to the stereotype of the Byronic hero. However, although these outcast figures are clearly identifiable in Scott's work, they are not intrinsically significant as in Byron, but function in a triadic system of discourse: lost hero, anarchronistic figure, outcast. The term 'outcast' itself, though undoubtedly crucial in defining a whole body of concerns in Romantic literature, cannot be used as if it were unproblematic: it is useful so long as one bears in mind that 'outcast' is the name for a bundle of myths, not a single theme. The complexity of the notion of outcast in Romantic literature can be brought out by indicating at least seven possible articulations of it – and they can obviously exist in combination. In the first variant, which can be thought of as Godwinian, an individual performs an act or action which serves to cut himself off from the rest of humanity – and it is primarily this separation that constitutes the moral wrong. Examples would include Godwin's *St Leon* and Goethe's *Faust*. The second variant is almost a transposition of this: the protagonist has committed a crime or great wrong which isolates him, but attention focuses on the crime (*The Rime of the Ancient Mariner*, *Manfred*). The third and fourth variants present characters who have not necessarily done any wrong but who do not belong in contemporary society. The weak form is that of Werther, the strong form that of Gotz, a man who has the strength of traditional cultural values to draw upon. A fifth variant is concerned specifically with the figure of the artist: his visionary consciousness, his imagination cuts himself off from the concerns and values of ordinary people. The sixth and seventh variants represent different ways of dealing with the situation of being isolated, alienated and adrift: one possibility is to embrace it (Byron *passim*), the other to seek to return to the social world and to one's fellow human beings (*Faust* Part II, *The Rime of the Ancient Mariner*). Scott's triadic presentation of lost hero, anachronistic figure and outcast is a way of embracing these multiple inflections. In effect, all three characters are confronted with the problem of alienation, but in different ways. The lost hero is in touch with the contemporary world, but he lacks a sense of community, a group with which he can identify, a stable place in the world. The anachronistic figure possesses a stable traditional culture and a basis for his values, but they often find themselves at odds with a world that rejects or undermines them. The outcast has affinities with both, but, unlike them, his fate tends to be disastrous or tragic: he finds himself completely at odds with the world and is thrown back completely on his own resources. While Scott's anachronistic figures are primarily a focus for nostalgia, his outcasts serve to dramatise the destructive processes of historical change, the shattering consequences of isolation for the individual. The outcast in Scott in a very real sense is also a *scapegoat*: he takes on his shoulders the stigma attached to a defeated group: his fate signifies that history is never neutral, but always partisan.

The accompanying table sets out this triadic structure of lost hero, outcast and anachronistic figure as it appears in Scott's major novels from *Waverley* to *The Fair Maid of Perth*. While

Novel	Lost hero	Outcast	Anachronistic Figure
Waverley	Waverley	Fergus MacIvor	Bradwardine
Guy Mannering	Harry Bertram	Mannering	Meg Merrilies
The Antiquary	Lovel	Lord Glenallen	Edie Ochiltree
Rob Roy	Frank Osbaldistone	Rob Roy Rashleigh	Rob Roy
Old Mortality	Harry Morton	Balfour of Burley	Old Mortality
The Heart of Midlothian	Effie/Jeanie	Sir George Staunton	David Deans
The Bride of Lammermoor	Edgar of Ravenswood	Edgar of Ravenswood	Caleb Balderstone
Ivanhoe	Ivanhoe	Richard	Cedric
The Monastery	Halbert Glendinning	Henry Warden	Martin the shepherd
The Abbot	Roland Graeme	Mary, Queen of Scots	The Abbot
Kenilworth	Tressilian	Amy	Sussex
The Pirate	Mordaunt	Cleveland	Norna
Peveril of the Peak	Peveril	Christian/ Ganlesse	Bridgenorth/ Countess of Derby
St Ronan's Well	Tyrrel	Etherington/ Tyrrel	Meg Dods
Redgauntlet	Darsie Latimer	Redgauntlet	Wandering Willie
Woodstock	Wildrake/Everard	Charles	Sir Henry Lee
The Fair Maid of Perth	Conachar	Rothsay/ Ramornay/ Conachar	Torquil of the Oak

this table does serve to emphasise the persistent, not to say ubiquitous, nature of this pattern of relationships, a number of qualifying remarks must be made in order to elucidate it and place it in perspective, since Scott does not simply repeat himself but rather makes this structure the ground upon which an endless variety of figures is woven. Apart from such shorter works as *A Legend of Montrose* and *The Black Dwarf*, where only the outcast figure is unmistakably present, this scheme significantly does not cover either *The Fortunes of Nigel* or *Quentin Durward*.

In the case of *The Fortunes of Nigel*, Nigel himself seems to assume all three functions: a lost heir, adrift in London, seeking friends whom he can rely upon; an anachronistic hero who brings claims of justice in a climate of opinion that is not propitious for a favourable outcome and in a courtly world that would prefer to forget the past; an outcast and fugitive from justice in Whitefriars. *Quentin Durward*, a major Scott novel, bears no obvious relationship to this triad of alienation. It is primarily a study in the contradictions of an age: the co-presence of violence and courtly traditions of violence and respect, the combination in Louis XI of rationalistic calcula-tion with extreme superstitiousness – which may well have been suggested by remarks of Ferguson. Quentin Durward himself is an extremely unproblematic figure, one of the few Scott heroes who acts with decision, confidence and determi-nation. Scott saw alienation, the psychological insecurity created in the individual estranged from a particular social group and living in a period itself riven by conflict, as characteristically modern (that is to say, post-Reformation) phenomenon. Henry Warden in *The Monastery* and Richard I in *Ivanhoe* are among the very few outcast figures who are not also seen as doomed. Warden, the Protestant preacher, points forward to the ultimate victory of the Reformation, while Richard is triumphantly restored to his rightful throne.

Similar considerations apply to *The Fair Maid of Perth*. The theme of the outcast is strongly asserted in the novel. The characteristic lost-hero role is filled by Conachar/Eachin MacIan of the Clan Quhele. Eachin fulfils the ancient prophecy that the tribe will be destroyed through 'a boy born under a bush of holly, and suckled by a white doe'. The relevance of this myth is that Eachin is separated from the tribe and spends his youth in the cultured city of Perth. Cut off from the warlike values of the group, he is unable to play his part in the fight to the death between the Clan Grattan and the Clan Quhele. This outcast figure is doubled by others: Sir John Ramornay, whose severed arm is the sign of his exclusion from society as punishment for the crimes he has committed, and his companion and friend the Duke of

Rothsay, who likewise becomes an outcast from the court. But the actual hero of the narrative is the courageous, stalwart and completely unproblematic individual, Henry Wynd, whose strong sense of identity is linked with the burgher community of Perth.

In *The Bride of Lammermoor* and *St Ronan's Well*, the predicament of the lost hero finds no satisfactory resolution and he himself becomes the outcast figure; for this reason these are amongst the bleakest and most tragic of Scott's novels. In *The Heart of Midlothian* and *Woodstock* the role of 'lost hero' is split between two characters. Jeanie Deans is a completely outgoing and stable personality, but her concern for her sister, Effie, places her in a complex and problematic situation, where she is constantly faced with a conflict of loyalties. In *Woodstock* neither Wildrake nor Everard is as insecure as the name 'lost hero' might suggest, but in combination Scott uses them to suggest the problem of loyalties in the Civil War: Wildrake the Cavalier leaning politicly to the Roundhead cause, Everard seeing much merit in the royalist argument and attracted to the daughter of a supporter of the King, but nevertheless firmly implicated in the puritan cause. Everard and Wildrake may not be psychologically lost, but they *are* characteristically indecisive.

The only other doubling of function occurs in *Rob Roy*, where *Rob Roy* is simultaneously anachronistic hero and outcast, a man at odds with the spirit of his age and hunted by the law. But Rob Roy is never in the position of being utterly alone; he finds great strength, encouragement and support from the people who follow him. Scott ends the novel with the comment of old Andrew Fairservice 'There were many things ower bad for blessing, and ower gude for banning, like Rob Roy'[58] – a formulation which implies that Rob's function as the transmitter of ancient Scottish values precludes that total interdiction which is the fate of the outcast. Scott maintains the anachronistic hero–outcast contradiction in perfect balance throughout the novel, and the scapegoat function is deflected onto Frank Osbaldistone's double, Rashleigh, who is slain by Rob Roy himself for his treachery to the loyalist cause. Finally, in *Old Mortality*, Old Mortality, the devoted stonemason who keeps alive the memory of the Covenanters by rechiselling the names of the martyrs on their tombstones, is an anachronistic figure who does not appear in the narrative as such, but serves as a framing device for it.

The triadic relationship of lost hero/outcast/anachronistic figure has complex implications for the reader of Scott's novels: it serves to present a multiple image of alienation in which each mirrors the predicament of the other in a transposed reflection: if modern man is alienated through his separation from the group and traditional sources of culture, the anachronistic figure also finds himself adrift in a world where the values he stands for are gradually but inexorably passing away. While both survive in most of Scott's novels through his use of the figure of the outcast, Scott both intensifies and generalises a sense of cultural defeat. Scott is obsessively concerned with defeat: he returns to this subject in novel after novel; the most characteristic and powerful moment in any Scott novel occurs when the hero finds that the whole world around him is crumbling to pieces. Yet the tragic nature and stature of Scott's fiction has been buried under a mass of often repeated cliches and doubtful half-truths. There is Daiches's insistence that 'Scott was never the obsessed artist, but the happy writer', the notion of Scott embodying the 'Augustan man' (A. N. Wilson), the 'middle-of-the-road' hero invoked by Daiches and Devlin, the invocation of Scott's 'age-of-reason outlook' (Cusac).[59] Even Lukács, who in other ways is so insightful and perceptive, is lured into the assumption that Scott's main concern is with the English success story. Much is wrong with the network of assumptions. We can no longer seriously invoke a homogenous 'age of reason': Scott owes a clear debt to Adam Ferguson, but this does not make him any more the disciple of Burke than of Rousseau or Voltaire. What relevance does the notion of 'middle-of-the-road' hero have to Roland in *The Abbot*, who is at odds with the world and without a firm footing in it until, partly through the agency of his mother, he is brought into an emotional involvement with the Catholic cause and with Mary, Queen of Scots, whose page he becomes? Roland aids Mary in her escape from Lochleven and is present at the battle of Hamilton Moor, when her troops suffer a shattering defeat:

> The column of the assailants, which has hitherto shown one dark, dense, and united line of helmets, surmounted with

plumage, was at once broken and hurled in confusion down the hill, which they had so long endeavoured to gain. In vain were the leaders heard calling upon their followers to stand to the combat, and seen personally resisting when all resistance was evidently vain. They were slain, or felled to the earth, or hurried backwards by the mingled tide of flight and pursuit. What were Roland's thoughts on beholding the rout, and feeling that all that remained for him was to turn bridle, and endeavour to ensure the safety of the Queen's person!?[60]

Scott here is not asking the reader to envisage what would be an appropriate middle-of-the-road response to such a situation, but is asking him to recognise what a catastrophic and traumatic experience this is for his hero: he has laboriously attempted to recover his identity and to find a place in the world where he will be both acknowledged and respected, and now, suddenly, of all this nothing is left. Undoubtedly the novel ends happily with the marriage of Roland to Catherine Seyton, but this cannot obliterate the image of defeat, any more than the marriage of Henry Wynd cancels the death of the Duke of Rothsay in *The Fair Maid of Perth*, or the reprieve of Waverley and Bradwardine blots out the memory of Fergus and Flora MacIvor. Too many critics of Scott write as if *Waverley* were the only Waverley novel; yet even here Scott referred in his postscript to his 'purpose of preserving some idea of the ancient manners of which I have witnessed the almost total extinction'.[61] There *is* a Whig interpretation of history, but Scott's relation to it has the character of a powerful anticipatory critique. Moreover, Scott writes not from a viewpoint of romanticising nostalgia, but, in the spirit of Ferguson, to bring out the characteristic strengths and limitations that are to be found in different types of society. The historical novel is nothing if not an inquiry into values.

The exploratory quality of Scott's fiction comes out even more strongly in the later novels, those subsequent to *The Monastery*. There has been a general tendency to disparage Scott's later work either on the grounds that he was never altogether at home when dealing with non-Scottish themes, or, more frequently, because his financial difficulties compelled him to write in a careless, slapdash manner. Scott's productivity was undoubtedly amazing: in 1822, for example, he published *The Pirate, The Fortunes of Nigel* and *Peveril of the Peak*, totalling in the Border edition some 2130 pages. *The Fortunes of Nigel* and *Peveril of the Peak* were supplied with prefatory epistles from Dr Dryasdust and Captain Clutterbuck, and all three novels were supplied with comprehensive historical notes comprising fifty-five tightly printed pages. Purely in financial terms so much effort was hardly necessary, for *Peveril* is nearly twice as long as *The Bride of Lammermoor*. One is struck rather by Scott's astonishing conscientiousness and by the degree to which he became so totally absorbed and involved in his historical materials that questions of expediency were virtually lost sight of. Moreover, from an analysis of his work as a whole it is perfectly clear that Scott was capable of publishing two full-length novels a year without any strain. Scott certainly does have his failures: *The Monastery* is virtually a complete disaster, *The Pirate* is not altogether satisfactory, *Peveril* is probably overburdened; but in general Scott keeps up a remarkably high standard and even his failures are instructive: they stem from his efforts to expand the range and scope of his fiction rather than from complacent pot boiling.

Undoubtedly, one consideration that shaped the direction of Scott's later work was a desire not to be exclusively tied down either to recent Scottish history or the struggle there between Protestant and Catholic. In *Ivanhoe* he sought to find an equivalent in the tension between Norman and Saxon culture at the time of Richard I, while in *The Monastery* and *The Abbot* he looked back to the Reformation, as a transition from medieval to modern times. Customs, folk-ways, the practice of the supernatural assume even greater importance. In *Old Mortality* Scott had described the Festival of the Popinjay, in *The Black Dwarf* the rituals of Border raiders, but in later novels the incorporation of such practices becomes even more profuse and more central to the action. In *The Pirate* he attempts to give density to the outlandish beliefs of the Orkney and Shetland Isles: the selling of favourable winds, the superstitious refusal to save a drowning man – an injunction twice broken, by Mordaunt Mertoun and Cleveland, each of whom saves the other. Quentin Durward infringes a French stipulation that the bodies of condemned men should be left hanging, since this is not the custom in his native Scotland, and consequently finds himself in serious trouble. In *The Abbot* the sport of falconry and the ancient ceremony of misrule, the traditional hobby-horse, the belief that evil spirits cannot enter a house uninvited are shown as established features of a world very different from that of Scott's own time; while *The Fair Maid of Perth* is almost entirely constructed around traditional practices of the Middle Ages: the frequent affrays and street battles, St Valentine's Day, the belief that blood from a murdered man will flow again if the murderer passes the body, trial by combat, the cry 'St Johnston's hunt is up', the funeral feast of a Highland clan. Scott's use of these customs does not stem merely from a desire to be quaint and picturesque but rather from a desire to deepen the cultural relativism of his earlier work. In novels such as *Rob Roy* and *Waverley* it was too easy for the reader to assign a normative significance to the modern commercial type of civilisation and to see the Highlanders simply as some kind of intriguing departure from it: to miss the crucial balancing of 'mischiefs' and virtues. By going farther back into time and by immersing both himself and his readers in a completely different phenomenological and social world, Scott enforced the recognition that reality can be perceived and structured in many different ways. Quentin Durward, in the novel of that name, serves as a focus of identification for the reader. Durward's inability to grasp or comprehend the specificity of other cultures is that of the generality of Scott's public and the development of the novel serves as an initiation for both:

'Are you a Christian?' asked the Scotchman.
The Bohemian shook his head.
'Dog!' said Quentin, (for there was little toleration in the spirit of Catholicism in those days.)
'No,' was the indifferent and concise answer of the guide, who neither seemed offended or surprised at the young man's violence of manner.
'Are you a Pagan, then, or what are you?'
'I have no religion,' answered the Bohemian.
Durward started back; for though he had heard of Saracens and Idolators, it had never entered into his ideas

or belief, that any body of men could exist who practised no
mode of worship whatever.[62]

In this way the boundaries of perception are clearly demar-
cated.

For Scott the presentation of magic, superstition and the
supernatural in his late fiction assumes a particular
importance – not simply because it is part of the system of
beliefs in a particular historical period, but also because it
serves to dramatise the complexity of the processes of
historical change. The figure of the necromancer, astrologer
or seer is one that recurs again and again: Alasco in *Kenilworth*,
Norna in *The Pirate*, Martius Galeotti in *Quentin Durward*,
Dwining in *The Fair Maid of Perth* and the hermit of Engaddi in
The Talisman. The point, however, is that for the most part
their prophecies fall far short of fulfilment. The role of the
seer is not so much to be right as to dramatise the type of
society and situation in which such a person acquires great
influence; to show how great a burden the obscurity of the
future imposed in cultures where there appeared to be no
rational basis for determining the most appropriate course of
action. Scott's use of superstition in fact forms an internal
critique of his former reliance on a *deus ex machina* figure – a
Rob Roy, Meg Merrilies or Edie Ochiltree – who served to
unravel the plot and bring the novel to a successful conclusion.
In the later Scott *deus ex machina* characters notoriously fail to
deliver the goods: Magdalen Graeme in *The Abbot*,
Touchwood in *St Ronan's Well*, Norna in *The Pirate* – each
finds the world resistant to his or her efforts to impose pattern
and meaning upon it. History is larger than the individual.
For this reason, Scott was rightly indignant at critics who saw
Norna as simply a rerun of Meg Merrilies:

> In one respect I was judged somewhat hastily, perhaps,
> when the character of Norna was pronounced by the critics
> a mere copy of Meg Merrilies. That I had fallen short of
> what I wished and desired to express is unquestionable,
> otherwise my object could not have been so widely mis-
> taken; nor can I yet think that any person who will take the
> trouble of reading the Pirate with some attention can fail to
> trace in Norna – the victim of remorse and insanity, and the

dupe of her own imposture, her mind, too, flooded with all the wild literature and extravagant superstitions of the north – something distinct from the Dumfries-shire gypsy, whose pretensions to supernatural powers are not beyond those of a Norwood prophetess.[63]

The difference between Norna and Meg Merrilies is made explicit within the novel: Norna herself believes in the action of mysterious forces but she is not capable of controlling them. As Cleveland says, 'I hold you for one who knows how to steer upon the current of events, but I deny your power to change its course.'[64] Superstition can be seen as a method of 'reading' history which, though not true, can at least provide a basis for action as far as the individual is concerned – though whatever he does occurs in a context of group activity and intra-group conflict, the outcome of which it is beyond the power of prophecy to determine. It signals the fact that Scott's narratives are no longer linear but polycentric.

Another plot device that suffers deformation in the later Scott is that of the appeal to the monarch, which occupies such a pivotal position in *The Heart of Midlothian*. In *Kenilworth* Amy Robsart implores Queen Elizabeth to save her from Varney, but this does not save her from a cruel death. Nigel intercepts Charles II in Greenwich Park in the hope that he will listen to his suit, but the King refuses to react in the appropriate way, will not listen and behaves in a manner that is altogether incongruous:

The poor king was frightened at once and angry, desirous of securing his safety and, at the same time, ashamed to compromise his dignity; so that, without attending to what Lord Glenvarloch endeavoured to explain, he kept making at his horse, and repeating, 'We are a free King, man – we are a free King – we will not be controlled by a subject – in the name of God, what keeps Steenie? And praised be his name, they are coming – Hillo, ho – here, here – Steenie!'[65]

For his pains Nigel is arrested as a traitor and transported by river to the Tower of London. Julian Peveril's efforts are equally anti-climactic. He sets out for London on a mission on behalf of the Countess of Derby, who fears that she and her family may be accused of involvement in the Popish Plot. He also tries to speak to the King, but is dismissed abruptly and, at a later audience, is told that the King himself is powerless to help, since he too is suspected of complicity. No character in later Scott is able to stand above the action. The monarch can be no arbiter, since he must always be responsive to the pressures and demands that are placed upon him. The limitation of power is continually stressed by Scott. Robert III, in *The Fair Maid of Perth*, deplores the spectacle of a clan battle to the death, but he observes,

> To little purpose is it to command what I cannot enforce; and although I have the unhappiness to do so each day of my life, it were needless to give such a very public example of royal impotency, before the crowds who may assemble to behold this spectacle. Let these savage men, therefore, work their bloody will to the uttermost upon each other; I will not attempt to forbid what I cannot prevent them from executing.[66]

The limitation is not simply a matter of character, since Louis XI, a strong and resourceful king, also finds himself in a position of weakness. In his later work Scott seems very preoccupied with the intrigues of court and polite society; this world is unfavourably contrasted with the primitive, heroic type of society where loyalty is one of the pre-eminent virtues. Yet, through his emphasis on the power of social groups, Scott came to minimise the dangers of despotism, which were such a central concern of Montesquieu and Ferguson. In *Quentin Durward* Oliver le Dain, Louis's agent, is able to secure

> the favour of many Burgundian nobles, who either had something to hope or fear from France, or who thought that, were the power of Louis too much reduced, their own Duke would be likely to pursue the road to despotic authority, to which his heart naturally inclined him, with a daring and unopposed pace.[67]

Admittedly, this is in the feudal type of society, where checks and balances are more likely to be found, but the whole spirit of Scott's work is to qualify the role of the individual in history – not to deny it, but to exhibit the objective and limiting historical circumstances in which this action is situated. Scott's view of history was thus far in advance of the historiography of his day. For even a Carlyle who attempts to show great popular movements in history distorts them by implying that the great man simply serves to express them, so that in some sense, Cromwell = puritan revolution. Moreover, Scott is free from the concept of history as a continuum of causes and effects: his analysis is not reductively event- and action-oriented, but recognises the importance of man's cognitive and conceptual orientation to the world. Conflict in history is generated not by the fact that historically important individuals pursue different ends but through the simultaneous existence of different ideologies and world views. Since each social grouping formulates its concept of itself and its relationship to others in its own way, communication becomes difficult, if not impossible. There can be no 'rational solution', since this would imply a common frame of reference. Relativism thus becomes the motor of history: ideas and social forces are indissolubly linked. The destruction of a set of values means the destruction of a social group and *vice versa*. The conclusion is pessimistic: Goethe's hope that we can learn from the example of Gotz is a vain one: Gotz, his values and his world are gone forever. For Scott the recovery of these values is a powerful and salutary aesthetic illusion; but it is an illusion none the less.

Thus, at the heart of the historical genre we find a paradox. The figure of the anachronistic hero is, initially, a device through which the emergent commercial, industrial and politically centralised form of culture can be relativised and called in question. The spectator or reader is asked to recognise that there are other values than those of the prevailing dominant culture; to acknowledge that the 'progressive' movement of history involves losses as well as gains and to identify wholeheartedly with the heroic individual even at the very moment when he recedes into the past. But, equally, the conclusion, rigorously drawn, that the values of any given community or culture are all of a piece and are closely bound up with a partaicular way of life leads inevitably to the conclusion that it is almost quixotic to lament a Rob Roy or an Edie Ochiltree: their effacement before the bourgeois legal order is inevitable and irreversible; and how can a denizen of this modern world in good faith empathise with precisely that which his culture is in the process of systematically eliminating? Perhaps Goethe and Schiller would not have accepted this formulation; their commitment to the moral autonomy of the individual was part of the heritage of the Enlightenment and it was too deeply rooted to be shaken. Goethe never doubted that the individual could transcend his age. But there is no such confidence in Scott. Scott cannot be casually linked with Burkian traditionalism for this very reason: he knew only too well from the experience of Scotland that the past does not automatically continue and survive. From *Waverley* onward his concern was with the disintegration and liquidation of worlds. There can be no going back.

In the later Scott there is a great consciousness of the transitoriness of human affairs. The problem for the novelist is simultaneously to show how certain concerns can acquire great vividness, urgency and immediacy, and to acknowledge within the context of the work itself the process of closure by which they have become sealed off from the present. Nowhere in Scott's fiction is the pathos of change more strikingly dramatised than in the Festival of Misrule, which is described in *The Abbot*. The spectacle of the monks and Catholic laity, whose monastery has already been pillaged and desecrated, attempting to continue with their ceremonials as masquers batter on the doors, serves as a powerful image of the moment of transition from the Catholic to the Protestant. But such an interpretation is immediately undercut. Sir Halbert Glendinning arrives and reproves the masquers for their behaviour:

> 'What is the meaning of this,' he said, 'my masters, are ye Christian men, and the king's subjects, and yet waste and destroy church and chancel like so many heathens?'
>
> All stood silent, though doubtless there were several disappointed and surprised at receiving chiding instead of thanks from so zealous a Protestant. The dragon, indeed, did at length take upon him to be the spokesman, and growled from the depth of his painted maw that they did but sweep Popery out of the church with the besom of destruction.

'What! my friends,' replied Sir Halbert Glendinning, 'think you this mumming and masquing has not more of Popery in it than have these stone walls? Take the leprosy out of your flesh, before you speak of purifying stone walls – abate your insolent licence, which leads but to idle vanity and sinful excess; and know, that what you now practise, is one of the profane and unseemly sports introduced by the priests of Rome themselves, to mislead and to brutify the souls which fell into their net.'

'Marry come up – are you there with your bears?' muttered the dragon, with a draconian sullenness, which was in good keeping with his character, 'we had as good have been Romans still, if we are to have no freedom in our pastimes!'

'Dost thou reply to me so?' said Sir Halbert Glendinning; 'or is there any pastime in grovelling on the ground there like a gigantic kail-worm? – Get out of thy painted case, or, by my knighthood, I will treat you like the beast and reptile you have made yourself.'[68]

At this moment the idea of anachronism is doubled: both Catholics and masquers are abruptly consigned to the world of the past, as symptomatic and reciprocal phenomena, not oppositional. The historical change into a puritan world is to be a qualitative jump, beyond the comprehension of the remaining actors on the scene. The idea of a doubled anachronism can also be traced in *Peveril of the Peak* – the whole of which novel, rambling and flawed though it is, can be seen as a study in the way in which the actors in a 'historical drama' are unable to comprehend the nature of the action or the stage on which they play their parts. Bridgenorth, Sir Geoffrey Peveril, the Countess of Derby, are all survivors from the struggles of the Civil War, steering their course by aged charts that no longer correspond to new circumstances. Consequently the parts they play appear incongrous. The false note struck by Sir Geoffrey when he appears before the king is characteristic. Scott observes, 'his dishevelled grey locks and half-arranged dress, though they showed zeal and haste, such as he would have used when Charles I called him to attend a council of war, seemed rather indecorous in a pacific drawing-room'.[69]

In *Peveril of the Peak* the anachronistic characters hover

between pathos and comedy; *St Ronan's Well*, however, endows the notion of anachronism with a genuinely tragic force. Scott bitterly satirises the shallowness and moral tawdriness of the polite society of St Ronan's Well and contrasts it with the decayed and desolate village of St Ronan itself. The village is essentially symbolic of the old traditional Scots way of life; the Well of the sophisticated, international polite society that is gradually increasing its scope and influence. The sense of hopelessness created by Scott's long opening description of St Ronan is intensified by his tale of Clara and Tyrrel, whose young dreams of happiness have been destroyed by a cruel deception. From the beginning there is no way out. As Clara says,

> We have run, while yet in our nonage, through the passions and adventures of youth, and therefore we are now old before our day, and the winter of our life has come on ere its summer was well begun. – O Tyrrel! often and often have I thought of this! – Thought of it often? Alas, when will the time come that I shall be able to think of anything else?[70]

Lord Etherington, who took Tyrrel's place at the wedding and who now tries to deceive Clara and her brother again, is himself a pathetic survivor, as doomed as any of the others. Scott concludes the novel on an ironic note:

> The little watering-place has returned to its primitive obscurity; and lions and lionesses, with their several jackals, blue surtouts, and bluer stockings, fiddlers and dancers, painters and amateurs, authors and critics, dispersed like pigeons by the demolition of a dovecot, have sought other scenes of amusement and rehearsal, and have deserted ST. RONAN'S WELL.[71]

Once again, the doubled anachronism; for the Well is now as deserted as the village was in the beginning. And yet the contrast is pointed: polite society can congregate elsewhere, but the traditional Scottish culture is gone for good.

But perhaps the most important characteristic of the later Scott is his *perspectivism*.[72] Scott had always focused his work around the conflict of cultures, but his use of a hero who

serves as shifter between them and as a point of identification
for the reader tends, in the earlier novels, to soften and tone
down the potential harshness of the contrast between them.
Characteristically, Waverley does not step straightaway into
the cave of Donald Bean Lean – we are led up to it gradually
via such stages as Tully-Veolan. And it is through Waverley's
eyes that we look. But in the later Scott the action lacks any
obvious centre, there are abrupt shifts of cultural milieu and
we recognise that there is no single perspective from which the
action can be viewed. Scott shows us that each social group,
each individual, sees things differently: there is a multiplicity
of possible vantage points. In *Kenilworth* and *The Fair Maid of
Perth*, in particular, Scott constructs fictions of unpre-
cedented virtuosity and complexity. In *Kenilworth* Scott presents
the struggle for the favour of Elizabeth between Leicester and
his supporters on the one hand and those of the Earl of Sussex
on the other. The moral universe of Leicester, with its secrecy,
ostentation and gambling for high stakes, is totally at variance
with the old-fashioned values of Sussex. Their worlds touch at
the court of Elizabeth but never meet. No one, not even the
Queen, sees all of the game. The novel is a series of
perspectival shifts from one character to another, from
Cumnor to Lidcote Hall, from the court to Kenilworth.
Varney, Leicester, Amy, Foster, Elizabeth: they are not, to use
a chess analogy, simply values but positions, and from these
positions the game is worked out by Scott with a ruthless and
rigorous logic. In *Kenilworth*, Scott synthesised the two main
tendencies of the Romantic period: cultural relativism and the
relativity and uniqueness of the subjective perception of the
individual. And for this reason Tressilian is one of the weakest
and most colourless of all Scott's heroes. We must register the
intricacy of the social labyrinth and not be led calmly through
it. Tressilian's perspective is just one of many. Only *The Fair
Maid of Perth* can rival *Kenilworth* in scope and intricacy of
construction. The reader cannot but marvel at the skill with
which Scott can delineate three completely distinct cultural
worlds, the court of Robert III, the burgher city of Perth and
the clansmen of the Scottish Highlands, bring them into
complex interaction with each other, and at the same time
show how the course of events in the novel, far from being a
factitious and picturesque method of yoking the dissimilar

together, is in fact produced by the tensions between them. Rothsay is a tragic victim of the disjuncture between the court and the city of Perth, Conachar/Eachin of the disparity between the Highlands and the lowlands. This can be expressed diagramatically:

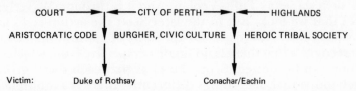

In *The Fair Maid of Perth*, there is a strong sense of a common world within which the drama is acted out, but at the same time there is a powerful sense of closure: the court is sealed off from Perth and the Highlands from both. The king does not understand how the citizens of Perth will react; Conachar has lost touch with his tribal culture. As Andrew Lang has said, *The Fair Maid of Perth* offers 'a series of brilliant and glowing scenes of stirring events'[73], but it does more than this: it shows, in the most poetically concentrated form, that culture is not an epiphenomenon but a lived-out reality.

PART III

The Figure of the Artist in Romantic Literature

5 The Folktale

The artist as poet, visionary, seer, prophet, outcast and exile is an obsessive and recurrent figure in Romantic literature. The semantic drift has grown so familiar that it is all but invisible: we take it as a matter of course that the writer should write about the artist's predicament – why, indeed, should he not? – or that in a poem the figure of the poet should obtrude upon the reader's consciousness in an insistent and self-dramatising way, presenting himself as a person endowed with transcendent consciousness and with a unique power to feel, interpret and understand. Yet such has not always been the case. Poets have often been assigned or have assigned to themselves the possession of divine inspiration, yet they have not always made themselves their own subject or suggested that the thoughts and feelings which they articulate are to be regarded not simply as deeply felt or experienced, but as specific to the person who assumes the role of artist. That is to say, the theme of the artist in Romantic literature has distinctive implications. It predicates a cleavage between the artist and the world and the work of art appears in the guise of resolution and absolution. The Romantic author does not address himself to a group of peers who will understand his point of view and orientation because they belong to the same stratum of society, but rather sees his work as a missive directed to readers who, though they may be presumed to be sympathetically disposed toward him, are nevertheless alien. He may seek to carry them along with him or win them over, to dissever them from bourgeois norms and values from which he himself is already estranged; but equally he may endeavour to protect himself by a posture of obliquity or indifference, sheltering his darker meanings in a symbolic cloud. It is often suggested that the difficulty of much modern – which might well be designated 'post-Romantic' – writing is attributable to the more complex meanings which the contemporary author has to express, a richer and more subtle capacity for deploying the possibilities of signification, and so on. But what is thereby overlooked is the changing basis of the compact between writer and reader: 'difficulty' is the mode through which the writer places in question the public domain and which itself renders his existence problematic; it is the stipulation that communication shall be on the writer's own terms: only adepts and initiates, who thus display their commitment to art against the world, shall be allowed to pass. The writing of the Romantic period is not in fact grounded in such a notion of 'difficulty', for the Romantic author himself attempts to overcome the gap that has opened up rather than leave that effort to the reader; but the sense of such a gap hovers oppressively over all his efforts. If the Romantic author is haunted by the prospect of a loss of the visionary, the registering of which was precisely the point of setting pen to paper in the first place, such a fear stems in part from the recognition that the vision may evaporate under a stolid, protracted and commonsensical bourgeois gaze.

Nevertheless, this matter of a 'lost vision' is a puzzling one, the more puzzling the more that we think about it. For if the notion of poetic genius is connected with a confrontation with some deeper and more mysterious self, and if the writer's claims on the reader's attention are based on some distinctive and deeply personal vision, it seems extremely odd that the Romantic artist should so often be found dispirited and empty-handed, beating the air in some vain attempt to recover the miraculous state of consciousness he once possessed. Moreover, it seems equally curious that readers should still throng to Romantic poetry in quest of the visionary, when the artist for the most part is as baffled as anyone else as to what has happened to it. The problem of loss is normally explained in biographical, circumstantial or psychological terms. The young Wordsworth was a person possessed of great poetic and imaginative powers which declined after 1805. Coleridge was prevented from completing 'Kubla Khan' by a person from Porlock who came knocking untimely at the door. But the phenomenon of the lost vision is so omnipresent and pervasive in Romantic literature, the list of incomplete and fragmentary works so extensive, that it becomes highly questionable whether the presupposition of the artist as a visionary source perennially subject to occlusion and interruption can be justified. It seems more logical and more consistent to regard the interrupted vision as itself a motif and thematic constant; to see such interruptions as necessary, composite and integral.

This examination of the figure of the artist in Romantic literature will be developed through a juxtaposition of English Romantic poetry with the German *Märchen*, or folktale, which in German Romanticism becomes a vehicle for imaginative speculation about the artist. Treatment of the artist in Romantic literature is highly codified: it does not simply involve self-consciousness on the part of the author, but is constituted out of a variety of generic materials, Gothic and historical, in addition to the folktale. Many of the problems surrounding the figure of the artist are clarified when we recognise that he is a person for whom there is no place: he is necessarily a wanderer between different worlds. This is logically entailed by the conception of the artist. If it were possible for the artist to be totally at one with nature he would not possess the self-consciousness that would enable him to write poetry. Harmony would render him mute. Similarly, if it were possible for the artist to dwell in an imaginary world and become totally possessed by his own vision, it would be so all-engrossing as to be incommunicable. Further, such an alienation from his fellow men would be morally harmful, as the recurrent notion of a bargain with the devil testifies: the artist's miraculous powers traumatically isolate him from the human world yet prove short-lived and unpredictable – he is always in some way cheated.

The artist is essentially a *mediator*, a go-between, who connects the natural with the civilised, the imaginary with the real; a shuttle threading back and forth between one and the other, endlessly in motion, never at rest. He himself has no place; the burden of connection which he takes upon himself excludes him from felicity. German writers took up the folktale, not simply because it was a possible source of an independent national literature, but because so many folktales focus on the problem of establishing a relation between two quite contradictory modes: the magical and the everyday. In the folktale the magical inserts itself into the actual in a tantalising way: the promise of blessing is fraught

with grave dangers and potentially catastrophic consequences. But many fairytales end happily. The danger of mixing
incompatibles and of constituting an explosive mixture is
successfully contained. But the Romantic writers who adopted
the *Märchen* form were more conscious of these dangers; they
twist the form to emphasise the incompatibility of art and life,
to show how difficult it is to reconcile one with the other. This
is exemplified by the story of Libussa, the legendary founder
of the city of Prague, which was retold by such writers as
Musaeus, Brentano and Grillparzer. Libussa possesses magical and prophetic powers, but this by no means assures that
her objective of doing good or of achieving personal happiness will be readily achieved; on the contrary, the magical
powers create endless difficulties and Libussa faces a sisyp-
hean struggle against innumerable petty obstacles. Libussa's
tribulations are those of the Romantic artist himself, a person
whose magic proves strangely ineffectual in a world that is
narrow, petty, mercenary and distrustful. The interrupted
vision therefore testifies to the incompatibility between the
imaginative and the real: the vision cannot be brought back
entire, since its *locus* is really somewhere else. The artist
returns bearing a fragment which serves as an authenticating
token of the validity of the imaginary, like the bone of an
apostle, but he is necessarily excluded from completeness.
Completeness is rather what categorises the world of the
imaginative as opposed to the world of the real, yet it can only
be invoked, it can never be shown. The artist remembers such
a plenitude and wholeness; his work establishes it not as a
presence but as the acknowledgement of a lack, which only a
person who has glimpsed the visionary can see. Paradoxically,
the unproblematic depiction of a vision would be a contradiction in terms, for this would indicate no incompatibility
between the imaginative and the real and consequently a
world in which the imaginative would have no function. Just
as the anachronistic hero only signifies in a world in which he
has no place and the hypocrite becomes a marker of the
existence of authenticity in a world that is degraded, so the
poet is most truly a hero in his moment of catastrophe and
loss, shattered by the insuperable and auto-destructive nature
of his own project. But actually this 'failure' is triumphant; it
becomes aesthetically transvalued because what it shows is *not*

the incompleteness of the vision, but the incompleteness of the everyday world, which will always and inescapably suffer from an impoverishing lack.

The problematic situation of the artist in the modern world is definitively broached by Goethe in his play *Torquato Tasso* (1790). Goethe chose for his artist hero not the calm, serene Ariosto, but Tasso, a demonic, obsessed and tortured figure; a man perennially self-doubting, yet also mistrustful of the world, who becomes convinced that people are trying to persecute him and who leaves Ferrara, the initial scene of his triumphs, in a restless search for peace. Tasso could never leave *Gerusalemme liberata* alone or regard it as complete and devoted an enormous amount of time and effort to its revision. Although these revisions had a predominantly conservative cast, reflecting Tasso's uncertainties about his poem's relation to neo-classical aesthetic theory, for Goethe they became symbolic of the questing spirit of the artist and of his reluctance to rest in any final solution. In this respect *Torquato Tasso* looks forward to Goethe's own complex and long-continued engagement with the Faust theme. But *Tasso* is also about the claims which the artist makes for himself and the claims which the world makes upon him. In presenting his poem to Duke Alfonso of Ferrara, Tasso makes a clear distinction between the contingent completion of the poem, which signifies its worldly guise, as a bid on the part of the poet for honour, fame and glory, and the fact that the poem is nevertheless to be regarded as unfinished. Tasso thinks of it as unfinished because the finishing of it corresponds to certain inward goals of which only he as poet is conscious and which only he is able to realise more fundamentally; therefore an end to the process of composing it would be a kind of spiritual death, an accommodation to the world of the intransigent claims of the spirit. Tasso is profoundly conscious that his aesthetic labours have not been acknowledged, which for him is the equivalent of their being slighted. In the modern world the poet cannot figure as a Virgil; his capacity to convey honour is doubtful, his place fragile and uncertain. Mentecatino, who wittingly or unwittingly provokes Tasso into the act of drawing his sword, a gesture which leads to Tasso's imprisonment by Alfonso, firmly takes the standpoint of reality. As far as he is concerned, art counts for little when weighed in the balance of ordinary affairs. A man's worth is not to be assessed by introspection and inwardness but by the part he plays on the stage of the real world. Tasso's quarrel with Ferrara can be seen not only as involving a complex misrecognition of a many-sided situation by all the parties concerned, but also as art's quarrel with a social milieu that assigns art and the artist no significant place. But, of course, Goethe has presented the issue in a more favourable light by articulating his theme in the context of the Italian Renaissance, where the artist *did* have a social position and where the poet enjoyed an honorific status above the painter. Goethe can thus present the issue in terms of a common courtly ethos, where Tasso, for all his genius, is, if anything, the more to blame, because his own devotion to art at the expense of life leads to his making serious misjudgements about people and their motives. In this sense *Tasso* also points forward to *Wilhelm Meister*. But to Goethe's contemporaries who enjoyed neither his aristocratic background nor his position of influence at Weimar the argument of *Tasso* must have seemed somewhat unrealistic. For them it was not so much a matter of wilfully abjuring an established position as an artist as of living in a world in which art had no acknowledged place and which, moreover, especially where Protestantism was influential, could be deeply suspicious of any claims made on behalf of art whatsoever.

In the *Märchen*, on the other hand, the status of the artist is always much more marginal and problematic. The deployment of the folktale as a fictional form becomes identifiably a form of discourse concerned with the situation of the artist. This is evident as early as the tale *Stumme Liebe* by Musaeus, which appeared in his *Volksmärchen* (1782). In this story, the young hero Franz, after the death of his father, a wealthy Bremen merchant, is rapidly brought to the point of bankruptcy through profligate living. As he takes up more humble accommodation, Musaeus observes to the reader that there was no popular fiction at that time and that the only arts on the agenda were epic and heroic poetry, which were solely for the cultivated. The point of these remarks is not simply that Franz has no alternative but to play the lute to while away the empty hours; it is also that his situation as the *déclassé* son of a merchant excludes him completely from the world of culture. Franz's playing of the lute establishes him as an artist at a time when it was not possible to be one. It might be added that for someone such as Musaeus such an existence was as problematic in the eighteenth century as ever it might have been in the Middle Ages. For he turned to writing after losing his position in the Church; but, after failing to make a living from it, was forced to fall back on more reliable employment. *Stumme Liebe* becomes an allegory of how the artistic sensibility can triumph in a world of recalcitrant fact. Franz stays one night in a haunted castle, but finds his sleep rudely disturbed by a ghost, who proceeds to shave his head completely bald. But Franz is completely unabashed at this unexpected experience and in playful retaliation shaves the ghost bald in return. Franz is surprised to find himself profusely thanked by the ghost, who proves to be a restless spirit, doomed to walk the earth tormenting people in his spirit existence as he had in life, until such time as he should find a person bold enough to treat him in the same outrageous fashion. Franz is rewarded by being shown the secret hiding place in his father's garden where the remainder of his treasure is buried. Franz does what no ordinary person would do: he takes the imaginary with the same seriousness as the real – thus both obliquely fulfilling his vocation as an artist and, at the same time, releasing himself from the marginality of his social situation.

The role of the artist is presented in quite another way in Brentano's *Die Geschichte vom braven Kasperl und dem schönen Annerl* (1817). The author encounters a grief-stricken old woman in the street and learns from her that Annerl is to be beheaded for killing her illegitimate baby. The story itself is deeply involved with questions of honour. On the one hand, Annerl's determination to make an honourable match leads to her seduction by an aristocrat; on the other, Kasperl's exaggerated military sense of his own honour leads him to commit suicide when he learns that his horse has been stolen by his own father and stepbrother. The critique of the cultural value of honour is reminiscent of Lessing's *Minna von Barnhelm*, but it is given an altered emphasis by the position of the writer himself in the narrative. For the writer, having no stable class position, is in a position to reject this value system and to protest at the fruitless suffering and sheer wastefulness to which it leads. He insists on seeing the Duke in the middle of the night, even though Grossinger (Annerl's seducer as it turns out) is adamant that it would infringe his honour to go against the Duke's explicit instructions that he is not to be disturbed. While the writer is not in a position to prevent the tragedy, he is in a position to *record* it, and thereby make a written protest against it. Significantly, Brentano's writer narrator is reluctant to admit his occupation to the old woman for fear that she will regard him as an idler, and he indicates a general reluctance on the part of authors to disclose the nature of their employment to the lower classes. Brentano describes himself as a *Schreiber* or 'penman', and does not use the usual term, *Schriftsteller* – a role he tries to live up to by recording and taking down the old woman's story. In this sense the writer *does* have a role, as the conscience of the nation.

In the development of the *Märchen*, Ludwig Tieck, co-translator with Schlegel of the works of Shakespeare, played a significant part. Tieck's literary career brings out clearly how rapidly Wertherism and Sentimentalism became exhausted, not just for Goethe but for everyone else as well. The fervid, narcissistic immersion in a morass of subjective impressions produced a mode of fiction in which self-dramatisation became an end in itself. The crisis that creates Wertherism, the displaced individual who attempts to create within himself the sense of worth that society denies, is necessarily static because its very subject is an agonising and irresolvable absence. Moreover, a Werther, or Tieck's William Lovell, is really a kind of artist, a person whose aesthetic responsiveness necessarily distances him from the day-to-day bourgeois world, but who is reduced to self-parody, because the novel implicitly takes up the standpoint of this bourgeois world and therefore cannot avoid presenting the hero as a person who is defined primarily through his inability to function effectively within it. He lacks a rationale. So both Goethe and Tieck were logically brought to the point where they had to make their hero an artist, a Tasso or Franz Sternbald. But, as we have already seen, it was not possible, nor, for Goethe, would it have been remotely desirable, for him to throw altogether in question the aristocratic and courtly ethos of the world of Ferrara. So in Tieck's hands the *Märchen* becomes the medium through which the everyday world can be rendered problematic by the imaginative – not simply because in Tieck's other world the mountains are always brighter, magical, luminous and more mysterious, but also because the ordinary world lacks authenticity and autonomy. It is shown to be parasitically dependent on the other, magical world, because the everyday world is inherently obscure and lacking in meaning. Man lives without recognising that the pattern of his existence has been laid down elsewhere; he is governed by fate precisely because he denies in his very existence the validity of the imaginative. In one of Tieck's most remarkable stories, *Der blonde Eckbert*, both the reader and Eckbert are shown how his banal and humdrum existence has been deeply permeated by the magical: the narrative takes the form of a progressive disclosure of this fact, with catastrophic and traumatic consequences for Eckbert himself. Eckbert has a close friend, Philip Walter, whom he seeks to bring into even greater intimacy by allowing no secret to remain between them. He asks his wife to tell Walter her story, which concerns her decision to leave home because of the cruelty of her father, and her journey through desolate rocks and mountains until she arrives in a rural paradise and encounters a mysterious old woman with a dog and a beautiful singing bird. There she spins and learns to read and is torn between a sense of contentment in her life of solitude and vague dreams of a life elsewhere. One day she leaves, taking with her the bird, which lays eggs that are filled with pearls and jewels. But when she returns to civilisation she becomes so incensed and tormented by the song of the bird, which poignantly evokes the joys of solitude, that she strangles it. At the conclusion of the story Walter mysteriously refers to the dog as Strohmian, a name which even Eckbert's wife herself had not been able to remember. The shock of this unexpected reference causes Bertha to sicken and die. During her illness Eckbert goes hunting and shoots Walter, almost without realising what he has done. He finds himself compelled once again to confess to a knight named Hugo. Tormented by his imaginings Eckbert sets out on a journey and encounters the old woman. She discloses to him that she was both Walter and Hugo; Bertha was his own sister, so that the home she originally left was his own. Eckbert, dying, in a dreamlike trance hears the old

woman speaking, the dog barking, the bird singing. The force
of the tale stems from its ingenious and sinister use of
repetition. Eckbert the humdrum everyday individual is
married to a woman who has known the mysterious and the
magical. His desire to disclose this to Walter represents a
desire to liquidate the magical by accommodating it to the
ordinary world, yet the tale shows that no such an accommodation is possible and that all that Eckbert's endeavours lead
to is a more convoluted involvement with the magical. Eckbert
is led by a fate over which he has no control to return to the
magical other world and to repeat the experience of his wife
and sister, and in consequence the truth of his existence is
communicated to him. Eckbert is destroyed by this truth
because his very existence denies the power of the magical and
the imaginative. Both he and his sister Bertha pay dearly for
their repudiation of the mysterious. In *Der blonde Eckbert* Tieck
shows the poetic other world not as insubstantial but as vivid,
potent and dominant.

The inescapable and tragic incompatability between the
magical and the mundane is represented even more forcibly
in Tieck's most suggestive and complex tale, *Der Runenberg*.
Here, Christian the young hunter, who appears in the midst
of the mountains, having left behind his family and friends to
seek his fortune, becomes a symbol of the artist who is forced
to sever all worldly ties in pursuit of his imaginative quest. The
price he pays for this is separation from the world of nature
and of natural human ties – emblematised by the mandrake
root, which groans as he involuntarily plucks it. Intuitively
Christian rejects the world of the everyday, which is all he has
ever known; the flat, unbroken plains of his childhood
depress him and he refuses to follow his father's occupation of
gardening. Instead his imagination is inflamed by tales of the
mountains, of hunting and of the exotic activity of mining.
The world he lives in is explicitly presented as a morally fallen
world in which the majority of people are conscious neither of
the poverty of their own existence nor of any higher ideal.
Christian obtains from a book directions for reaching the
mountains, where he encounters an exhilarating new world.
He takes up the occupation of huntsman, but is nevertheless
perplexed by an unaccountable feeling of melancholy.
Prompted by a mysterious stranger, he hurries in the direc-

tion of the Runenberg, where he sees a strange and compelling vision: a beautiful maiden who disrobes before him and hands him a magical inlaid tablet, glittering with precious stones, asking him to take it in remembrance of her – thus figuring as an erotic and aesthetic equivalent of the Old and New Testaments. But when Christian recovers consciousness the tablet is nowhere to be found and Christian himself is in a state of mental shock and confusion, unable to determine the validity of what he has seen.

This loss of the visionary moment is a crucial and pivotal experience in the narrative. Henceforward Christian is a man possessed, unable to reconcile himself with the world more than temporarily. He descends from the mountains and reaches a small, peaceful village, where a harvest festival is in progress. He falls in love with a girl he sees there called Elizabeth and whom he eventually marries, despite the fact that he is fully aware that she falls far short of the ideal vision he once had. He also exchanges his hunter's costume for that of a farmer. All this represents an attempt on his part to come to terms with the everyday world, and he appears even more worldly and materialistic when he buys land and property using some gold which the mysterious stranger had left with him for safekeeping. But Christian again becomes restless: he is conscious of a struggle between externalities and the profound, involuntary impulses of his own deeper self. His desire to return to the mountains appears in an ambivalent light. To his father it is a sign of a craving for the discordant, the shifting and the barren, a rejection of peace. For Christian, on the other hand, the rocks are types and symbols of the eternal as distinct from nature, which is transitory and subject to decay. By marrying Elizabeth he has forsworn his commitment to the infinite and given himself over to the temporal and the finite. In a wood he meets a hideous old woman and finds again the magical tablet; but his father warns him that it is cold, malignant and inhuman and tells him to throw it away. Christian departs in search of mysterious treasures and returns many years later after his wife has remarried. He is a wild, bearded, dishevelled figure, carrying a sack over his shoulder. He opens the sack and produces from it gravel, pebbles and stones, which in his apparent madness he describes as uncut jewels. He kisses his wife and daughter and disappears once more, returning to the woman he had seen in his vision.

Christian is the type of the artist and of the terrible price that he pays for his visionary quest. It is of the essence that he has a vision that he loses but which he must nevertheless seek to recover. A relativism is inherent in the very nature of his rejection of the perspective of the everyday; the tablet appears threatening and sinister to Christian's father, but this is simply because it is alien to ordinary human concerns. Christian's desire to regain his vision of the maiden necessarily appears odd from the point of view of a common-sense that has never even craved such a vision, let alone been granted one. The stones which Christian produces from his sack do not appear to be the wonderful things he takes them for, but, as I have already suggested, the imaginative cannot be brought back into the context of the everyday without losing its specific quality of pertaining to the imagination. So it is logical that only Christian should see the mysterious fire which the stones contain and that this should not be visible to anyone else. But here also is the dilemma of the artist: the vision which haunts him and obsesses him, which even he has lost, is equally the very thing that he cannot communicate to others, or even indicate why it should be important to him. He can only become a mad, distracted wanderer, impelled by motives that are impenetrable, perverse, opaque. Both Christian and the tablet in the ordinary world figure as a pointless and incomprehensible cypher. Between art and ordinary life, between the mysterious and the mundane, there can never be any accommodation. Their claims are totally irreconcilable.

This is also the conclusion of Novalis's *Heinrich von Ofterdingen* (1799), though Novalis's presentation of this theme is less tortured, more lyrical and serene. In *Ofterdingen* we become very conscious of the symmetry of the presentation of the artist with that of the anachronistic hero. Novalis's story is set in the medieval period, when, as Novalis himself insists, there was a far stronger sense of the miraculous and the sacred than is to be found in the contemporary world. Novalis's unfinished work is a prolonged meditation on the role of the artist and on the possibility of art. Novalis is obsessed with the loss of the 'Golden Age'. In the Golden Age the arts flourished: artists were, as for Hölderlin, priests, prophets and the source of law and authority; they enjoyed a position and status in society which they all too notably lack in the modern period. Heinrich's journey to the joyous and harmonious southern city of Augsburg is a frame for a series of allegories and fables which relate to this central concern. The story of Arion, who is thrown into the sea by his greedy fellowship-passengers and saved by a whale, signals both the incompatibility between the artist and the cupiditous commercial world, and his harmony with the world of nature from which his fellow men have become estranged. Symbolically this is also the Fall. This fable is counterbalanced by another in chapter 3, which depicts the return of the Golden Age. The princess of a great kingdom falls in love with a humble youth who has devoted himself to the natural sciences and the study of nature. The princess disappears for a year and returns with a baby and the youth who is its father, who sings wonderful songs about the secrets of the universe and of the return of the Golden Age. The sharp contrast between a utilitarian and commercial spirit and the pure and disinterested desire for knowledge recurs in the fifth chapter, where Heinrich encounters an old miner. The miner is accused by the others of greed, but he is motivated rather by a spirit of wonder and curiosity. Mining is symbolic of a moral and spiritual quest. The miner must be dedicated, attentive and persistent in pursuing the veins and seams along their mysterious and unpredictable courses. He is led to an awareness of the complexity and wondrousness of the universe and to a cognate exploration of his own inner world, in which precious metals as objects of barter and exchange cease to figure. He is interested in the minerals for their own sake, as products of nature; the minute they are transformed into commodities they cease to have any interest for him. Mining becomes linked with the study of history, since both are concerned with sources, beginnings, origins. Novalis insists that only the poet can be a historian, or, at least, that the historian must be a poet, since the writing of history involves a process of aesthetic ordering, an imaginative and intuitive entry into the life of remote and distant ages. Against Goethe, who, in *Wilhelm Meister* and *Torquato Tasso*, had made a forceful distinction between the world of art and the world of action, Novalis insists that the poet himself is a hero, since he creates aesthetically the possibility of heroism and is capable of inspiring others with it. After Novalis it was possible for Carlyle to include both the poet and the man of letters in the roster of heroes of *Heroes and Hero Worship*, along with Mohammed and Cromwell. Heinrich's own personal visionary quest is linked with a mysterious blue flower which he sees in a dream, enclosing the face of a beautiful girl. Subsequently this dream is made real when in Augsburg Heinrich encounters Matilda, the lovely daughter of the poet Klingsohr, whose face resembles a lily that leans towards the sun. But at the very moment when Heinrich and Matilda pledge their mutual love the vision is threatened, for Heinrich dreams that Matilda drowns, sucked down into a whirlpool. This vision is also prophetic, for in the second part of *Heinrich von Ofterdingen*, which is unfinished, Heinrich appears in the guise of a lonely and disconsolate pilgrim, who has lost Matilda and who has nothing left but his recollection of those visionary moments. He imagines that he hears Matilda's voice, and, as he again sees her in a vision, he recovers an inner calmness and serenity. The world only becomes precious to Heinrich at this moment of estrangement and loss. At this point there is no reason for the novella to continue, since the loss of the visionary, the return to the world, is precisely the mode in which it must end, even though such an 'ending' is necessarily unfinished. The poet must simply come to terms with the necessary incompatibility between the imaginative and the actual, as Heinrich is able to do with the fading of his vision. Notes for the 'conclusion' of *Ofterdingen* were found by Tieck amongst Novalis's papers after his death, and these suggest that the expectations of the first part were to be completed by a fulfilment in the second part. But the actual unfulfilment of the work, the very impossibility of completing it, is suggested by the mysterious book which the old hermit shows Heinrich in chapter 5, which contains pictures which represent Heinrich in scenes in which he has yet to appear. The ending of the book is missing. How could it be otherwise? For completion would only be a loss of another kind.

Resolutions can only be offered in a context which renders their fictive nature transparent. The conclusion to the first part is an allegory narrated by the poet Klingsohr, which presents the destructive and vindictive nature of a world that is dominated by an arid rationalism and a magical apotheosis in which peace, love, imagination and wisdom will be brought into a harmonious unity. But by implication this unity is to be looked for not in the real world but in literature and poetry. The return of the Golden Age is a proposition the ontological character of which is shifting and uncertain. But, since it involves a derealisation of the real and a triumph of imagination, it would be a recurrence in which all such distinctions would cease to exist.

Though both Tieck and Novalis are deeply preoccupied with the role of the artist, it is E. T. A. Hoffmann who turns this preoccupation into an obsession and who inserts the tale of the artist into such a central position in the literature of Romanticism. This concern is also highly significant because it represents one of the principal ways in which the values of English and German Romanticism are transmitted to other cultural contexts, such as France or Russia. The writers most involved in the generalisation of values of the Romantic period are Byron, Scott and Hoffmann: in all three great prominence is given to heroic figures who are alienated from the everyday bourgeois world. In Byron and Hoffmann the position is one of absolute intransigence; no resolution is possible. And even Scott, for all his legendary common-sense, finds no possible resolution for all those characters of his – perhaps not always technically heroes – who capture the reader's imagination, such as Redgauntlet, Rob Roy and Fergus MacIvor. For the very qualities that make them heroic are at the same time qualities that set them apart from the world, that set them against the tide of history – which, of course, is merely to reiterate that in Romantic literature after Goethe the idea of heroism becomes transformed. The hero is a hero not because of his ability to function in the world but because such a limited capacity is precisely what he lacks; any rapprochement would be a sign of his degradation. This was also Goethe's view in *Götz von Berlichingen*, but it was one that he modified almost to the point of *volte-face* in *Tasso* and *Wilhelm Meister*. For Hoffmann the artist is not just the hero: he is the only possible type of hero.

This is not to say that Hoffmann never puts the nature of the artistic endeavour, as he defined it, in question. On the contrary, in a number of stories the destructive implications of his quest are fully articulated, but this in no way derogates from his heroism. Hoffmann's relation to his fellow exponents of the *Märchen* can best be brought out with reference to his tale *Die Bergwerke zu Falun* (1819). This story is an imaginative fantasia on the symbolism of mountains, mining and treasure-seeking deployed in *Der Runenberg* and *Heinrich von Ofterdingen*, reminiscent of Novalis in its imagery, but closer to Tieck in its sinister tone. This said, it must be added that Hoffmann's story is a virtuoso performance, whose complex legerdemain with signifying possibilities depends on a pre-existing set of codified meanings. It thus also serves to demonstrate that such complexity is to be attributed not just to creativity on the part of the individual writer, but to a 'snowball' effect in the genre itself. The field of possibility gets larger, and as the ball gets bigger so does it become easier to pick up new material and to establish more complex imaginative connections. The dream of Elis Frobom at the start of *Die Bergwerke zu Falun* condenses all the symbolic interconnections of Novalis's story. Elis dreams he is on a ship, sailing through sparkling waves. He sees above him a dome of shining minerals, metal plants of miraculous beauty and within them smiling maidens. But, unlike Novalis's *Ofterdingen*, this vision of harmony is troubled by a more sinister note. The dome seems flawed, since the stars can be seen shining through a crack in it and Elis also sees the imposing face of a woman, referred to as 'the Queen', which fills him with fear and against whom he is warned by a voice. Thus the dream itself is already split and Hoffmann's further development of its imagery in the narrative takes the form of rendering its contradictions more acute. The most obvious of these is the sky–earth opposition. Elis believes that his search for precious metals is a spiritual question, associated with redemption and a transcendence of the actual. To go down into the mine, seen truly, is to ascend. Things found in the earth are the sign of higher values. But at the same time Hoffmann also suggests that the descent into the mine may signify not redemption but damnation. The mine of Falun is vast, desolate and intimidating – actually compared by Hoffmann with Dante's Inferno. This split is intensified by the fact that Elis dreams not of one woman but of two: a maiden who tries to save him, whom he subsequently identifies with Ulla, the daughter of the chief official of the district, whom he falls in love with and marries; and the sinister Queen associated with mining. Elis is divided between his desire for earthly happiness, represented by Ulla, and his longing to pursue his obsessive vision, represented by the Queen. As in *Der Runenberg*, Elis is unable to discriminate, to know whether he is sane or mad, and, of course, the everyday world provides no criteria for deciding, since it is not exposed to the contradiction which the artist figure experiences. Elis does not know whether he should accept the happiness he enjoys with Ulla as 'true' or whether he has in fact settled for a lower order of values and priorities, thus abandoning his own best self, which sought for the subterranean Queen. In a second dream he again sees the Queen, who pulls him 'downward' in a way that appears to signify his destruction, but at the same time he experiences a mystical interior vision. On his wedding day Elis insists that he must return to the mine to bring Ulla a precious jewel, but the mine collapses and he completely disappears. Many years later his body is recovered. As Ulla, now an old woman, embraces him, his body crumbles to dust. Symbolically Elis's quest has meant a choice of death over life and an alienation from his own humanity; but the contradictions in the story are too easily resolved simply by suggesting that Elis is deluded. The point is that, once Elis has glimpsed the visionary possibilities of the mine, he can never be at peace. Just as the figure of woman is split into Ulla/the Queen, so Elis himself is split, craving each at the expense of the other. The visionary manifests itself as a negativity in the real, but this negativity may only be an effect of the real rather than a property of the visionary. The mysterious red stone cannot be given by Elis as a wedding gift, since such a purpose binds it into the contingent and cancels its transcendent meaning. Elis will always be torn between the two, as Torbern, an old miner, tells him. The switch in the colour coding of the dream is also suggestive: from blue to red, i.e. from the pure vision of Novalis to the menacingly ambiguous obsession of Tieck, from flower to stone.

In *Die Bergwerke zu Falun* Elis's behaviour appears to be mad to the more 'normal' people around him, but, more generally, Hoffmann suggests that madness is the price that the artist must pay for enduring the contradiction between the ideal and the real. In *Der Sandmann* Nathaniel pays such a penalty for his dedication to the world of the imagination. He falls in love with Olympia, a beautiful automaton created by the sinister Coppelius, and in consequence becomes estranged from his childhood sweetheart, Klara. The conclusion of the tale is foreshadowed in a poem in which Nathaniel describes how, as he is standing with Klara at the altar, Coppelius touches Klara's eyes, which spring into his own breast, burning and scorching. This image is subsequently developed by Hoffmann in a complex and paradoxical way. For it is true that in his obsession with Olympia, the dream of ideal beauty, Klara loses her attraction for him and, in some sense, ceases to be real for him, since he is convinced that only the ideal is real. But, at the same time, the ideal itself proves deceptive and the implications of the eye image are developed in another way, when, in a traumatic encounter, Nathaniel discovers Olympia as only a lifeless doll, with no eyes in her head, but only black holes. In the story the human eye is a shifter. The eye represents life as opposed to death and the human as opposed to the inert and mechanical, but at the same time the eye is associated with the possibility of ideal beauty. Loss of eyes signifies derealisation – the loss of value whether in Klara's case or Olympia's. So Nathaniel's dream signifies the pain introduced into his life by Coppelius, who degrades his love for Klara. Olympia only appears as beautiful because she has human eyes, but no mortal woman could be as beautiful as she. Significantly, it is Olympia's eyes that exert the greatest fascination upon Nathaniel, so that he is able to overlook defects in her that to others identify her as rather odd and inhuman. The eye is the locus and intersection of an ideal of transcendent beauty, which is part human and part imaginary; thus, the transference of eyes is a crucial motif in the narrative. At the end of the story Nathaniel, like a madman, shrieks at Klara 'Whirl, wooden doll', as he had to Olympia, for the real woman has become as hollow and debased to him as his own vision of the transcendent. The malignant fascination of the ideal is that it proves both a chimera and at the same time renders the real intolerable, driving Nathaniel to self-destruction that is compounded out of guilt and despair.

Another victim of this contradiction is Berthold the painter in *Die Jesuiterkirche in G*. This story prominently underlines the Protestant orientation of the artist thematic. For the characteristic concern of Jesuit architecture is for an elegance and refinement that the narrator views as decadent and worldly. Professor Aloysius Walter, who complacently rejects the gloomy and solemn spirit of Gothic architecture, is seen as a man who betrays the true spirit of Christianity, to which Gothic profoundly gave a material substance – the striving for ideality beyond the limits of the merely sensual. The one individual who sees this, the only man who is capable of infusing the Church with a sense of spiritual values, is Berthold, the mad painter. Berthold's whole life has been a struggle to achieve the ideal, which, at the same time, has brought him much suffering. As Berthold himself says, any man who has ever tried to achieve the ideal can never be free from pain. This is precisely Hoffmann's definition of the artist. In a series of equations which form a continuous loop, art = the ideal = suffering = alienation from the world. In Italy Berthold struggles to achieve higher values. While he is painting landscapes, which seem to him the only way to a realisation of this goal, he meets a mysterious stranger – one of many such mentor figures in Hoffmann – who tells him that mere copying of nature is not enough. It is the *inward* recognition of the sublime in nature (precisely the sublime as conceived by Kant) that the artist must strive to express on canvas, a transcription not of the external but of the internal. Berthold is able to attempt one sublime canvas, which represents the beautiful Princess Angiola as the Virgin Mary, but this is possible only as long as Angiola is a vision to him, which he reconstructs from memory. Later he meets her again, saves her life and marries her; but as a result he destroys the ideality which she represents for him. Hoffmann hints that Berthold has actually murdered his wife and child, precisely because they can no longer lead him towards the ideal, but have become insuperable obstacles, blocking the way towards it. Berthold finally finishes his unfinished masterpiece and then kills himself. It takes a great deal of life to create only a little art; these multiple sacrifices appear as the price to be paid for just one masterpiece.

Hoffmann's most lyrical and optimistic presentation of the quest for the ideal is to be found in *Der goldne Topf*, where the young student Anselmus is finally united with his love,

Serpentina, whom he first sees in a vision, as one of green and golden snakes, twisting and twining in the branches of an elder tree. In this story, as in Tieck's *Der blonde Eckbert*, the world of the miraculous dominates the actual. Hoffmann convinces the reader that the struggle of the salamander against the black dragon and the union of the salamander with the snake have a cosmic import and significance that the prosaic objective of becoming a court councillor lacks. But, unlike *Eckbert*, the consequences are benign, because in the subordination of the actual to the imagination the conflict between them disappears. Veronica is Anselmus's worldly love as opposed to his spiritual one, but she is forced to turn to magic in an effort to regain Anselmus from Serpentina. Crucially, Archivist Lindhorst, simultaneously scholar and salamander, functions as a shifter who is simultaneously at home in the real and the imaginative world and who elides the contradictions that might exist between them. Like his fellow searchers after the ideal, Anselmus too fears that he may be mad, in succumbing to an infatuation for a green and gold snake, but when he confides this fear to the Archivist he is relieved to find that he not only does not find this strange, but, on the contrary, finds it perfectly natural. The Archivist's grounding in the world of the actual – his association even with the attainment of such worldly objectives as becoming a court councillor – paradoxically also serves to validate ambitions in the enchanted realm of the imagination to which he is also connected.

Anselmus's apprenticeship to Archivist Lindhorst as a copyist of manuscripts becomes symbolic of the transcendental quest of the writer. Like Berthold as a painter of nature he begins with faithful and literal transcription, but as he progresses he is called upon to undertake more complex and intricate tasks. He has to reproduce incredibly convoluted calligraphic forms, resembling plants, mosses and stones: this clearly corresponds to the advice which the mysterious gentleman gives Berthold in *Die Jesuiterkirche in G*, to reproduce nature not literally, but on a higher and more imaginative plane. But for Hoffmann the imaginative has its dangers as well as its wonders. The anxiety always is that the imaginative will lose its vital, dynamic creativity and be transformed into a fixation on the dead and inert. In *Der Sandmann* this manifests itself through Olympia the doll automaton, who represents a false transcendence even though Nathaniel's idealisation of her has a visionary quality. In *Der goldne Topf* it takes a different form: the confinement of Anselmus in a corked crystal bottle. This fate, brought upon him by his failure to copy the most complex of the manuscripts and by his dropping ink on the original, is a sign of his difficulty in coping with the excruciating demands which the imaginary imposes. Hoffmann himself makes the same point in more than one of his stories. In *Der Sandmann* a narrative interpolation raises the problem of writing in precisely these terms: the fear that in the act of writing the inner mental picture has been lost and that the words that are designed to convey it are lifeless and dead, that language is inadequate to render the brilliant colours of the inner vision. Similarly, in the twelfth vigil of *Der goldne Topf* the narrator despairs of ever being able to do justice to the magical world of Anselmus and Serpentina. For Hoffmann this world is always characterised by colour and movement, by sinuous motions that are manifestly erotic. In Elis's dream there are curling plants and interlocked female bodies, in Anselmus's vision there are the shimmering, glistening, twining snakes. The golden pot itself exhibits endless magical reflections, including, significantly, one of Anselmus himself, with arms outstretched towards Serpentina. The golden pot is a crucial symbol in the tale of the possibility of an imaginative transcendence of the actual; it is therefore highly relevant that the witch, at the instigation of Veronica, Anselmus's materialistic and worldly love, should struggle to deprive Archivist Lindhorst of it. However, in Anselmus's one moment of weakness, as he partially succumbs to the influence of the black magic, he actually confuses Veronica with the transcendent Serpentina and momentarily doubts the existence of the visionary world.

Nevertheless, Anselmus's triumphant apotheosis into the mystical other world does leave Hoffmann with a problem – which is how the tale and the trajectory of the narrative are to be reinserted in the everyday. In the concluding vigil the narrator becomes anxious about his ability to complete the work – necessarily so, because such a completion involves a return to reality and a consequent bracketing of the imaginative. But he receives a letter from 'Salamander Lindhorst' encouraging him to finish the project and, on visiting his house, is vouchsafed a vision of the blissful union of Anselmus and Serpentina. But with its fading the narrator is affected by a deep sense of grief and tormented by the contrast between the bliss which he has witnessed and his own depressed and downtrodden state as he faces a return to his lonely garret. But the Archivist consoles him by saying that the poetic itself represents such a realm of harmony and that therefore the story of Anselmus is to be read as a metaphor of the artistic quest. This saving consolation, the shift between actualising the imaginative and viewing it as a noble fiction, but a fiction none the less, makes explicit what was only implicit in Novalis's *Heinrich von Ofterdingen*.

Nevertheless, this tempered optimism appears almost euphoric in the context of Hoffmann's work as a whole, where the artist is seen in a desperate struggle against the world, where the need to retain his integrity often takes the form of extremity and violence. A note of pessimism was sounded in Hoffmann's first published work, the sketch *Ritter Gluck*. The opening paragraph sets the tone: the narrator endeavours to give himself up to a pleasing reverie, to enter into an imaginary dream world, but he is continually dragged back to the hateful and banal quotidian, with its trivial gossip and talk about money, by the raucous and inharmonious sounds of the café orchestra. Disharmony characterises the ordinary world, just as harmoniousness characterises the imaginary. The mysterious man of fifty who identifies himself in the very last words of the story as 'Ritter Gluck' is not to be completely identified with the real, historical composer Gluck, a composer whom Hoffmann much admired, but rather with the higher, more spiritual and transcendent side of Gluck – the true artist, as opposed to the historical individual who was forced to make compromises destructive of his genius. He reveals himself to be Gluck's best self by his extraordinary knowledge of and affinity with Gluck's work, by the fact that from blank pages he can play the work with complete fidelity and at the same time transform it and transmute it into something that is both imaginatively more complex and more emotionally powerful. This transcendent music, according to Hoffmann, was the form which it took when Gluck received it from the visionary other world; but Gluck betrayed and compromised the visionary and for penance is doomed to go on haunting this world – the artist as wanderer. The designation *Ritter* carries with it a heavy irony: on the one hand it suggests worldly rank and status (knight), yet it points to a higher nobility than the world can actually embrace, the nobility of the artist. A parallel irony is to be traced in the story *Rat Krespel*, where the eccentric Krespel, a virtuoso maker as well as player of violins, is believed to be both insane and tyrannical, because of the mysterious hold which he exercises over a young girl, Antonia, whom he keeps confined in his house. Like Hawthorne's *Rappaccini's Daughter*, the story ironically reverses the reader's expectations. Krespel has been endeavouring to save or prolong the life of his daughter, for whom singing will mean death, by protecting her from the harsh intrusion of the mundane world and by translating onto his violin the beauty that she would otherwise have expressed through her voice. The intervention of the outside world nevertheless brings about her death. There is clearly more than a touch of autobiographical irony in the appelation 'Rat', or councillor, as applied to Krespel, since the truth of his existence is no more to be summed up by that designation than was Hoffmann's by the title of judge.

The enmity between the artist and the world is brought most sharply into focus in *Signor Formica* and *Das Fraulein von Scuderi*. The close of the former tale identifies the bitter parodist and mordant theatrical mime, Signor Formica, as the artist Salvator Rosa in disguise. In this story art is shown as triumphing over life, as Signor Pasquale Capuzzi, another Bartolo figure, who exercises malign guardianship over a beautiful young girl, is subsequently made into a figure of public ridicule through his inability to distinguish art from life in Formica's brilliant impersonation. The story also implies the subterranean nature of the artist's social criticism: he does mock and criticise society, but through the medium of a double, wherein his own identity is masked and veiled. But, of course, it is the figure of Cardillac, the demonic creator of beautiful jewellery in the age of Louis XIV, that is the occasion of Hoffmann's most extreme statement. Cardillac resents his social subordination to the aristocracy and the necessity that forces him to abandon his most beautiful creations when he has completed them; for they are then transformed into mere articles of commerce and erotic commodities for people who have no conception of their aesthetic merit or of the artistry that went into their construction. Cardillac takes his revenge by murdering his customers and retrieving the jewellery. Clearly, this story, for all its vehemence and bitterness, points to a truth, since many artists have endeavoured to retain their best work and have gone to extraordinary lengths to recover treasured creations that they have been forced by necessity to sell – Picasso is only the best known example. But for Hoffmann the implications are more metaphysical: the jewellery represents the artist's own precious vision, which must not be compromised or sullied by the actual; even murder can seem legitimate in this highest cause. Hoffmann does not present Cardillac in an altogether sympathetic light, though he does make his motivation recognisable. Nevertheless, Cardillac is yet another instance of the Superman figure on which Romantic literature converges: a man who is a law unto himself, whose values are incommensurable with those of the everyday world; and who not only refuses to submit to its dictates, but scornfully rejects and repudiates them. In his own eyes everything that he contemplates must be permitted, no matter what the cost.

Hoffmann's ultimate definition of the artist, which makes manifest the transformations to which the idea had been subjected within a relatively brief time-span, is contained in his last work, the complete–incomplete novel *Kater Murr*. The novel purports to have its source in a manuscript retailing the experiences of a tomcat, Murr, written on the back of scrap paper narrating the story of the artist Kreisler. Murr was the name of Hoffmann's own favourite cat, but the real meaning of the juxtaposition is rather different, for *Kater Murr* is the last and most damaging attack by the Romantics on Goethe's self-image as an artist. The opposition Murr/Kreisler must be translated as Goethe/Hoffmann. Murr, the complacent, self-important cat, convinced of his own genius, his profundity and of the importance of his studies and researches, all too clearly represents Hoffmann's view of Goethe. The identification is reinforced by many sly digs which the novel contains at Goethe's expense. Murr's amours recall those of his illustrious predecessor. He describes the stroking which he receives from a servant girl in language which recalls Faust's description of

Gretchen. Goethe is invoked in the opening sentence of the novel, which paraphrases, then cites, Egmont's delight in existence, in the sheer joy of living. Murr's scientific theories also parody Goethe. Murr's belief that dog and cat are just rays cast from a single prism mocks Goethe's theory of colour, just as his conviction that the language of cats and dogs stems from a single source is a joke at the expense of Goethe's notion of the *Urpflanz*. Murr also deploys the idea of the 'beautiful soul', which is formulated in *Wilhelm Meister*, while the whole bogus structure of *Murr* in terms of a *Bildungsroman*, involving such notions as 'apprenticeship', 'maturity' and 'the sublime', is unmistakably aimed at both *Wilhelm Meister* and *Werther*. By contrast, the depiction of Kreisler, which, of course, is the more earnest aspect of the novel, despite the fortuitous and fragmentary nature of its appearance, has strongly autobiographical elements. Kreisler loses his position as councillor as did Hoffmann, his love for Julia was also Hoffmann's and all his principal compositions referred to in the text are actually works which Hoffmann composed. The purpose of the Goethe–Hoffmann contrast is not so much to exalt Hoffmann as the type of the artist, though that is certainly involved, as to call in question the idea of artistic genius associated with Goethe. For Hoffmann, what defines the artist is his alienation and his capacity for suffering.

Kater Murr is virtually a text book in the varieties of literary irony. Friedrich Schlegel's definition of romantic irony in terms of a foregrounding of the literariness of the work and rapid switches of style and mood is evident in the structure of *Murr*, which jolts the reader from the self-satisfied narcissism of Murr to the agonies of Kreisler and back again. Moreover, these are also distantiation devices, which permit Hoffmann to establish an aesthetic gap between the work and his own experience. But there are other ironies as well. For to ironise Goethe as Murr is also to ironise Hoffmann as Kreisler, a fugitive and and elusive absence, flickering behind the others' obtrusive presence. Hoffmann brackets his subject to give it a greater emotional force, just as Pirandello made the sufferings of his six characters seem the more acute by his insistence on their fictive nature.

In the figure of Kreisler all the caveats with which Goethe surrounded his Faust are abolished. Kreisler is the striving, struggling, questing figure, driven onward and tormented by a vision of the ideal, but he does not thereby lose contact with human feeling, because his sufferings are all too intense and real. Kreisler is also a Superman figure: if he kills a man in self-defence, if he acts in ways that may seem bizarre and even cruel, this is justifiable because of the intensity of the emotions that he feels, the pressure of the contradictions to which he is subject, as a free artist who is also a man placed in a position of subjugation. Goethe's concern with renunciation is also criticised. Kreisler recognises that he does not fit in with the world, but he nevertheless refuses to abjure it and insists on the secular nature of the emotion – his love for Julia – which led him to compose his Mass. Hoffmann insists that the artist is not to be judged by the standards of the world; on the contrary, the artist is the measure of all things, a scale and standard to set against the shallowness and superficiality of the mundane world.

Kreisler's experiences at court, reminiscent of *Torquato Tasso*, enable Hoffmann to show how true, deep and tender feeling is inhibited and interdicted in such an aristocratic context, how this setting itself induces Kreisler's bitter and mocking changes of mood. For Kreisler is loved by both Princess Hedwige and Julia, though he loves only Julia. Kreisler and Julia sing a duet which makes the depth of their love for one another only too explicit, yet, upsetting as it is to Julia, Kreisler is forced to follow the 'number' with a light comic song, so as to restore the Princess's favour and to suggest that the emotions have been aesthetic, not real. Kreisler's position of subservience makes any relationship between himself and Julia out of the question – incredible even; yet, at the same time, it is possible for Prince Hektor to arrive on a mission to marry Princess Hedwige and force his unwanted attentions on Julia at the same time. The theme of lost love, of the artist haunted by a vision of the ideal, represented for him by a woman, recurs once again in *Kater Murr*; for Kreisler's hopeless love for Julia, destroyed by the evil Prince, is paralleled by Meister Abraham's love for Chiara, the charming young girl whom the Meister, in his guise as Severino the conjuror, featured in his 'Invisible Maiden' illusion. Through the intervention of Prince Ignatius Chiara becomes truly lost to him and Abraham now experiences in reality the loss of which his illusion was only the type. The artist is seen as engaged in a desperate but vain struggle against a hostile world, in which even the dignity and integrity of his own feeling is subject to casual destruction. The fate of the manuscript dealing with Kreisler only parallels the fate of its actual subject. The artist is victim, perhaps only artist when he is a victim. Such notions are now deeply embedded in Western culture. When T. S. Eliot referred, almost as a matter of course, to the mind that 'suffers' and the mind that 'creates', he nevertheless drew on a conception, of the artist as sufferer, which before the Romantic period was a far from inescapable equation.

Hoffmann's best known opera, *Undine*, was based on a story of the same name by Friedrich de la Motte Fouqué, a Prussian aristocrat, whose Protestant family had left France to escape religious persecution. At first sight *Undine*, though undoubtedly a *Märchen*, is not a tale of the artist, since it concerns the love of a medieval knight, Huldbrand, for the water-sprite Undine. But a poem which prefaces the work refers to the author's long-standing fascination with a vision of Undine and concludes by identifying the author with the knight, which makes it more than legitimate to interpret the tale in that light. Huldbrand is torn between affection for his worldly love, Bertalda, and his deeper passion for the mocking, wilful, yet tender Undine. Undine herself is a shifter between the terrestrial and magical worlds, because, although a water nymph, she nevertheless possesses a soul and the capacity to feel. The relationship between Huldbrand and Undine is threatened both from the worldly and from the other-worldly side; for Undine is distrusted by humans and plagued and tormented by her wicked uncle, the malevolent water spirit Kühleborn. In this world Huldbrand loses Undine because he is unworthy of her: he cannot help but mistrust her, despite her integrity and her persistent efforts to reconcile the contradictions imposed on her existence. She disappears into the Danube, but returns to reclaim Huldbrand in death. The Bertalda–Undine opposition reasserts the priority of the imaginative over the actual. Undine is the ideal woman of Huldbrand's imagination and Fouqué compares him with Pygmalion, who brings his statue to life. But the tale asserts the impossibility of domiciling the visionary in the everyday

world. The vision necessarily disappears and is accompanied
by a deep sense of loss. It can be truly possessed only in death.

Another German writer of French extraction was
Chamisso, author of *Peter Schlemihl's wundersame Geschichte*
(1813). Chamisso was a good friend of Fouqué – the idea of a
man losing his shadow is said to have sprung from a
conversation between the two men after Chamisso had lost
most of his belongings on a journey. Both were members of
Hoffmann's celebrated drinking club, the Brotherhood of
Serapion. Chamisso's tale of an unfortunate man (a *Schlemihl*)
who agrees to exchange his shadow for a purse that can never
be emptied seems to possess an obviously allegorical character, yet it is strangely resistant to interpretation. As an
expatriate, Chamisso may well have felt that he lacked social
weight in Germany and German society, equivalent to not
possessing a shadow, but nothing in the story itself points to
this as a particular concern. The obvious assumption that loss
of a shadow is equivalent to a loss of virility would seem to be
confirmed by the fact that Schlemihl feels unable to marry;
but, since by the end of the narrative the loss no longer figures
as an unmitigated disaster, such a reading involves quite a
substantial conceptual forcing and misrecognition of the text.
It is also tempting to see Schlemihl either as a Godwinian
fable of the way in which a man can lose his place and be cut
off from human society, or as a Faustian warning against
going beyond what is permitted. However, if the story is
approached without such preconceptions its meaning seems
quite clear – in fact, deliberately to reverse many of the
signifying conventions of its own time. The tale does not
criticise the individual from the standpoint of society, but
criticises society from the standpoint of the individual. The
shadow is the individual's real self, his deeper personal
identity. To thrive and prosper in society he needs money (the
purse of Fortunatus) and in exchange for it he must give up
his real self. But society cannot grasp the significance of this
deeper self, the shadow. In society having a shadow is simply
part of the proprieties, a prerequisite which simply makes a
person respectable and just like everyone else. But for
Chamisso, as for Edward Young, to understand the shadow
self in this way is wholly to nullify the mysterious sources of
identity, to be involved in a moral forgetting, a spiritual

emptiness. The moral of Chamisso's tale therefore is that one should not concern oneself too greatly with the shadow itself (appearance), but be concerned only what it represents: the deeper non-socialised sources of one's identity. Significantly the purse brings Schlemihl no happiness but only endless trouble, discord and exploitation by others. But finally, when he is completely isolated and alone, he chances upon a pair of seven-league boots. At this point the tale clearly becomes an allegory of the artist. For, if in society he loses his identity and becomes powerless, away from it he regains power, energy and confidence and a wonderful new imaginative world opens up before him. Schlemihl becomes not a bracketed questing figure like Faust but one whose mission has transcendent value, as he endlessly spans the earth, making scientific, geographical and botanical discoveries. The meaning of the tale is spelt out in its closing sentences: the individual should pay no heed to social appearances ('the shadow') or to money, but live for his inner self, the reality of which the shadow is only a shadow!

In the *Marchen* so far discussed the artist characteristically figures as a man whose gifts and inclinations separate him from the world, but Eichendorff's *Aus dem Leben eines Taugenichts* portrays him in the populist rather than the elitist mode, though Eichendorff himself came from a wealthy family. Eichendorff's Taugenichts ('Good-for-nothing') is a man of the people, whose songs and violin-playing gladden the hearts of those he encounters; they are expressive not of a private *Angst* but of spontaneity, joy and a spirit of good fellowship. The contradictions between ideal and real are presented in *Taugenichts* only to be abolished. Taugenichts does indeed see an image of a beautiful maiden which haunts him all the way through the novel and whom he believes to be a countess far above his social station; but, after many accidents and intrigues in Italy, he returns to his German homeland to find that the girl who obsesses him is only an orphan, a footman's niece, and that there can be therefore no obstacle to their marriage. Eichendorff was a devout Catholic, and, while there can never be simple equations made between beliefs and artistic motivations, in this instance it would seem that the orientation of Eichendorff's work does imply a critique of the unbridled subjectivism and cult of genius that is found in Hoffmann. The artist figures who appear in the Italian section of the narrative are shown to be excessively narcissistic and overly concerned with the aesthetic. The notion of the disruption of the aesthetic by the real, which is the theme both of Hummel's painting *Company in an Italian Inn* and of Hoffmann's story *Die Fermate*, where the arrival of the innkeeper with the wine disrupts the singing of an exquisite cadence, is parodied in *Taugenichts* – Eichendorff suggests that reality must always take priority over the aesthetic. Eichendorff implies that the artists in their self-preoccupation have lost touch with the ordinary people – not the last time that such a charge was to be levied. Eckbrecht, who acts as spokesman for the cult of genius, says that the artists are leaving the people behind as they stride towards eternity in their seven-league boots – a remark which is surely also a dig at Chamisso. For Eichendorff there are grave dangers in this moral hubris. *Aus dem Leben eines Taugenichts* has a narrative just as convoluted and intricate as a story by Hoffmann, but it points not so much to the action of a sinister and impenetrable fate as to the existence of a benign and all-seeing Providence to which the individual should resign himself, in a complete and unhesitating confidence that all will be for the best. Taugenichts always displays a devil-may-care attitude; he does not greatly concern himself about where he is, what is happening or what people's motives are. He simply lives exuberantly from moment to moment and allows destiny's pattern to unfold according to its own laws and in its own time. Undoubtedly, Eichendorff does not merely see his hero as careless and irresponsible; he is rather a holy fool, whose trust and faith in the world are confirmed by the course of events. In *Taugenichts* the contradiction between art and life is shown to be a moral error. The Czech musicians whom Taugenichts encounters on his journey home wander from one place to another, playing and enjoying themselves. Their art is at one with nature and with the world. Eichendorff does not discount the ideal but suggests that in the joyous celebration of life of such a figure as Taugenichts the two worlds can commingle and ultimately fuse. For the ordinary world is transfigured by an artistic radiance, and art becomes humble and reverent as it finds its place in the world. But did it have such a place? For the problem posed by Hoffmann was far from imaginary and Eichendorff's tale is the imaginary solution to a real dilemma, which, by virtue of his temperament, background and social position, he himself did not experience.

This analysis of the tale of the artist in Romantic literature would not be complete without reference to its translation to another cultural context, that of France, in the work of Balzac, one of the greatest and most influential exponents of the genre. His tales of the artist, *La Peau de chagrin* and *Sarrasine*, are amongst his earliest works and are exactly contemporaneous with the official broaching of the Romantic–classical controversy in France through Victor Hugo's *Hernani* (1830) and *Notre-Dame de Paris* (1831). Balzac was widely read in German literature, but the contrast which it predicated between the visionary and the actual could not with him assume the same form. For Balzac was writing not in a divided and economically backward country, burdened by tolls and taxes which inhibited the development of commerce, but in Paris, with its sharp contrasts between the splendours and the miseries of the world, where the capitalist was king and where the most fantastic visions of grandeur could be transcribed into hard fact. The sumptuous banquet which Balzac describes early in *La Peau du chagrin*, the extraordinary elegance and brilliance of its setting, the costly food and wines, its culmination in a display for the delectation of the guests of exquisitely beautiful women from every part of the world, is no scene from Part II of *Faust* in some extraterrestrial location, but one set in the Paris mansion of the wealthy capitalist Taillefer. Consequently it is necessary for the meaning of the visionary, and of the compact that the artist makes on its behalf, to be redefined. Indeed, Balzac parodied the original notion of a contract with the Devil in *Melmoth reconcilié*, which plays with the notion that in France Melmoth, far from finding it impossible to find someone to change places with him, would, on the Bourse, be confronted by an *embarras de richesse*!

At the outset of *La Peau de chagrin*, Raphael, a young artist who has lost all his remaining funds at the gaming tables, wanders in the streets of Paris contemplating suicide. He enters a strange old shop, clearly identified by Balzac as a world of the ideal as opposed to the real, where he sees many wonderful things, including the wild ass's skin, possession of which can realise all the possessor's dreams, but only at the cost of shortening his life. With every wish the skin shrinks until nothing is left and the owner dies. This myth strongly asserts Balzac's conviction that the artist is necessarily a man who thrives through excess, who pays the price for his own creativity as he is driven and destroyed by the acting out of his own desires. The skin, for Balzac, is also a sign of the essential mysteriousness and wonder of the world, which will always remain impenetrable before scientific knowledge. Raphael has the skin subjected to innumerable tests by scientists, but throughout it remains untouched, unmarked, inscrutable. But the deeper significance of the mysterious skin is not that it can realise possibilities, but that it serves to demarcate the visionary from the actual, to show that the visionary is not be achieved in social terms. The story is structured around the opposition between two women: Pauline, a simple, humble, loving girl, and Foedora, the writer's obsession, a glamorous but superficial woman of society. To begin with, Raphael neglects Pauline, whose love for him is transparent, in favour of the glittering and enigmatic Foedora, even taking money from Pauline to entertain his idol. For Raphael, Foedora is the occasion of a semiotic torture; he is unable to decipher the meaning of her words, her gestures, her behaviour, to know whether she loves him, could love him, or indeed possesses any feelings at all. He is even driven to voyeurism. Observing her behind the curtains, he discovers that her existence is entirely self-centred, that she has no intention of marrying, that her being is entirely external and social and that the deeper Foedora, the real woman of feeling that he has sought to decipher, does not exist. Nevertheless, he still loves her. The significance of the wild ass's skin as a talisman is that, by giving Raphael great social power and wealth, he is liberated from the fetishised eroticism of a class society. He discovers that he no longer loves Foedora, her power over him is broken, and that he really loves Pauline, whom he failed to recognise at her true worth. The contrast between Foedora, the social and external, and Pauline, the ideal and inward, is echoed in Henry James's *The Portrait of a Lady*, where Madame Merle is similarly opposed to Isabel Archer. Raphael does not gain Pauline's love through the magic skin; he possesses this already. The skin is rather a mechanism through which Pauline is transposed into the visionary – a vision which the artist must necessarily lose but which becomes the more intense and supremely transcendent at the moment of its loss. Raphael must die to possess Pauline with the purity of a vision, because only in this way can the absolute distance between worldly love and ideal love be signified. To ask what happens to Pauline, as the imaginary interlocutor does in the Epilogue, is absurd, because Pauline is to be seen not as a real person but as the epitome of the transcendent; she is a dream, an apparition which must remain intangible and therefore incorruptible. And Foedora, as Balzac says, is society – the negation of both the artist and his vision.

Such also is the conclusion of *Sarrasine*, but it is the more tragic because the artist Sarrasine is unable to distinguish what pertains to society from what pertains to art. The story is composed of two linked narratives, one about Paris society and one about the artist, each of which sheds light on the other. The opening section poses the problem of the origin of the fabulous wealth of the Lanty family and suggests that the resolution of the enigma is to be found in the figure of the mysterious old man who is present at their parties and who is treated by them with considerable deference. The narrative of Sarrasine describes how the young sculptor falls in love with a beautiful singer, La Zambinella, who represents for him the ideal of feminine beauty. The story ends with a twist and an identification. Sarrasine is mortified to discover that Zambinella is a male castrato, and he is punished for his error by being stabbed to death on the orders of Count Cocognara, Zambinella's patron. The old man is identified as this castrato, source of the Lanty fortune. The story parades a series of transformations. A man becomes a castrato and appears on the stage as a woman; this is transformed by the painter Vien into a painting of Adonis, ideal beauty as a man. Zambinella's singing in Rome is transformed into wealth for the Lantys in Paris; sterility in art creates sterility as wealth. Artifice creates money creates artifice. Origins are masked through the process of transformation.

Like *La Peau de chagrin*, *Sarrasine* has the character of a revelation. Just as Raphael, behind the curtains, discovers the truth about Foedora, so the narrator of *Sarrasine*, seated in a window recess behind a silk curtain, in his position of an observer is able to disclose the truth about the old man – and also to recognise that the dance of life is, in reality, a dance of death. The old man displays the truth that was hidden from Sarrasine.

What is striking about his appearance is the discrepancy between body and clothing. He is a little old man with a stooped back, bony legs and thighs, emaciated jawbone and skull, yet he wears a blond curled wig, lace frills, ornaments hanging from his ears and a watch-chain as dazzling as a woman's necklace. This discrepancy was, of course, precisely what Sarrasine could not and did not see. Zambinella's features were smooth, soft and feminine. The paradox about Sarrasine's involvement with Zambinella is that he does not recognise that the clothing she wears, the delicate slippers, bodice, floral dress, bonnet and lace blouse, are veils and obstacles in the way of his imaginative constitution of her *essence* of feminine beauty in the nude as sculpture; that they are, rather, what constitute 'her' as *appearance*, dictated by a particular set of social and theatrical conventions. Just as Raphael endeavours to decipher Foedora, to read in her signs and gestures the evidence of genuine feeling, so does Sarrasine interpret Zambinella, but without the knowledge that she is a castrato that would explicate the riddle. Sarrasine finds everywhere in Zambinella the markers of femininity, in her delicacy, weakness, reserve. His sensibility as an artist betrays him as a man. Zambinella is both Foedora and Pauline: she expresses the emptiness and hollowness of social being, where there is nothing that lies behind the exterior – and 'rien' is precisely the reproach that Sarrasine hurls at Zambinella in the moment of unmasking – yet Zambinella is also the basis for Sarrasine's vision of an ideal woman.

Sarrasine is very much a tale of the artist and of the contradiction between the ideal and the actual. Roland Barthes's study of the story, *S/Z*, for all its ingenuity, misses the importance of this, because it focuses so narrowly on the narrative itself as a self-sufficient entity, instead of recognising that its codification is established in terms of a signifying practice constituted socially and culturally and not solely in the act of writing. *S/Z* is corrupted by an aestheticism, which, despite Barthes's disclaimers, is indeed very like trying to see a whole landscape in a coffee bean. The point of *Sarrasine* is that the male–female mistake is the horrendous marker of an equally serious category confusion: of imagining that the degraded and false world of social appearances can be the source of an ideal vision. In making a sculpture Sarrasine has made a copy of a copy; he cannot transcend his original because he was as much in bondage to the world of fashion as was Raphael when he took Foedora as a sign for the beautiful. The revelation of difference is simultaneously a pointer to the abolition of difference. Instead of becoming separated from the world, the visionary has become entangled with it, and in the process is mocked, parodied and rendered impotent. Artifice produces money, but it cannot produce art, for it is counterfeit by nature. The nude, as truth, as the beautiful reality behind appearances, does not exist. Art cannot exist as a genuine possibility in bourgeois society, since bourgeois society knows only artifice, illusions and false appearances which it does not seek to go beyond. The Lantys are triumphant; Sarrasine is destroyed.

These early works of Balzac suggest an opposition between art and society that is scarcely consonant with the tenor of Balzac's work as a whole; for Balzac's great project was to analyse and exhibit the working of a society. He could not have undertaken it and carried it through with such pertinacity had he himself adopted such an unequivocally visionary standpoint. Nevertheless, the terms of the antithesis can still be traced even in the midst of the dense social thickets of *La Comédie Humaine*. In *Les Illusions perdues* Balzac describes how the young poet and novelist Lucien Chardon struggles to make his way on the literary and social scene of Paris. But his early dreams of making his mark by the sheer force of genius and sensibility are dissipated and his spirit is ground down by the brutal rebuffs and discouragements he receives. He finds it impossible to maintain his sense of vocation in the context of malice, back-biting, opportunism and intrigue. He returns to the provinces, where he becomes known for his fashionable way of dressing, the only real triumph, Balzac notes, which he was to achieve. Lucien, oppressed by a sense of his own unworthiness and failure after David Séchard, the printer, is thrown into a debtor's prison on his account, contemplates suicide. He plans to drown himself and goes off wearing his most elegant clothes. Although he is saved from this act by a mysterious Spanish priest, Carlos Herrera (in fact the master criminal Vautrin in disguise), the moment is clearly symbolic. For Lucien the poet, sensitive, reflective and idealistic, is dead, and all that is left of him is social externals. He dies not by drowning but by stepping into the coach bound for Paris with Herrera and taking his gold pieces. The false suicide in *Les Illusions perdues* prefigures Lucien's actual suicide in the sequel, *Splendeurs et misères des courtisanes*, but the Lucien who is there reborn is quite another person from the youthful poet.

But if society has its dangers for the artist, so does the road to the absolute. In Balzac's late story *Le Chef-d'oeuvre inconnu*, the old painter Frenhofer, in his desire to create a sublime and transcendental work of art that will go far beyond the mechanical reproduction of form through line drawing, has so overlaid his canvas with layers of paint that no subject can be distinguished. Frenhofer's insistence that volume is created only through the action of light, that outlines must not be definite and that it does not matter if the picture is a blur from close to if it comes into focus when you stand back, is strangely prophetic of developments in painting – we might take Frenhofer's picture to be an Impressionist work or a late Turner. But Balzac clearly intends the story as a critique of an expressive rather than representational theory of art. Like the mysterious stranger in Hoffmann's *Die Jesuiterkirche in G*, Frenhofer insists that the aim of painting must not be to copy nature to express its spirit, to communicate his own visionary world. To this objective the young Balzac was sympathetic. But at the close of his fictional career he emphasised the problematic nature of the visionary. The artist loses any reference point and becomes a law unto himself; he enters a private world where there are no markers or bearings and he is unable to separate what he wishes to achieve from what he actually has achieved. The Superman, who abandons all worldly criteria and follows his own dictates, nevertheless lives in torment, the torment of having no basis for assessing what he is doing. Just as Hogg's Justified Sinner has no way of knowing whether his certainties are from God or the Devil, so Frenhofer is unable to stand back from his visionary ob-session. His confusion is expressed in his final gestures: he accuses the young painters of envy and drives them from his studio, but the same night he kills himself and burns his canvases. Frenhofer lives in a mysterious world, he is beyond the limits of ordinary human nature; but the further he progresses the more equivocal his achievement becomes. Henry James, who knew Balzac's story well, certainly must have had Frenhofer in mind when he gave the artist Dencomb in *The Middle Years* the words 'We work in the dark – we do what we can – we give what we have. Our doubt is our passion and our passion is our task. The rest is the madness of art.' For art, truly, is a madness, where the artist seeks to produce something like that which has never existed. If the work itself illuminates that darkness it can never do so for the artist himself. Frenhofer's vision has a definite pathos, even for Balzac, because it is also a lost vision. That is to say, Frenhofer's conception has a certain sublimity even if that conception cannot be materialised into paint. So, although the canvas is a failure, there is nevertheless something impressive about Frenhofer the visionary, a man whose compulsion for the sublime is so intense that he can reject his own remarkable work as inferior. *Le Chef-d'oeuvre inconnu* points up the paradox of Romantic art with remarkable force and lucidity, in a way that both parallels and counterpoints Pater's later discussion of Leonardo da Vinci. The artist stands or falls by his vision, yet that vision can never be adequately communicated, rendered or translated; it remains, constantly, maddeningly out of reach.

6 The Figure of the Artist in English Romantic Poetry

The role which the poet or author plays in society and the functions that are assigned to him are not everywhere the same. Authorship is a complexly codified notion which is not solely marked by the appearance of a name in a particular position on the spine of a book. It is from the Romantic period that we derive our notions of the author as an emitter or source, the issuing of a distinctive viewpoint from a delocalised source into the arena of public discourse. The author's subject becomes simultaneously his own property and at the same time the index of a distinctive individuality. Symptomatic of these tendencies in poetry is Cowper's *The Task* (1785), which begins with the words, 'I sing the sofa.' On the face of it this opening is not very different from that of Dyer's *The Fleece* (1757):

> The care of sheep, the labours of the loom,
> And arts of trade, I sing.

The one difference would seem to be the element of anti-climax supplied by the word 'sofa', which suggests mock epic in the style of *The Rape of the Lock*:

> What dire offence from amorous causes springs,
> What mighty contests rise from trivial things,
> I sing.

All three refer back to the example of Virgil: the announcement of a poetic subject, accompanied by the locution 'I sing'.

But to appear before the public in the capacity of an artist is to place oneself in an equivocal social position, a grey area of uncertainty, where there are no definitive guidelines. In

228

I. Day's *Scenes for the Young* (1807), a work designed to promote good manners and the love of virtue in children, a dialogue takes place between young William MacKenzie and his mother, Mrs MacKenzie, who endeavours to enlighten him on the qualities and credentials required to make a gentleman. William asks, 'Let me see; then bishops, doctors, judges and barristers are gentlemen by profession. And are not merchants and artists looked upon as such?' – to which his mother answers, 'the first merchants and the first artists always are; but not the lowest, as in professions'.[1] As far as the artist is concerned his status is not purely a function of his artistic ability but is closely bound up with social acceptance: what finally validates him as a gentleman is the decision taken by people of quality to accept him as a person of similar status to themselves and his own disposition to comport himself like a gentleman and act in a manner calculated to win their approval and respect. Many of Blake's problems as an artist arose from his failure or refusal to see that genius alone was not enough; it was requisite that he should act in conformity with notions of how a society painter should behave and furnish society with appropriate artistic services. Art is one of the service industries. In the Romantic period the writer and artist become a perennial source of embarrassment: they draw attention to themselves in ways that are unseemly; they insist on their genius and on the uniqueness of their vision in a way which, if it does not smack of self-advertisement, appears incongruous, disproportionate, not to say mad; if gentlemen, they act in ways likely to bring their class and themselves into discredit; if not gentlemen, they comport themselves with the effrontery and vulgarity of social upstarts.

It is such a note of personal flamboyance that marks the opening of Cowper's ostensibly modest poem. For, with Dyer, he places his subject first and thereby assigns it a certain priority, while the expression 'I sing', because traditional, is fairly colourless; it in no way draws attention to the author. Moreover, to write of sheep, flocks and shepherds is well established as a genre of pastoral poetry. It is a characteristic neo-classical assumption that the subject itself has a certain status and that the poet must subordinate his muse to the theme. Thus, for Shaftesbury, the writer's determination to address himself to an audience and explicitly to communicate with it alters the whole aesthetic relationship and deflects attention away from the subject:

> This is the Coquetry of a modern Author; whose Epistles Dedicatory, Prefaces, and Addresses to the Reader, are so many affected *Graces*, design'd to draw the Attention from the Subject, towards himself; and make it be generally observ'd, not so much *what he says* as what he appears or *is* and what figure he already makes, or hopes to make in the fashionable world.[2]

This portrait of the author as an importunate social climber is one that becomes even more familiar in the Romantic period. Cowper as such has no such ambitions, but his manner of writing displays characteristics to which Shaftesbury would certainly object. For in his opening line the whole relation between author and subject has been transposed: it is not the author who answers the subject's bidding but the author who decides and determines topics and endows them with literary status. It is from this annunciatory 'I' that the subject, 'the sofa', flows. Moreover, there is something strangely prosaic and unaffected in the form of this locution that does not parade the disproportion of a mock epic; and, indeed, *The Task* is not a mock epic. What is rather implied is a certain homology between the author and his subject; his choice points to an idiosyncratic, yet homely and comfortable personality which the work itself will in due course reveal. But that foregrounding of the poet is the only certainty that this introductory gesture affords. The subjects that the poem will handle are at the poet's entire discretion.

After Sterne the author, his life and work become an expressive totality, which teases and tantalises the reader to complete the portrait, of which the works themselves form only a pencilled outline. In his *Blumen-, Frucht- und Dornenstücke* Jean-Paul Richter alludes to the interest that readers have in every trait and peculiarity of great writers – to know what clothes they wear and what kind of food they like to eat.[3] And some writers told them. The Romantic period lacked only that indispensable medium of our own time, the interview (though conversations there were even with the great man), to supply full and complete answers to every nagging problem, for the essay as practised by Lamb and Hazlitt raised as many queries as it answered. Thus, the literary code of complete revelation contradicts a social code of modesty and discretion. In his review of *Childe Harold's Pilgrimage*, Scott, with more than a trace of misgiving, observed, 'although we do not pretend to ascertain the motive on which Lord Byron acted in bringing the peculiarity of his own sentiments and feeling so frequently before his readers',[4] but nevertheless went on to say that 'it is with no little admiration that we regard these extraordinary powers'.[5]

Scott's indulgence was not shared by other critics writing on other writers. The author's foregrounding of his own sensibility and his insistence on its importance were felt to be an impertinence. John Wilson Croker, reviewing Coleridge's *Biographia Literaria*, felt it incumbent upon himself to awaken the author from any inflated misapprehension as to his own public importance: 'It is impossible to read many pages of this work without thinking that Mr. Coleridge conceives himself to be a far greater man than the public is likely to admit; and we wish to awaken him from what seems to us a most ludicrous delusion.'[6] But these were kindly words by comparison with the strictures of Robert Hunt on Blake. Hunt has no objection to Blake's being an 'unfortunate lunatic' provided that he absents himself from the public gaze – that, after all, was the very point of the burgeoning mental institutions – but he does object to his making a spectacle of himself by his pretentions to genius: 'The praises which these gentlemen bestowed last year on this unfortunate man's illustrations to Blair's *Grave* have, in feeding his vanity, stimulated him to publish his madness more largely, and this again exposed him, if not to the derision, at least to the pity of the public.'[7] The author's message is necessarily discordant because it does not sufficiently express the standpoint of genteel society; but from the type of person that Blake is that is hardly to be expected and blame must rather be laid at the door of his gentlemanly sponsors who have failed to grasp the fact that discourse to be literary discourse must first and foremost be socially acceptable discourse. By this crucial criterion Blake's claims to genius do not so much qualify him as disqualify him. The reviewer in *Blackwood's* makes no bones about the nature of his objections to Leigh Hunt (which, of course, apply equally well to Keats), since, if good writing is to be construed as the absence of vulgarity, it follows that no vulgar person can be a good writer: 'All the great poets of our country have been men of some rank in society, and there is no vulgarity in any of their writings; but Mr. Hunt cannot utter a dedication, or even a note, without betraying the *Shibboleth* of low birth and low habits. He is the ideal of the Cockney poet.'[8]

Wordsworth, though not as vulgar as Hunt, nevertheless breaches propriety by presenting opinions to the reader from the standpoint of a person of lowly status. It is bad enough, according to Jeffrey, that the representation in *The Excursion* is low mimetic: 'The other persons of the drama are, a retired military chaplain, who has grown half atheist and half misanthrope – the wife of an unprosperous weaver – a servant girl with her natural child – a parish pauper, and one or two other personages of equal rank and dignity';[9] but Wordsworth compounds the felony by the central importance and moral stature which he assigns to the person of the old pedlar: 'Did Mr. Wordsworth really imagine, that his favourite doctrines were likely to gain anything in point of effect or authority, by being put into the mouth of a person accustomed to higgle about tape, or brass sleeve buttons?'[10] To have made them really convincing Wordsworth should have backed them up with the authority of a peer of the realm, barrister at law, member of parliament or justice of the peace – or, if a cleric, at least a bishop. Wordsworth's mistake is that he fails to see that such persons as an old pedlar, since they possess no status, cannot have a standpoint at all, let alone one that would be suitable for literary discourse. To foreground the pedlar in this way exposes Wordsworth to the charge of 'revolting incongruity'[11] – an incongruity which pertains not only to the poem but also to the poet himself as transgressor and disruptor of social codes.

To place himself on the right footing with his readers the author needs a little diplomacy and finesse, partaking no doubt more than a little of the *outré* but not identifying himself too closely with his artistic materials nor insisting too forcibly on his visionary powers. De Quincey's *Confessions of an English Opium-Eater* by skilfully combining the insalubrious with a recognition of the requirements of decorum, strikes an appropriate note:

> I here present you, courteous reader, with the record of a remarkable period in my life; and according to my application of it, I trust that it will prove, not merely an interesting record, but, in a considerable degree, instructive. In *that* hope, it is that I have drawn it up; and *that* must be my apology for breaking through those restraints of delicate reserve, which, for the most part, intercept the public exposure of our own errors and infirmities.[12]

Although De Quincey's work is simultaneously confessional and visionary, the author does not celebrate or glory in the fact but rather apologises for it in advance. Its real purpose is to be instructive, and it is to this end that the author reveals himself, as well as to defend himself from the damaging imputation of being a Coleridge. If the opium-eater fears and trembles, the book will have accomplished its task. The visionary and the confessional are simply a by-product. Or so De Quincey pretends.

The Romantic author who managed things best was Scott. The transparent *incognito* proved the most ingenious of strategies. 'The author of *Waverley*', 'The great unknown' – these were mysteries of authorship to whet the appetite of the time, to provoke speculation about the enigmatic source of these vastly popular works; yet at the same time the early recognition that Scott was the probable author, combined with the persistence with which the said author appeared before the public with a new work, ensured that the trail before the barking hounds never went stale. Scott almost certainly saved himself a great deal of hostile criticism as a result, since, although identified, the author of *Waverley* could never be disparaged with quite the personalising snub administered to a Wordsworth or a Keats. Also, in his capacity as a novelist Scott need only appear in the guise of an entertainer, without any presumption or obligation to foist himself on the sorely tried patience of a refined public as the self-important possessor of a socially incongruous vision. As Carlyle subsequently put it,

> From the first most people suspected, and soon after the first, few intelligent persons much doubted that the author of *Waverley* was Walter Scott. Yet a certain mystery was still

kept up; rather piquant to the public; doubtless very pleasant to the author, who saw it all; who probably had not to listen, as other hapless individuals often had, to this or the other long-drawn 'clear proof at last' that the author was not Walter Scott, but a certain astonishing Mr. So-and-so; – one of the standing miseries of human life at that time. But for the privileged author it was like a king travelling incognito. All men know that he is a high king, chivalrous Gustaf or Kaiser Joseph; but he mingles in their meetings without cumber of etiquette or lonesome ceremony, as Chevalier du Nord, or Count of Lorraine: he has none of the weariness of royalty, and yet all the praise, and the satisfaction of hearing it with his own ears. In a word, the Waverley Novels circulated and reigned triumphant; to the general imagination the 'Author of *Waverley*' was like some living mythological personage, and ranked among the chief wonders of the world.[13]

To whit, in the immaculate conception of anonymity Scott escaped the attribution of any stigmatising source; the world could acknowledge his genius without having to reckon with the person, and Scott was thoroughly and universally famous before anyone could snatch a fire-extinguisher to damp down the dangerous flames of literary adventurism.

In the poetry of William Blake we find many parallels with the literature of German Romanticism – the contradiction between imagination and a world that resists it, the artist as hero, the sense of a lost vision – but with an important difference. For in the German *Märchen* the contradiction between the visionary and the actual – with the important exception of Novalis, who, like Blake, did believe in the possible restoration of the Golden Age – is presented virtually as a theoretical given; whereas Blake, in his earlier poetry at least, anticipated a realisation of his prophecies in the field of the historical and the immediate present: the American and and French revolutions heralded the coming of a new age in which all systems of domination, religious and political, would be overthrown. *America* and *Europe* are rightly seen as prophetic books: they gesticulate dramatically in the direction of the actual. However, the status of Blake's major long poems, *The Four Zoas*, *Milton* and *Jerusalem*, is rather different. They belong to a later period in which the Reign of Terror in France coupled with severe political repression and the persecution of radicals in England had made the realisation of such a vision much more problematic. In these poems we find a complex synthesis of the religious, the political and the aesthetic, in which Blake assigns a key role in the transformation of consciousness and the transformation of the world to the imagination and to the artist who is its vessel. What makes Blake so enormously suggestive and illuminating as a poet is his awareness of ideology; he recognises the hold that systems of ideas have over people's minds and the extent to which such structural formations are a major obstacle in the way of human progress. The relevance of Blake's 'I must Create a System or be enslav'd by another Man's' is not simply autobiographical. It points to the importance in the poems themselves of overcoming and deconstructing an oppressive system of ideas. But 'system' is rather a misleading word when applied to Blake's writings themselves – not because they are inconsistent or unsystematic, but because it suggests the very kind of mental lock which Blake himself was trying to break. They should therefore be thought of rather as a counter-discourse in which terms and polarities are reversed, realigned or switched to dramatise the very arbitrariness of the discourse it brings into question. When Blake wrote in *Jerusalem* that 'Poetry's Fetters Fetter the Human Race' he alluded not only to the chains of conventional versification but also to the numbing effects of a poetry that only reproduces and retransmits, without ever questioning or challenging. Blake was such an uncompromising poet because he saw no possibility of adjusting the inward to the external: the inward can make no concessions whatever to worldly dominance, or the divine vision will be lost . More than this poetry is also lost, because what makes the poet superior to the priest is that his vision is pure and uncorrupted, whereas institutionalised religion loses the divine vision through its immersion in externals. So, although from a certain point of view poetry is the only true expression of a religious spirit, at the same time it is the very opposite; for religion necessarily loses touch with the divine vision and is transformed into Antichrist. In Blake the Protestant legacy appears in its starkest and most radical form – an aesthetic rejection of religion itself in the name of the inner light:

Prayer is the study of Art,
Praise is the Practise of Art,
Fasting & c, all relate to Art,
The outward ceremony is AntiChrist.

The Four Zoas is a scenario in which Blake represents the loss
and recovery of unity. *The Four Zoas* is not innocent: rather it is
a conscious reworking of Christian eschatology and Milton's
Paradise Lost in terms of the artist and the imagination. In
place of a schema which presents a cosmic struggle between
the principles of Good (God) and Evil (Satan) centring on the
existence of man as a free moral agent, Blake develops a fable
concerned with the loss of *vision*, which becomes the decisive
category – 'In Eternity All is Vision'. In Blake's version of the
Fall, Albion is split into Four Zoas – Urizen, Orc, Los and
Tharmas – each of whom has a feminine emanation, from
whom he also becomes divided. Of these, Tharmas, who
represents pity, mercy and compassion (i.e. Christ-like virtues) is most strongly connected to the moment of unity.
Tharmas is associated with the moment of the Fall, since his
compassion for Enitharmon, the emanation of Los, leads to
the jealousy and departure of Enitharmon, whom he then
forlornly seeks, like Orpheus in search of Eurydice. But,
equally, Tharmas expresses the interconnectedness, the possibility of unity between the Four Zoas – a possibility which
only Los, representing the imagination, can actualise; so that
Los's relation to Tharmas is crucial for the reconstitution of
the original unity of being. All this is perfectly expressed by
Blake's depiction of Tharmas through imagery of the sea: as
unity the sea is placid, calm, unruffled, peaceful; but when
disturbed it becomes choppy, fragmentary, chaotic, its calm as
in a storm transformed into violence and rage. The other
three Zoas have a certain correspondence, albeit in the form
of parody, with the figures of *Paradise Lost*. Urizen, who for
Blake is the principle of a destructive rationalism, is Milton's
God, but at certain points in Blake's narrative he is transvalued into the position of Milton's Satan: in Night the Sixth
he wanders through a bleak, forbidding and alien universe,
which his own propensity for domination has created, thus
reproducing the wanderings of Satan in *Paradise Lost*; on
Night the Eighth, also like Satan, he falls 'a grovelling serpent

on his belly prone'. Orc, or passion, emotion, is Blake's equivalent of Milton's Satan and Blake is disposed to see passion as more creative than reason; but the crucial perspective of *The Four Zoas* is that both Urizen and Orc represent an urge to dominate and become godlike, which is unhealthy and contrary to man's nature. Divinity is a temptation and a lure. In the course of Night the Ninth of *The Four Zoas* Blake stresses that the movement of his poem is toward the recovery of the human position, which has become lost; the project is to 'resume the image of the human', since in 'Attempting to become more than Man we become less'. The grave danger with both reason and passion is that they rapidly get out of control and create a disproportionality that becomes incredibly difficult to rectify. Los, the imagination, the artist, represents a golden mean; for, while Urizen is the cold illumination of light without heat and Orc a fire that rages out of control, only Los is associated with the ideal state, a steady but controlled burning. It is important to recognise that in *The Four Zoas* Los occupies the human position, that of Adam and Eve in *Paradise Lost*. Only Los, who has remained on the human plane, can recover man's lost humanity, and only Los as the imaginative principle can reconstitute the lost unity with his emanation, Enitharmon, whose very name suggests the possibility of harmony.

However, the structure of the poem can also be seen in terms of a series of betrayals by Los, who at crucial moments compromises his integrity and capitulates to alien powers. Here, Blake's division of the poem into nine nights, like Young's *Night-Thoughts*, is important, because it points to the poem's meditative structure. Like *Night-Thoughts*, the poem involves the facing of darkness and despair on eight successive nights until the gloom is finally dissipated on the last. Los fails to act in the disunity that breaks out in Night the First; he acquiesces in the domination of Luvah (Orc in his unfallen form) and allows him to be imprisoned. His rejection of Tharmas (i.e. the possibility of reconstituting the primal unity) leads to a splitting of his own identity into two. Faced with the task of rebuilding the ruined world created by the one-sided domination of Urizen, his hammer, symbol of creativity, falls. For Blake this is the cardinal crime of the imagination: to approximate the world rather than to trans-

form it in terms of one's own inwardness – Los 'became what
he beheld'. Although the birth of Orc, or passion, presided
over by Los and Enitharmon, is an important step towards the
recovery of unity, Los again commits an act of betrayal by
binding Orc in the Chains of Jealousy. Los's power is even
more deeply threatened in Night the Seventh, where Los and
Enitharmon, by eating the fruit of the Tree of Mystery
(corresponding to the eating of the fruit of the Tree of
Knowledge by Adam and Eve) compromise the imaginative
principle. They have been corrupted by rationalism: the reign
of mystery for Blake signifies the reign of Antichrist, the
domination of churches and rationalistic or natural religion.
The reign of Antichrist will only be brought to an end with the
Last Judgement, which represents the recovery of unity and
an end to the domination which the one-sidedness of reason
or passion induces.

The puzzles which *The Four Zoas* raises centre primarily on
the status which Blake assigns to the stages which occur in the
poem. For Milton's *Paradise Lost* is undoubtedly located
in historical time. *Paradise Lost* has no happy ending,
even though such an ending is distantly envisaged and Adam's
own position between Eden and the Last Judgement is
homologous with that of Milton many hundreds of years later.
Just as Adam must come to terms with the expulsion from
Paradise, so Milton must come to terms with the defeat of the
puritan revolution. The ending is so historically remote that
the consolation it offers is somewhat notional. *The Four Zoas*,
on the other hand, is a hypothetical description of certain
successive states of consciousness, which may well correspond
to man's historical development but whose connection to it is
far more ambiguous. Here, the parallels with Hegel are rather
striking. Hegel also presents a schema involving successive
states of consciousness and progressive transformations in
which conflict is seen as creative rather than destructive, but
there is also an ambiguity in his writing as to whether the
stages he outlines definitely correspond to certain determinate states of affairs. These hypothetical transformational
models seem, therefore, highly characteristic of Romantic
discourse: they represent fields of possibility, which leaves
open the question of how they are actually to be realised. We
may say that this progression represents a logical and neces-

sary progression, but the precise mode and manner of its working out cannot be foreseen.

For Blake the problem of the artist's relationship to a particular social context and ideology had now become an urgent one, since it touched on very immediate personal concerns. The task of realising his own freedom under the doubtful guardianship and sponsorship of Hayley created a continual tension in his mind; under Hayley, Blake felt his genius continually rebuked. At the same time he was grappling with the conceptual difficulty posed by contradictions in Milton's work: how could it be that Milton had written so much better and with a keener prophetic insight than he was consciously capable of, while failing to grasp the nature of his own vision? The solution to this problem is formulated by Blake in terms of vision *versus* imaginative betrayal. Where Milton is faithful to his own inner imaginative world he is capable of transcending the dominant ideology and of recognising the warping and distortion of values. He can even render this as an incarnate poetic vision, though he himself dwells in a world of shadows:

> Silent Milton stood before
> The darkened Urizen; as the sculptor silent stands before
> His forming image (he walks round it patiently labouring),
> Thus Milton stood forming bright Urizen, while his mortal
>   part
> Sat frozen in the rock of Horeb, and his redeemed portion
> Thus formed the clay of Urizen; but within that portion
> His real human walked above in power and majesty
> Though darkened . . . .

The historical Milton was always prone to a sliding away from his own truth into an imaginative betrayal in which he becomes identifiable with Satan; it is Blake himself who will express the truth that the name Milton designates or can designate. That is to say, Blake can be pure artist – the imagination uncompromised, the divine vision held fast.

Blake's sense of the centrality of the role of the poet and his readiness to ascribe to him a crucial cultural role may well have been influenced by John Brown's *History of the Rise and Progress of Poetry* (1963), which made a major contribution to discussions of the role of 'the Bard' in the later eighteenth century. For Brown the coming about of a situation in which the Bard lost his indispensable place at the court of kings and became a voice that progressively went unheeded was inevitably and inescapably associated with decadence and cultural decline. As far as the Hebrews were concerned, Brown saw Solomon, as the last poet king, marking a turning-point;

> After him the *complex* Office of *Legislator* and *Bard* seems to have *separated*: The peculiar Causes which had so long upheld it in the Jewish State, now began to cease: For *Idolatry* more and more prevailed, *Manners* became *corrupt*, and public Misery and Ruin ensued. The *Prophets* and *Bards* were no longer found in the Courts of Kings, or among the Rulers of the People: Yet still they continued to throw out the Emanations of prophetic and moral Truth, accompanied with the Enthusiasm of *Song*, in the more retired and yet uncorrupted situations of private Life: And such were the *later Prophets*, whose writings still remain in Scripture.[14]

For Blake, as for Brown, poetry and prophecy are one and in Blake's poetry the opposition corruption/poetry is constantly deployed; only poetry offers a remedy for the social ills of the time, since only poetry is beyond culture.

In the last section of Book II of *Milton* Blake/Milton appears in majesty to awaken Albion/England from the darkness of rationalism and natural religion:

There is a negation, & there is a contrary:
The negation must be destroyed to redeem the contraries.
The negation is the spectre, the reasoning power in man.
This is a false body, an incrustation over my immortal
Spirit, a selfhood which must be put off & annihilated alway.
To cleanse the face of my spirit by self-examination.

To bathe in the waters of life; to wash off the not-human
I come in self-annihilation & the grandeur of inspiration,
To cast off rational demonstration by faith in the Saviour;
To cast off the rotten rags of memory by inspiration;
To cast off Bacon, Locke and Newton from Albion's covering;
To cast off from poetry all that is not inspiration,

That it no longer shall dare to mock with aspersion of madness
Cast on the inspired, by the tame high finisher of paltry blots
Indefinite, or paltry rhymes, or paltry harmonies.

Against the purity of the inner mental and imaginative world
the external appears as degraded and compromised, as does
the tradition of scientific inquiry that formulates itself in
relation to it. *Milton* thus makes it crystal clear how crucial the
figure of the artist/visionary is for Blake; only he can pierce
the veil of mystery and ideology and even he may become
seriously confused and compromised in his attempt to struggle against it; the prophetic–poetic side of his personality is
always at risk from the man himself, living in a degrading and
betraying material world. Only the artist can redeem the
world, since only the artist can see that redemption is needed
and envisage the form it should take.

Thus the importance of *Milton* for Blake was that it clarified
for him the centrality of his own role as artist and encouraged
him to write the apocalyptic poem *Jerusalem*, in which Blake
Los would figure as his own hero: Blake's sense of himself as a
man set against the world was, of course, intensified by the
curious episode of the fracas in Blake's garden involving the
soldier Scolfield, which subsequently led to Blake's facing
charges of sedition. Yet, despite this, and other humiliating
experiences, Blake writes of England/Albion more in sorrow
than in anger, though anger is undoubtedly present. Though
Jerusalem, like all of Blake's poetry, presents the reader with
many difficulties, it is nevertheless simpler in design and
argument than *The Four Zoas*: it is essentially a prolonged
lamentation by Blake over the fallen state of Albion, culminating in a final triumphant vision of transcendence and redemption. The poem gives us a far stronger sense of Blake's own
time: we cannot fail to be aware of England as a country at war
with France, as a country that is developing industrially,
where the systematic exploitation of the poor goes hand in
hand with the propagation of a moral creed committed to
ideals of benevolence, sociability, charity and the general
good. The poet is firmly anchored in a real world:

> I heard in Lambeth's shades:
> In Felpham I heard and saw the visions of Albion;

I write in South Molton Street, where I both see and hear
In regions of humanity, in London's opening streets.

It is the poet's task to report on the world as he sees it and at
the same time to open up the prospect and possibility of a
world that can and must be other. The poet is 'Striving with
systems to deliver individuals from those systems'.

Yet in the context out of which Blake is writing, that of a
repressed and repressive England, struggling simultaneously
against France and against her own people, optimism was
hardly easy. War leads to the warping and distortion of all
moral values; false imperatives appear self-evident and simple
truths are lost sight of:

Then left the sons of Urizen the plough & harrow, the loom,
The hammer & the chisel, & the rule & compasses; from
    London fleeing
They forged the sword on Cheviot, the chariot of war & the
    battle-axe,
The trumpet fitted to mortal battle, & the flute of summer in
    Annandale.
And all the arts of life they changed into the arts of death in
    Albion.
The hour-glass contemned because its simple workmanship
Was like the workmanship of the ploughman, & the water-
    wheel
That raises water into cisterns, broken and burned with fire
Because its workmanship was like the workmanship of the
    shepherd.
And in their stead, intricate wheels invented, wheel without
    wheel;
To perplex youth in their outgoings, & to bind their labours in
    Albion
Of day & night the myriads of eternity, that they may grind
And polish brass and iron hour after hour, laborious task!
Kept ignorant of its use, that they might spend days of wisdom
In sorrowful drudgery, to obtain a small pittance of bread:
In ignorance to view a small portion & think that all,
And call it 'demonstration', blind to all the simple rules of life.
'Now, now, the battle rages round thy tender limbs, O Vala!
Now smile among thy bitter tears: now put on all thy beauty.

Is not the wound of the sword sweet, & the broken bone
  delightful?
Wilt thou smile among the scythes when the wounded groan
  in the field?
We were carried away in thousands from London, & in tens
Of thousands from Westminister & Marylebone in ships
  closed up;
Chained hand and foot, compelled under iron whips
Of our captains; fearing our officers more than the enemy.'

In these extraordinarily powerful and eloquent lines Blake
paints a picture which invokes no theoretical cosmology but
the brutal facts of class oppression during the Napoleonic
wars: the destruction of a peaceful way of life and the ruthless
press-ganging of men into military service, with war and battle
pursued under the impetus of fear and coercion. Blake is also
extraordinarily perceptive in suggesting how technology
creates its own *raison d'être*, since the purposes for which
machines, whether of death or of any other kind, are built
appear unproblematic. Technology becomes ideological because it encourages men to view the world in a limited and
essentially operational way. Only the poet, who sees all, can
also see a way out.
  But *Jerusalem* is not solely concerned with war; it also
continues the struggle against natural religion and its func-
tional role in a class society. The churches promulgate
religious values in a way that is hypocritical and manipulative;
they play a crucial part in the subjection and domination of the
working class:

The twenty-eight cities of Albion stretch their hands to thee,
Because of the oppressors of Albion in every city & village.
They mock at the labourer's limbs, they mock at his starved
  children,
They buy his daughters that they may have the power to sell
  his sons;
They compel the poor to live upon a crust of bread by soft
  mild arts;
They reduce the man to want, then give with pomp and
  ceremony.
The praise of Jehovah is chanted from lips of hunger & thirst.

The point could not be made more incisively. The Church
abases man and takes away his dignity, self-confidence and
self-respect so that he is in a position where any pitiful
offering will be accepted with grateful thanks. Blake's Divine
Vision defines itself in direct opposition to this: it appeals to
the divinity in every man as the only possible source of
redemption:

Then Los grew furious, raging: 'Why stand we here trembling
    around,
Calling on God for help and not ourselves in whom God
    dwells,
Stretching a hand to save the falling man?'

Man has lost sight of his higher capabilities and his sense of the
field of possibility is vastly curtailed:

The visions of eternity, by reason of narrowed perceptions,
Are become weak visions of time and space, fixed into furrows
of death.

For to lose contact with the inner imaginative world is to be
spiritually dead – the threat that hovered over the poet
Milton. It is Blake's mission as a poet to reawaken in his
readers their sense of the power of the creativity that lies
within them:

Trembling I sit day and night; my friends are astonished at
    me.
Yet they forgive my wanderings, I rest not from my great
    task –
To open the eternal worlds, to open the immortal eyes
Of man inwards into the worlds of thought – into Eternity
Ever expanding in the bosom of God, the human imagination.

As Blake himself saw it, his task was a far greater one than that
of Milton; for Milton had simply to disclose the working out of
a providential design in the universe, a design that might
often seem obscure, but of which, nevertheless, there were
many and evident signs. But Blake as poet and visionary is
engaged in a struggle against ideology and false consciousness,

to introduce light into a world of darkness, obscurity and death. To turn Albion into Jerusalem is as difficult as to turn water into wine. In other words, Blake is pretty well on his own: like a solitary Old Testament prophet he can speak and testify but there is no guarantee that anyone will listen. In his isolation he carries an enormous responsibility upon his shoulders. Blake's final vision of the regeneration of Albion did not come easily; it has the character not, as with *The Four Zoas*, of a cosmic scenario, but of a deeply pondered personal affirmation.

In his best-known work, *Songs of Innocence and Experience*, however, Blake is also a poet of the lost vision. The double structure of the work, with its liquidation of the simple, naïve expression of the first set of poems and its replacement by a spirit of negativity, repression and frustration, has a notable poignancy. The Songs of Innocence tease the Songs of Experience with their very frivolity; yet the Songs of Experience also seem to parody their predecessors by their uncompromising bitterness. The parodic relation is bivalent – precisely because each inhabits a world that totally excludes the other. There can be no compromise or mediation as Blake presents us with stark alternatives: 'the Two Contrary States of the Human Soul'. The Songs of Innocence appear almost intolerable, because they verge on the impossible; for the nightmare of the Songs of Experience is that of an endless cycle of corruption and degradation from which there can be no point of exit:

> I wander through each chartered street
> Near where the chartered Thames does flow,
> And mark in every face I meet –
> Marks of weakness, marks of woe.
>
> In every cry of every man,
> In every infant's cry of fear,
> In every voice, in every ban,
> The mind-forged manacles I hear –
>
> How the chimney-sweeper's cry
> Every blackening church appals,
> And the hapless soldier's sigh
> Runs in blood down palace walls;

> But most through midnight streets I hear
> How the youthful harlot's curse
> Blasts the new-born infant's tear
> And blights with plagues the marriage hearse.

The word which functions with such power in this poem is the word 'every', repeated no less than than six times. The vision of desolation presented in the poem is *every*where – its omnipresence dictated by the 'mind-forged manacles' that proscribe freedom and pleasure. So Blake's sense of loss is not suffused with a mood of regret so much as a mood of anger and indignation: the lost innocence is to be taken not as inevitable and inescapable but as a human responsibility and a cultural crime. On the other hand, *The Songs of Innocence and Experience* do not themselves offer a resolution. The lost world *is* lost, though Blake does include an appeal to the future:

> Children of the future age,
> Reading this indignant page,
> Know that in a former time
> Love, Sweet love, was thought a crime.

Wordsworth is also a poet of loss, perhaps quintessentially a poet of loss, since it is when he invokes the loss of a personal vision that his verse becomes most immediate, powerful yet intimate. And it is also around Wordsworth that the paradoxes surrounding Romantic poetry most thickly cluster. For Wordsworth was a source of puzzlement to nearly all his great poetic contemporaries: Blake, Coleridge, Keats, Shelley. For Blake, Wordsworth's offence was to ascribe his poetry to the influence of natural objects, since the source of the visionary could only be within. For Coleridge, the source of wonder lay in the fact that Wordsworth, though faced with a predicament very like that of Coleridge himself, the loss of vision and visionary powers, could nevertheless go on making inspired poetry out of that very loss. For Keats, the problem was to be located in Wordsworth's own equivocal relation to his subject-matter. For if it really was the world of nature that was important, and if it was its capacity for 'tranquil restoration' that Wordsworth sought to celebrate, then surely Wordsworth's own personality was incidental. As I have noted elsewhere, the aesthetics of Romantic poetry are oriented towards content and subject-matter, and it is just this that is the basis of Keats's objection to Wordsworth:

> It may be said that we ought to read our Contemporaries – that Wordsworth &c. should have their due from us. But, for the sake of a few fine imaginative or domestic passages, are we to be bullied into a certain Philosophy engendered in the whims of an Egotist – Every man has his speculations, but every man does not brood and peacock over them till he makes a false coinage and deceives himself. Many a man can travel to the very bourne of Heaven, and yet want the confidence to put down his half-seeing. Sancho will invent a Journey heavenward as well as any body. We hate poetry that has a palpable design upon us – and if we do not agree, seems to put its hand in its breeches pocket. Poetry should be great and unobtrusive, a thing which enters into one's soul, and does not startle or amaze it with itself, but with its subject.[15]

This formulation is crucial, particularly in its accusation of self-deception, since it sounds a note that is to be repeated in much Wordsworth criticism. The problem is to define just what it is that Wordsworth is offering the reader. If he claims merely to be exhibiting the power of natural objects, he denies his own genius and imagination; if he offers himself as a visionary then he is in bad faith, since he is no longer in possession of the visionary moment; if his philosophy, this is itself too insubstantial; if his personality, this is irrelevant. It seems that there is no way that Wordsworth can win. But the betrayal which Wordsworth's contemporaries felt, in their different ways, has a common source: which is that Wordsworth's poetry is indeed that of a personal vision – as Keats said, of the 'egotistical sublime' – and yet Wordsworth is extremely reluctant to admit that this is so – partly out of a kind of modesty, which itself is possibly false, perhaps partly out of deference to the decorum of the times, and partly because he fears that this might detract from the universality and relevance of his poetry. Yet, in truth, the teacher is *not* nature, but Wordsworth. Indeed, it is Wordsworth who institutionalises the poet as teacher and sage.

It would be easy to conclude that the figure of the poet as

presented in the works of Wordsworth has the quality of
self-evidence – surely, we postulate, the poet just describes
things as he sees them, his poetry is the record and articulation
of moments of consciousness. However, a careful study of
Wordsworth's verse shows that the 'poet' as revealed in such a
poem as 'Resolution and Independence' is a *construct* developed in the process of writing. Much Romantic poetry owes
an important debt to parallel forms in drama and prose, and
Wordsworth is no exception. His early play *The Borderers* was
heavily influenced by Schiller's *Die Räuber*, and Wordsworth's
poetry relies equally on a deployment of mythological figures
from the historical genre: anachronistic figures who reflect
the moral values of a bygone age, as Michael and the Old
Cumberland Beggar, and the outcast wanderer who becomes
gradually transposed into the figure of the poet himself. A
pertinent note is struck by Marmaduke at the end of *The
Borderers*:

> a wanderer *must I* go,
> The Spectre of that innocent Man, my guide.
> No human ear shall ever hear me speak;
> No human dwelling ever give me food,
> Or sleep, or rest: but over waste and wild,
> In search of nothing that this earth can give,
> But expiation, will I wander on –
> A Man by pain and thought compelled to live,
> Yet loathing life – till anger is appeased
> In Heaven, and Mercy gives me leave to die.

Here we find a strain of guilt, anguish and remorse that is
considerably more lurid than anything we shall find in
Wordsworth's non-dramatic poetry, but there nevertheless
remain several features that are worthy of comment. The
wanderer, traveller and itinerant poet is a figure who continually recurs in Wordsworth's poetry, and he is not an observer
pure and simple: he is himself a complex figure in search both
of human contact and of some personal redemption or
illumination; in the final analysis he is not so very different
from the Byronic hero, who combines a sense of severance or
separation from the world with a longing for communication
and the desire to escape from an inner melancholy and deep

sense of oppression. In this way Wordsworth's poetry has a dialectical character: it develops a dialogue between the poet and the object of his perception and the development of the poem has a double function – to exhibit to the reader both what the poet perceives and the poet himself in the process of perceiving it. In 'Resolution and Independence', for example, the poem presents the reader with the figure of the old leech-gatherer, but it simultaneously discloses the figure of the poet himself, who makes the leech-gatherer the subject of his meditation. Initially, before the revelation of his missions, the author of the poem is presented as a traveller:

> I was a Traveller then upon the moor;
> I saw the hare that raced about with joy;
> I heard the woods and distant waters roar;
> Or heard them not, as happy as a boy:
> The pleasant season did my heart employ:
> My old remembrances went from me wholly;
> And all the ways of men, so vain and melancholy.

It is in such a context that such an apparently disreputable and undoubtedly dishevelled figure as that of the leech-gatherer can acquire significance. For the old leech-gatherer, far from being a 'mighty Poet', occupies the very lowest situation in human affairs and is engaged in an occupation that is degrading, boring and even potentially dangerous. Yet he *does* have an exemplary importance for the poet: since both poet and leech-gatherer are wanderers who live on the fringes of human society and must draw on a deep reservoir of inner fortitude if they are to go on facing the world. Indeed, the leech-gatherer may well be viewed as a poet *manqué*, with his 'Choice word and measured phrase, above the reach/of ordinary men.' Yet, in talking to the leech-gatherer the poet's main object is to appropriate him symbolically. Half the time he scarcely attends to what the old man is actually trying to say to him:

> The old Man still stood talking by my side:
> But now his voice to me was like a stream
> Scarce heard

and he wanders off into an internal reverie both about his own future and about the leech-gatherer as prototype of the wanderer. As the 'sea-beast crawled forth' and lying inert beside the pool, the old man seems scarcely real and Wordsworth has to concentrate mentally to grasp the truth of what he really signifies, rather than be misled by how he actually appears. The leech-gatherer, unprepossessing as he is, is the type of the poet; what he can do, Wordsworth can do also.

The poet with his 'greater knowledge of human nature' and 'more comprehensive soul' is able by a process of imaginative involvement to generalise the particular into the universal; to endow the objects of his attention with a higher and more philosophical significance than they would otherwise have found. The poet is a transmitter and mediator between his subject and his readers; his concern, that nothing of consequence shall be overlooked or given insufficient stress. The poet redresses the balance between contingency and value by gesturing emphatically in the direction of the unperceived significant. Wordsworth will not allow the reader to overlook his interpretative presence. In telling the story of the Idiot Boy he interjects,

> I to the Muses have been bound
> These fourteen years, by strong indentures:
> O gentle Muses! let me tell
> But half of what to him befell;
> He surely met with strange adventures.

The need for the Muses' assistance, the fear of their desertion, serves the purpose of an urgent arm-waving on the part of the poet as he summons the reader in the direction of a subject which it is imperative that he reflect upon. To tell the tale of an idiot is morally just as important as to sing of arms and the man; if the tale itself is naive this is not to say that the poet himself is a simpleton – rather it is an artful simplicity, born of wisdom and experience. The same rhetorical device was deployed by Wordsworth in the Prologue to 'Peter Bell', in the form of a dialogue between the poet and his 'little Boat' of the imagination. The boat reproaches Wordsworth with his faintheartedness in being so reluctant to adopt a fanciful theme; to which Wordsworth answers,

There was a time when all mankind
Did listen with a faith sincere
To tuneful tongues in mystery versed;
Then Poets fearlessly rehearsed
The wonders of a wild career.

Go – (but the world's a sleepy world,
And 'tis, I fear, an age too late)
Take with you some ambitious Youth!
For, restless Wanderer! I, in truth,
Am all unfit to be your mate.

Although the direct object of these observations was to suggest that Wordsworth's purpose was to show 'nobler marvels' in 'life's daily prospect', his general sense of foreboding was all too apt. For Wordsworth presents the poet in the light of an anachronistic hero, telling of the marvellous to an age so unresponsive and prosaic that it is scarcely conscious that the marvellous exists. This sense of the poet as anachronistic and as at odds with his own time pervades all of Wordsworth's poetry, from the time of the Preface to *Lyrical Ballads*, where he despaired whether poetry written in a natural and simple style could ever hope to make its way in a corrupted and sensation-hungry urban world, right on up to the writing of *The Excursion*. In the second book of *The Excursion* Wordsworth drew a poignant contrast between the honorific status of the minstrel in days gone by, who was showered with gifts, recognition and praise, and his 'obscure Itinerant', the Wanderer who must pursue his lonely vocation in 'these our unimaginative days'. The rural life that Wordsworth celebrates represents a suspension of time, whereby genuine virtue can persist into an unheroic age. The life of the shepherd lad invoked by the Wanderer in Book IV is untouched by triviality as he remains consistently out of tune with the modern:

Imagination – not permitted here,
To waste her powers, as in the wordling's mind,
On fickle pleasures, and superfluous cares,
And trivial ostentation ...
                              a Man so bred
(Take from him what you will upon the score

> Of ignorance, or illusion) lives and breathes
> For nobler purposes of mind: his heart
> Beats to the heroic song of ancient days.

In a fallen world the poet's high function as bearer of the Truth is crucial. For if the Truth is always self-evident and unconcealed the poet must nevertheless alert his contemporaries to it since they will pass by it without seeing it. As conscience of the age Wordsworth in *Michael*, against the bleak and seemingly unmarked landscape of Greenhead Ghyll, arrests the reader to unfold the deep moral signifiance of the 'straggling heap of unhewn stones' that is Michael's grave. The poem is a reminder, a recollection and a reproach.

Certainly the marvellous as manifested in 'Peter Bell' made Wordsworth the object of widespread ridicule. Yet in 'Peter Bell' Wordsworth was setting himself a task which to him was highly important: it was an attempt to synthesise the different aspects of *Lyrical Ballads* within a single poem; to show how the power of nature can transform a corrupted individual into a good and honest man, but to do it without any use of the miraculous. As Wordsworth wrote to Southey,

> The Poem of Peter Bell, as the Prologue will show, was composed under a belief that the Imagination not only does not require for its exercise the intervention of supernatural agency, but that, though such agency be excluded, the faculty may be called forth as imperiously, and for kindred results of pleasure, by incidents within the compass of poetic probability, in the humblest departments of daily life.[16]

Yet the wonders of *The Rime of the Ancient Mariner* continue to command respect, while the relative 'probability' of 'Peter Bell' has fallen under an irreparable cloud, despite the fact that their theme and moral orientation are the same:

> And now that Peter taught to feel
> That man's heart is a holy thing;
> And Nature, through a world of death,
> Breathes into him a second breath,
> More searching than the breath of spring.

The rhyme scheme of the poem is certainly unfortunate, and Wordsworth's attempt to simulate the manner of Coleridge regrettable, but it would be wrong to conclude that 'Peter Bell' is inherently risible. Contemporary and subsequent dissatisfaction with the poem has a more fundamental cause. Readers of poetry had become accustomed to forms of poetic discourse – by Wordsworth himself, amongst others – in which the figure of the poet was placed in the foreground and in which the act of interpretation by the poet had its own specific import and significance. The idea of a transparent, self-evident narrative structure was no longer feasible – a repetition of the *Ancient Mariner* was a rash endeavour, because it was now in conflict with the very idea of poetry as it was coming to be understood. A poem could be written about a leech-gatherer or a potter (Peter Bell) but only from the point of view of a *Poet*, whose own insight would validate them as the subjects of poetic discourse, not in a purely empathic or descriptive mode. The distance that Wordsworth establishes between himself and the leech-gatherer is critical. The collapse of such distance in 'Peter Bell' permits Shelley to present Wordsworth himself as his hero:

> And yet a strange and horrid curse
> Clung upon Peter, night and day;
> Month after month the thing grew worse,
> And deadlier than in this my verse
> I can find strength to say.
>
> Peter was dull – he was at first
> Dull – oh, so dull – so very dull!
> Whether he talked, wrote, or rehearsed –
> Still with this dullness was he cursed –
> Dull – beyond all conception – dull.

The belated publication, then, of 'Peter Bell' was a mistake, because of changes in poetic taste, where naivety no longer had the redeeming charm of novelty. In other poems Wordsworth describes characters who are equally simple, but he is careful to maintain a distance from them: to point towards and celebrate the simplicity, honesty and integrity of Michael or the Old Cumberland Beggar as *figures* and *types* rather than to try to represent their consciousness from within. The description of the beggar and his progress leads into a lengthy apostrophe, spoken by the poet *in propria persona*, in which the moral significance of the spectacle is spelt out:

> But deem not this man useless. – Statesmen! ye
> Who are so restless in your wisdom, ye
> Who have a broom still ready in your hands
> To rid the world of nuisances; ye proud,
> Heart-swoln, while in your pride ye contemplate
> Your talents, power, or wisdom, deem him not
> A burthen of the earth! 'Tis Nature's law
> That none, the meanest of created things,
> Of forms created the most vile and brute,
> The dullest or most noxious, should exist
> Divorced from good . . . .

The beggar as anachronism is an embodiment of a spirit of goodwill and friendship from a bygone age, when people were ready to help others and think beyond their own immediate and selfish purposes. In this poem the distinct role of the poet emerges with exemplary clarity: there is the old beggar whose significance may be neglected and overlooked in the self-importance of the modern age; there is the reader who must be awakened to it; between them the poet as connector and transmitter, who shows him what the beggar is and what he represents. The reader is placed by Wordsworth in an evocatively depicted context where the beggar actually is ignored and overlooked, where even the dogs cannot be bothered to bark at him, so that he is also forced into the role of participant and a guilty one at that. Wordsworth enforces his message of acceptance and toleration by a series of repeated injunctions:

> Then let him pass, a blessing on his head . . . .
>
> And let him, *where* and *when* he will, sit down . . . .
>
> As in the eye of Nature he has lived,
> So in the eye of Nature let him die.

The poet renders the invisible visible; and, having done so, he comments and interprets.

The same can be said of Wordsworth in his capacity as poet of 'absent things'. Although it would be wrong to suggest that Wordsworth readily accepted his own loss of vision – he could not have been the poet that he was if he had – he developed the best strategy for coping with the situation. He became a mediator and a go-between, operating in the gap between his visionary sense of a harmony with nature and a world that was excluded from it, as he himself was. In his poetry Wordsworth eternalised simultaneously the vision and its loss; as he wrote in the 'Elegiac Stanzas Suggested by a Picture of Peele Castle, in a Storm, painted by Sir George Beaumont': 'The feeling of my loss will ne'er be old'. In many of Wordsworth's poems absence and presence become intricately interlaced. In his moving sonnet, 'Surprised by joy' Wordsworth intuitively looks for his daughter, Catherine, to share in his emotion only to recall that that she is now dead. But this recognition of absence triggers off another: his realisation that this presence in his mind is only so vivid because he has allowed her to be absent from his mind. Yet this secondary absence, although a cause for self-reproach, pales into insignificance against the absence itself that can never be rectified. All that is left is the presence of absence, as in 'The Solitary Reaper', where 'The music in my heart I bore/Long after it was heard no more'. In some sense the loss itself becomes part of the vision: the awareness of loss serves to intensify the imagined sense of the presence of the visionary. Wordsworth's poetry at its most poignant and intense moments is a poetry of presence and absence simultaneously; a moment of illumination whose divine incandescence is certified by its very fragmentariness and evanescence:

There was a time when meadow, grove and stream,
The earth, and every common sight,
To me did seem
Apparelled in celestial light,
The glory and the freshness of a dream.
It is not now as it hath been of yore; –
Turn wheresoe'er I may,
By night or day,
The things which I have seen I now can see no more

Here also is the deepest truth of the poet's image of himself as a wanderer: his wandering is a spiritual journey back and forth between the here and now and the 'absent things' of the visionary imagination, often accompanied by a tormenting sense of isolation – since the poet's memory of his own visionary experience excludes him from any unthinking immersion in the actual; yet his necessary existence in 'the light of common day' is a disbarment from the transcendent. The act of writing is an attempt to overcome these disjunctures simultaneously. The poet, in writing of his feeling for nature and the experiences connected with it, is able to share his emotions with others and confer a value upon them, while in the process of writing the experiences themselves flare momentarily out of the darkness of memory.

For Wordsworth *The Prelude* was an inescapable project and we also recognise it as crucial to the definition of Romantic literature; for the poet himself has become the most important subject-matter for poetry, and a poem which deals with the growth of a poet's mind is an endeavour that can simultaneously exhibit the power of genius and explain it. And yet the moment the poem is initiated its puzzling and contradictory character becomes manifest: for it is a work which shows Wordsworth moving towards something, being a poet, while at the same time moving away from nature and the very experiences that are to make him one. Moreover, Wordsworth is unable to be a poet in the traditional epic style; the 'lofty themes' evoke no response: 'I feel the imaginative power Languish within me.' Wordsworth seems suspended in a limbo; excluded both from the role of poet and cut off from his own experience. *The Prelude*, we should never forget, begins, as with Baudelaire, with the poet's inability to write a poem. It presents his delays, uncertainties, frustrations and perplexities. In theory Wordsworth's childhood was one which was especially favourable for the poetic vocation, yet Wordsworth seems unable to capitalise on or make use of his good fortune. So that the poem itself as we know it appears as nothing more than a vast digression, introduced by:

> Was it for this
> That one, the fairest of all rivers, loved
> To blend his murmurs with my nurse's song,

And, from his alder shades and rocky fall,
And from his fords and shallows, sent a voice
That flowed along my dreams?

which, as it were, serves to explain that Wordsworth *really should* have been able to write a great poem – as, in the process of explaining, he did. Yet the invocation of childhood seems to issue from another voice, from one that was truly there and which therefore knows neither the agony of the poet straining between conception and language nor the hiatus between self and vision. In the dissolves and flashbacks that take Wordsworth into the heart of his earlier self it is as if the poet himself dissolves in the process of writing. Thus, Wordsworth's initial invocation of his loss of power is especially provocative in that we are bound to mull over why the same sense of discrepancy should not also apply to a poem about his own childhood experiences. If Wordsworth has irretrievably lost his childhood vision, how will he be able to find the words to give substance to that sense of plenitude as he drifts further and further away from it? In the final analysis Wordsworth is unjustly accused of the 'egotistical sublime', since his desire to attribute, ascribe and dedicate his poetry to nature had the effect of eliminating any sign of the struggle to compose it. Wordsworth's achievement in actualising his visonary sense in *The Prelude* is extraordinary, since that task is entirely distinct from the visionary experiences themselves. Wordsworth, in establishing the poet as his own subject, simultaneously dematerialised him as author! The presence of the poet is displaced.

Despite this, Wordsworth never doubted that he *was* a poet or failed to see himself in such a light; he had a massive confidence in his own role that is in marked contrast with Coleridge. Considering that Coleridge possessed what Wordsworth lacked – a theory of the nature of the poetic that addressed itself to the literary artefact rather than to the poet himself – and that his admittedly small body of work had nevertheless been praised by a number of contemporaries, his uncertainty seems disproportionate. Yet Coleridge repeatedly bewailed his loss of the visionary in catastrophic terms, most notably in this letter to William Godwin, written on 25 March 1801, when Coleridge had not even reached the age of thirty:

The Poet is dead in me. My imagination (or rather the Somewhat that had been imaginative) lies like a cold snuff on the circular rim of a brass candlestick, without even a stink of tallow to remind you that it was once clothed and mitred with flame. That is past by! I was once a volume of gold leaf, rising and riding on every breath of Fancy, but I have beaten myself back into weight and density, and now I sink in quicksilver, yea, remain squat and square on the earth, amid the hurricane that makes oaks and straws join in one dance, fifty yards high in the element....[17]

Obviously, one way of discussing this self-conception of Coleridge is to relate it to the very real problems and difficulties which he faced at the time; yet they really provide no explanation, since a great many poets and writers have had such experiences and have made use of them in their own work. What is notable in this passage is the way in which Coleridge views his poetic self as a double, another self now absent, a 'stranger within' who is no longer to be found. In 'Dejection', written the following year, Coleridge expressed similar feelings in terms even more provocative, though less frantic:

> There was a time when, though my path was rough,
>   This joy within me dallied with distress,
> And all misfortunes were but as the stuff
>   Whence Fancy made me dreams of happiness:
> For hope grew round me, like the twining vine,
> And fruits, and foliage, not my own seemed mine.
> But now afflictions bow me down to earth:
> Nor care I that they rob me of my mirth,
>   But oh! each visitation
> Suspends what nature gave me at my birth,
>   My shaping spirit of Imagination.
> For not to think of what I needs must feel,
>   But to be still and patient, all I can;
> And haply by abstruse research to steal
>   From my own nature all the natural man –
>   This was my sole resource, my only plan:
> Till that which suits a part infects the whole,
> And now is almost grown the habit of my soul.

For this, after all, is one of Coleridge's better poems, and it deals with a subject that Wordsworth also made into a centre of poetic concern, yet without thereby excluding himself from the ranks of the poets. It is difficult to resist the conclusion that an important and paradoxical source of Coleridge's pessimism about his own work was his own conception of the poet and of poetry. As a result of his reading of Kant, Coleridge identified the 'shaping spirit of imagination' with the act of poetic composition itself. It was in the very process of composition that the imagination made its impression felt – that is to say, Coleridge's definition allowed no scope for a gap between vision and expression, which Wordsworth was certainly conscious of, writing in 'Tintern Abbey' 'I cannot paint/What then I was'. For Coleridge such an inability would be proof of a loss of poetic power. His subsequent definition of the poetic activity in terms of a unifying power that is able to achieve a complete fusion of all elements is necessarily totalistic:

> The poet, described in *ideal* perfection, brings the whole soul of man into activity, with the subordination of its faculties to each other, according to their relative worth and dignity. He diffuses a tone and spirit of unity, that blends, and (as it were) *fuses* each into each, by that synthetic and magical power, to which we have exclusively appropriated the name of imagination.[18]

This, indeed, posits a state of ideal perfection, but that is just the trouble, for in terms of Coleridge's theory it is hard to see how poetry is to be written in any other way, for there can be no halfway house between the fused and the unfused, the disparate and the unified. Either the poem is completely and perfectly achieved or it can scarcely be viewed as a poem at all. Thus Coleridge is a martyr to his own philosophically grounded theory of poetry: the conception of poetic achievement which he sets out is so terribly daunting that Coleridge sees it as stretching very far beyond his own capabilities. Coleridge's anxiety as a poet stems as much from the inordinate demands which he makes upon himself as a poet as from his own existential sense of a personal crisis. For, while the work he has been doing may fall back from the level of his best, through his theorising poetry itself recedes from him with frightening speed, like infinitely distant stars in an expanding universe. The problem is compounded by the fact that, since Coleridge views inspiration as a kind of possession, it follows that even the poet's achievements cannot really be regarded as being his own. When Coleridge refers to 'fruits, and foliage, not my own' this is a very significant declaration, since it suggests that he has no conviction that the poems he composed, when inspired, were truly his. So long as he believed himself inspired he was the other that wrote them, but with the loss of that certainty he feels himself to be an imposter and a fraud. Their very imaginative glitter and the belief that they are not the product of conscious volition only serve to intensify his conviction that he cannot really have written them. With Wordsworth having the vision is one thing and finding the words another, but for Coleridge the very ability to find the words is threatened, since he believes he cannot find them if not possessed by the imaginative other. The ability to write such a great poem as *The Rime of the Ancient Mariner* had the perverse effect of so torturing Coleridge with a sense of his own unworthiness that he no longer believed he could be a poet. For Coleridge the mind that created was entirely separate from the mind that suffered; he could see no way of connecting the two.

In 'Kubla Khan' Coleridge painted his own picture of the artist and his vision. The exotic world of Xanadu is one characterised simultaneously by enclosure and fertility. The river runs underground, Xanadu is enclosed by forests, walls and towers; yet the ground is fertile, with incense-bearing trees, and there is a huge fountain that hurls out fragments of rock – a sign of energy and power. It is a world that encompasses all contradictions, peaceful yet violent, sunlight and ice, energy and containment. The focus of the vision is the damsel, representative of the artist's poetic sensibility; in recreating her song he would also recreate the visionary world. Thus the vision both contains the song and *is* the song. Such is the task of the artist; but it is one that will only lead to his being mistrusted by the world, since the visionary and the real are ultimately incompatible. Therefore the fact that the poem ends as it does seems attributable to more fundamental causes than the arrival of a person from Porlock. For what the poem states is that the vision cannot be brought back from the imaginative other world. The task of recreating the visionary, though hypothetically possible, is really in vain. The caves and the dome cannot be transported without destroying what they signify, an alternate scene of possibility. The vision belongs only in a dream – or a fragment!

The Rime of the Ancient Mariner is Coleridge's greatest and most imaginative poem; yet perhaps too much attention has been paid to the processes of imaginative fusion associated with its composition, which has had the unfortunate effect of virtually assigning authorship of the poem to Coleridge's unconscious and of effacing its connection with his other work. Yet the theme of the poem, the expression of an acute sense of isolation and alienation and the sudden change of heart that brings with it the realisation that, since nature is omnipresent, man is always closely connected with other phenomena in the universe, even when he is least aware of it – this is just as clearly articulated in a relatively humdrum poem, 'This Lime Tree Bower, My Prison', as on the cosmic canvas of the *Rime*. Much of the power of Coleridge's *Rime* derives from his linkage of the various mythological structures of Romanticism that have been analysed in these pages. The Mariner is an outcast and wanderer, a man accurst, who for his crime against nature must do penance and seek redemption. At the same time he is afflicted by a split between two sides of his personality: one which seeks grace struggles against a perverse, darker side which resists. In this the Mariner parallels both the cosmic rebel figure, such as Schiller's Karl Moor, and the Gothic hypocrite. The Mariner's loss of all capacity to feel signals an identity crisis of the most traumatic type; for, if feeling is the source of one's deepest identity, then beyond that there is no further source of appeal. Everything disintegrates:

> The many men, so beautiful!
> And they all dead did lie:
> And a thousand, thousand slimy things
> Lived on; and so did I. . . .
>
> I looked to heaven, and tried to pray;
> But or ever a prayer had gusht,
> A wicked whisper came, and made
> My heart as dry as dust.

The Mariner's sense of his spiritual death is reminiscent of Coleridge's own personal crisis: he is oppressed both by a sense of his own unworthiness and by his own emptiness. The fountain of his very being has dried up and he no longer knows who he is. So one may surmise that such feelings were not new to Coleridge, that his self-doubt had about it a tendency to compulsive repetition, in which an anxiety-produced introspection produces not certainty but further anxiety. But the Mariner experiences a mysterious and inexplicable change of heart; at the sight of the water-snakes he becomes reborn and he discovers new resources of humanity within himself:

> O happy living things! no tongue
> Their beauty might declare:
> A spring of love gushed from my heart,
> And I blessed them unware.

So the nature of the Mariner's deepest self is inscrutable and highly equivocal. Are there layers on layers of personaltiy which the most trying and testing experiences will progressively unpeel? To what extent is the Mariner's perdition or redemption his, since both his rejection of God and his acceptance are generated from beyond his own conscious volition? The Mariner has no unified personality but is a theatre of contending forces. His trials on the sea correspond to the turmoil of his own interior odyssey.

The Ancient Mariner should also be seen in the light of the figure of the artist. The Ancient Mariner is himself the source of the poem and his attempts to stop the wedding guest and compel him to hear his story are akin to the struggle of the Romantic poet himself, who brings his readers tales of the wonderful and the miraculous, which they are distinctly reluctant to hear. The poet is disruptor of the social ritual and the ceremony of the everyday. Moreover, the Mariner's very contact with the miraculous makes him a poet, since it endows him with a 'strange power of speech', like the gift of tongues that was given to the apostles. Like the poet the Mariner returns from a visionary journey which he is under a deep inner compulsion to communicate and relate, while the poem itself is a desperate attempt to overcome his sense of isolation.

If he brings to his auditors a message of harmony, its impact is nevertheless strangely dissonant and unsettling, because it involves an exposure to paranormal experiences. In the everyday world the poet cannot figure other than as a molester and an intruder, his demands for attention melo-dramatic and importunate.

In the poetry of Keats the sense of a lost vision has no less poignancy. Indeed, it is perhaps even more intense, since with Keats the vision is not so much lost as always trembling on the point of being lost, like joy in the 'Ode on Melancholy', 'whose hand is ever at his lips/Bidding adieu'. The word 'fade' and its derivatives carry a special resonance in Keats as the fabric of the imaginative other world suffers a loss of substance despite all Keats's strenuous efforts to render it palpable. In the 'Ode to Psyche' he writes of 'Olympus's faded hierarchy!'; in the 'Ode on Indolence' he writes how the visions he saw 'Then faded', again 'They faded', 'Fade softly from my eyes' – a triple repetition that receives further emphasis from the fact that each phrase appears at the beginning of a line. In the 'Ode on a Grecian Urn' the lover depicted on the vase is consoled with the reflection that, although he will never kiss his beloved, 'She cannot fade', while in the 'Ode to a Nightingale' the rep-etitions come thick and fast: Keats longs to 'fade away into the forest dim', to 'Fade far away, dissolve, and quite forget'; he writes of the 'Fast fading violets cover'd up in leaves' and in the final stanza addresses the nightingale by saying, 'Adieu! adieu! thy plaintive anthem fades.' To fade is at once the desire to escape from the quotidian into a world of ease, oblivion and voluptuousness, and the escape of that dream itself from the clutching fingers of consciousness. Keats's visions have a distinctive pathos not so much because they are lost as because they are evanescent: they torment the sensi-bility by their capacity to elude it; they tease and provoke by their dissolving tangibleness. Consequently it is rather misleading to insist on the quality of concreteness in the poetry of Keats without further specifying that this capacity for rendering phenomena vivid and immediate through language is con-cerned to capture them at the very moment of their loss. Keats is not a celebrator of the material world pure and simple; he is the poet of the transition from presence to absence, in which the visionary becomes material, the material visionary. Keats's poetry cannot escape from this alternation between the real and the imaginary; from *Endymion* onward it has the character of a closed system.

The paradox of *Endymion* is that it presents the reader with a series of enchanting visions which nevertheless have the character of a recurrent nightmare. The poem is a set of Chinese boxes: each vision encloses a further vision, and so on. Keats describes a serene and radiant world where Endymion, the shepherd king, dwells with his enchanting sister Peona. Yet this is not fulfilment enough for Endymion, who is obsessed with the beautiful Cynthia, whom he has encountered in a dream and who figures as a 'Dream within dream'. But Endymion, by falling asleep within the dream, loses his vision and awakens to a disenchanting and tawdry reality. This slippage of levels is inherent in the very nature of dreaming, since dreaming is characterised by a sense of powerlessness in which it is the suspension of ordinary volition that is the condition of the dream itself. In submitting to the dream the dreamer must submit. *Endymion* can have no genuine progression or development, since an obsessional alternation between dream and reality is its actual theme. In Book II, Endymion again encounters Cynthia, representative of his ideal vision, and again loses her. This impossibility of fixing the vision with any permanency is seen by Keats as a function of the predicament of the modern artist, who lives in an age when such a heroic celebration of the ideal is no longer possible:

> Aye, the count
> Of mighty poets is made up; the scroll
> Is folded by the Muses; the bright roll
> Is in Apollo's hand: our dazed eyes
> Have seen a new tinge in the western skies:
> The world has done its duty. Yet, oh yet,
> Although the sun of poesy is set,
> These lovers did embrace, and we must weep
> That there is no power left to steep
> A quill immortal in their joyous tears.

The sense of absence created by Keats in the poem is complex and multiple. For *Endymion* is not only a meditation on the theme of 'Et in Arcadia Ego' – the presence of sorrow, greed and loss even in Arcady; it is further intensified by the distance that separates us from such an Arcady and further still by a lack in language which makes it impossible to communicate even a glimmering of what such an existence could be. For Wordsworth loss was a fact he had to come to terms with, for Coleridge a personal catastrophe, but with Keats the lost vision has the character of an inescapable necessity; the poet is separated from it by a multiplicity of quivering veils. It is at best 'A hope beyond the shadow of a dream'. The visionary cannot be 'used', no moral can usefully be drawn from it, since for Keats the sense of loss is too powerful, the feeling of betrayal too intense:

> No, never more
> Shall airy voices cheat me to the shore
> Of tangled wonder, breathless and aghast.

Keats's intense desire is that the visionary shall forever be tangible, and his poetry is a struggle with the fact that this can necessarily never be the case. In *Endymion* the oscillation between visionary presence and absence that can only go on being repeated is inherently frustrating. The cycle continues in Book III, where Endymion meets old Glaucus, who similarly laments the loss of his Scylla; while, in Book IV, the transposition of his more earthly love, the Indian maid, into Cynthia, the moon goddess, appears less a fulfilment than a mutual cancellation. To ensure progression Endymion disappears into the vision, like Anselmus in Hoffmann's *Der goldne Topf*; but without any frame for the tale or any narrator to restore us to the actual this ending seems unsatisfactory, a consummation that figures as a lack.

The logic of Keats's tale is of an endless and unbreakable cycle of repetition. But *Endymion* is nevertheless complex in conception and textually rich in the manner of its working out. It expresses perhaps more adequately than any other poem the welter of contradictions in the situation of the Romantic artist and the difficulty of any resolution of the dilemma by which the artist can neither melt into his vision nor come to terms with the melting of that vision. So for Keats the vision is most truly captured at the moment of loss. The validity of this seems confirmed by the Hyperion poems. Ostensibly this is a suitable subject for Keats, since they deal with the theme of lost immortality; but there we find only the note of absence without presence. They cannot unlock the true poignancy of the Romantic visionary, but remain imprisoned within a perennial and invariant note of Ossianic regret – surely the reason why Keats could finish neither poem.

Keats's gift for rendering his visions palpable is exquisitely exemplified by 'The Eve of St Agnes'. The richness of texture and detail with which mood and atmosphere are evoked, the vividness of the Beadsman, Porphyro and Madeline are notable; yet the poem aims not so much at realism as to make tangible a dream within a dream, the dream of the young lovers within the dreamlike world of the poem:

> Beyond a mortal man impassion'd far
> At these voluptuous accents, he arose,
> Ethereal, Flush'd, and like a throbbing star
> Seen mid the sapphire heaven's deep repose
> Into her dream he melted, as the rose
> Blendeth its odour with the violet, –
> Solution sweet.

The aesthetic contrast between the warmth of the young lovers and the chill of St Agnes' Eve symbolises the contrast and contradiction between the visionary and the real; that vision is threatened in the poem, just as the world impinges on the vision which the poem renders immediate. The poem plays with the fact of its own possibility, steadily glowing into an intensity, the more lambent because it necessarily must fade. Madeline awakens to find that her dream is not true. Yet the moment of its being rendered true is just the moment at which the lovers are lost to both the poet and his readers:

> She hurried at his words, beset with fears,
> For there were sleeping dragons all around,
> At glaring watch, perhaps, with ready spears –
> Down the wide stairs a darkling way they found. –
> In all the house was heard no human sound.
> A chain-droop'd lamp was flickering by each door;

The arras, rich with horseman, hawk, and hound,
Flutter'd in the besieging wind's uproar;
And the long carpets rose along the gusty floor.

These lines focus many of the contradictions of the poetic project. The vision escapes detection by the 'sleeping dragons' of the factual, everyday world that could not permit or countenance it and becomes lost without more than the most residual trace, felt only in a flickering, a fluttering and gusts of wind. This loss, by its suddenness, becomes a sign not of absence but of presence. For the vacancy is only a vacancy of closure that can be refilled by a repetition of the poem. The arras, 'rich with horseman, hawk, and hound', symbolises the poem itself as a richly woven aesthetic artefact, the flickering lamp the transitoriness, yet truth, of the visionary. The young lovers are gone but the poem remains as testimony of a dream that is forever absent/present.

The contradiction between the rational and the imaginative is made more open and explicit in 'Isabella' and 'Lamia'. Lorenzo and Isabella represent the artistic sensibility, feelings of tenderness and delicacy to which the harsh material world is inimical. Lorenzo is slain by Isabella's unscrupulous brothers. Isabella, in preserving her lover's head in a pot of basil, becomes representative of the artist, who takes painful, bitter, yet cherished experiences and preserves them in language that will give them immortality. The basil plant is the poem itself, a growth nurtured by love and human feeling:

And so she ever fed it with thin tears,
Whence thick, and green, and beautiful it grew,
So that it smelt more balmy than its peers
Of basil-tufts in Florence; for it drew
Nurture besides, and life, from human fears,
From the fast mouldering head there shut from view:
So that the jewel, safely casketed,
Came forth, and in perfumed leafits spread.

The poem is the organic connection between beauty and pain, rooted in the truth of experience creating plenitude out of a lack. Lamia is for Lycius the truth and beauty of the visionary; she signifies the possibility of a purer and more enduring love than the world can contain or comprehend, like the song she sings, 'A song of love, too sweet for earthly lyres'. But Lamia, as the visionary, is incompatible with the rationalistic, every-day world. Lycius, symbolic of the poet, can enjoy happiness and complete fulfilment with her alone, but he cannot seek to introduce her to the social world, for the vision will vanish and he himself will be destroyed:

> Philosophy will clip an angel's wings,
> Conquer all mysteries by rule and line,
> Empty the haunted air, and grimed mine –
> Unweave a rainbow, as it erewhile made
> The tender-person'd Lamia melt into a shade.

The visionary cannot be defined by reason; though real enough, it does not have the character of permanence. The rainbow, as Wordsworth says, 'comes and goes', but it is none the less real for that. 'Lamia' and 'Isabella' also exhibit the elevation of the aesthetic over the moral. The revelation that Lamia is a 'serpent' is not a factual but a moralistic category which cannot comprehend the fact that Lamia is nevertheless transcendentally beautiful. The beautiful is feared and hated because it is alien to ordinary life. In this way values become warped and perverted.

For Keats the evanescent had become the quintessence of the beautiful. He managed to express this even in his 'Ode on a Grecian Urn', where we might expect the urn to figure as an instance of the eternal, pure and simple. But for Keats it is not merely that the figures on the vase are seen as composing the series of suspended moments, transitory and fleeting; there is also the question of the relationship of the urn to the spectator. The figures invoke actions and events that are puzzling and tantalising; what they represent is an enigma that can never be entirely resolved, so that the problematic nature of the urn's figural representation is also an important part of its complex aesthetic fascination: 'What leaf-fringed legend haunts about thy shape.' The Grecian urn finally suspends all questioning that its appearance provokes: 'Thou, silent form, dost tease us out of thought'; but it is never an eternalisation of the eternal, which would, indeed, be superogatory and tautologous, but an aesthetic arrest of the transient. Beauty is not fixity but a beauty that eludes fixity even in its apprehension. The representation of the urn is both there and not there and the imagination both rests in it and goes beyond it. The implied equivalence of beauty and truth is surely to suggest that that truth is not to be construed as an insatiable quest for knowledge and possession but as a recognition of absence, lacuna and enigma as inescapable, which is why to know this is to know enough and more than enough.

Transience is also the theme of the 'Ode to a Nightingale', where the fleetingness of life and the imminence of death are linked with the transience of vision. The simultaneous brevity yet plenitude of the nightingale's song, the 'full-throated ease' that nevertheless become a 'plaintive anthem' that fades is a token of life and of the ecstatic moment of vision, an image of the poem itself – all are subject to the necessity of suspension and closure. Autumn is the season celebrated by Keats, because it is the season of abundance and of terminations; it corresponds to the task of the visionary poet, which is to articulate presence and absence simultaneously – to show presence in the light of absence, and absence in the light of presence: 'Season of mists and mellow fruitfulness'. Autumn is characterised in terms of sounds because they create in language the equivalent of the dying echo, the moment of sound that is both presence and absence, yet truly neither one nor the other – a fading that can nevertheless be held. Pedalled into a consonance by the multiple verbal and sonic echoes of the poem, Keats *delays* the visionary into the real in a fixed–fleeting moment that is his definite resolution of the dilemma of *Endymion*.

In his conception of poetry and the role of the poet, Shelley was often very close to Keats, an affinity that found definitive expression in the writing of *Adonais*. Poetry, for Shelley, is a paradoxical synthesis of the enduring and the fleeting. If, as he writes in *A Defence of Poetry*, poetry is 'the form and splendour of unfaded beauty', the circumstances that pro-duce it are mysterious and transient:

the mind in creation is as a fading coal, which some invisible influence, like an inconstant wind, awakens to transitory brightness; this power arises from within, like the colour of a flower which fades and changes as it is developed, and the constant portions of our nature are unprophetic either of its approach or its departure. Could this influence be durable in its original purity and force, it is impossible to predict the greatness of the result; but when composition begins, inspiration is already on the decline, and the most glorious poetry that has ever been communicated to the world is probably a feeble shadow of the original conceptions of the poet.[19]

The words in their eloquence are affirmative, but even Shelley's poetics are tinged with melancholy at the mutability of human affairs. Shelley has no simple belief that poetry automatically situates itself on the ground of the eternal; the very process of poetic composition is a last minute struggle against transience and time. Poetry may be defined as a *trace*. In relation to the circumstances that produced it, as a representation of 'evanescent visitations of thought and feeling',[20] it figures not so much as a simulacrum or expression with the character of fullness and adequacy as as a vestige: 'its footsteps are like those of a wind over the sea, which the morning calm erases, and whose traces remain only, as on the wrinkled sand which paves it'.[21] Sand inevitably bears no guarantee of permanence – in 'Ozymandias' the 'lone and level sands' before which all marks of grandeur and glory become insubstantial is a sign of effacement. Poetry for Shelley dreams no dreams of gold, bronze or marble; it is to be seen rather as a momentary infusion of radiance or colour, a trace, dye or stain.

If Keats, in his 'Ode to a Nightingale', only implied a parallel between the song of the nightingale and the poet, Shelley in *A Defence of Poetry* made the connection explicit:

Even in modern times, no living poet ever arrived at the fulness of his fame; the jury which sits in judgement upon a poet, belonging as he does to all time, must be composed of his peers: it must be empannelled by time from the selectest from the wise of many generations. A poet is a nightingale, who sits in darkness, and sings to cheer its own solitude with sweet sounds; his auditors are as men entranced by the melody of an unseen musician and softened, yet know not whence or why.[22]

It is doubtful whether the contemporaries of Pope or Dryden would have felt the force of this comparison; for both men were personally well known to many of their readers and their poetry took for granted a public role. But Shelley's metaphor encapsulates a new situation, of the poet as an invisible and unidentifiable source. Shelley's categorisation must, of course, be taken in conjunction with his bold claims for poets as 'unacknowledged legislators of mankind'[23] and 'mirrors of the gigantic shadows which futurity casts upon the present',[24] but it nevertheless confirms the alienation and isolation of the artist in the Romantic period. His relationship with the reader is that of the literary marketplace and the printed page; unknown and unseen by those who read him, his poetry springs first and foremost from his own condition, of which it is simultaneously articulation and solace. Generated by isolation, the song incorporates it as consolation and cure. Shelley offers a similar definition in his ode 'To a Skylark', where he sees the bird as being

> Like a poet hidden
>   In the light of thought,
> Singing hymns unbidden,
>   Till the world is wrought
> To sympathy with hopes and fears it heeded not.

The skylark is a symbol of the freedom of the poet; he sings of his own volition rather than producing music to order, yet, because of the compelling power and beauty of his song, he cannot be ignored. The poet as skylark is more than a little reminiscent of Coleridge's Ancient Mariner, who buttonholes the wedding guest so that 'He cannot choose but hear'. The poet sings unbidden and unasked, but the world gradually comes to listen and to enter into a sympathetic involvement with 'hopes and fears it heeded not', just as the wedding guest has his horizons extended by the Mariner's narrative and is brought to see life in a more complex light. The task of the artist is above all to compel the world to listen: 'The world should listen then – as I am listening now'.

Shelley's world-view is a curious synthesis of Platonism with the Enlightenment thought of such as Diderot and Voltaire. It opposes history with the visionary. History is very largely the record of the crimes, follies, treacheries and deceptions of mankind. It is a story of tyranny and oppression and the mystification of the masses by hypocritical priests. A reading of history offers few consolations; if it instructs it is very largely through abreaction; though a better future can be envisaged, its arrival can by no means be guaranteed. Shelley's view of history is extremely pessimistic; his answer to it is located in the figure of the poet, who is able to see and recognise the pure and eternal forms that are obscured and distorted in the medium of historical experience. Plato's views are, of course, bound up with an espousal of philosophy that is at poetry's expense, but Shelley overcomes this by arguing that Plato was a poet, while such poets as Shakespeare, Dante and Milton are to be regarded as 'philosophers of the very loftiest power'.[25] Language is crucial for Shelley's conception of poetry and the poet. The Tower of Babel is an influential symbol for his thinking, since it points not so much to the origin of languages as to the corruption of language. In *Prometheus Unbound*, a work which itself implies that the unbinding of Prometheus would signify a loosening of the cords of the historical that bind every generation, Prometheus says,

> Names are there, Nature's sacred watchwords, they
> Were born aloft in bright emblazonry;
> The nations thronged around, and cried aloud,
> As with one voice, Truth, Liberty, and love!
> Suddenly fierce confusion fell from heaven
> Among them: there was strife, deceit and fear:
> Tyrants rushed in, and did divide the spoil.
> This was the shadow of the truth I saw.

Here Shelley shows an awareness of ideology. Words become corrupted and transposed into their opposite as forms of power and structures of domination. Names, 'Nature's sacred watchwords', are for Shelley marks and signs of the eternal that are placed in the guardianship of poets. Though they may continually be corrupted, poets will always rise up to breathe life and truth back into them again; but 'if no new poets should arise to create afresh the associations which have been thus disorganised, language will be dead to all the nobler purposes of human intercourse'.[26]The corruption of language is also the corruption of sensibility; for all T. S. Eliot's disparagement of him, Shelley was certainly the progenitor of many of the latter-day poet's reflections on that subject – for Shelley, corruption 'begins at the imagination'.[27] In lines reminiscent of John Brown, who described how, even in ages of moral corruption, poets still continued to 'throw out the Emanations of prophetic and moral Truth',[28] Shelley writes that in these last days, 'poetry ever addresses itself to those faculties which are the last to be destroyed, and its voice is heard, like the footsteps of Astraea, departing from the world'.[29] Thus, poetry stands for the perennial possibility of renewal and regeneration. The poet can save man from the detritus of history.

The contradiction between poetry and history is well represented by Shelley's long poem *The Revolt of Islam*, and Mary Shelley's description of the circumstances of its composition affords a clue to the felt hiatus between them. Shelley composed the poem in idyllic circumstances – it was written in 'his boat, as it floated under the beech-groves of Bisham' – but at the same time in nearby Marlow the circumstances of the labouring poor were troubling his mind:

> With all this wealth of Nature which, either in the form of gentlemen's parks or soil dedicated to agriculture, flourishes around, Marlow was inhabited (I hope it is altered now) by a very poor population. The women are lacemakers, and lose their health by sedentary labour, for which they were very ill paid. The Poor-laws ground to the dust not only the paupers, but those who had risen just above that state, and were obliged to pay poor-rates. The changes brought by peace following a long war, and a bad harvest, brought with them the most heart-rending evils to the poor. Shelley afforded what alleviation he could.[30]

The Revolt of Islam is a complex allegory of tyranny, freedom and revolt, but it can never remain solely within the realm of the historical or rest in a description of the fact of tyranny and oppression. The boat, symbol of the journeying and exploratory imagination, must always travel beyond this or the poet will have failed in his task. Shelley did represent contemporary methods of manipulation and domination:

The Tyrant knew his power was gone, but Fear,
The nurse of Vengeance, bade him wait the event –
That perfidy and custom, gold and prayer,
And whatsoe'er, when force is impotent,
To fraud the sceptre of the world has lent,
Might, as he judged, confirm his failing sway.
Therefore throughout the streets, the Priests he sent
To curse the rebels. – To their gods did they
For Earthquake, Plague, and Want kneel in the public
    way.

But at the opening and close of the poem Shelley insisted on the importance of grasping transcendent truths whatever the immediate exigencies and whatever the consequences:

Truth's deathless voice pauses among mankind!
If there must be no response to my cry –
If men must rise and stamp with fury blind
On his pure name who loves them, – thou and I,
Sweet friend! can look from our tranquillity
Like lamps into the world's tempestuous night, –
Two tranquil stars, while clouds are passing by
Which wrap them from the foundering seaman's sight,
That burn from year to year with unextinguished light.

At the end of the poem, the poet on his visionary journey by enchanted boat is vouchsafed the recognition

that virtue, though obscured on Earth, not less
Survives all mortal changes in lasting loveliness.

Although Shelley did believe in the power of the poet to transcend the actual; although he has the most exalted conception of the poet and his function of any of the English Romantic poets with the possible exception of Blake – much of his poetry is nevertheless highly pessimistic. Although the vision itself guarantees, the vision is not guaranteed as far as the poet is concerned. When faced with the loss of the visionary, Shelley's sense of desolation is nothing less than overwhelming, and unlike Wordsworth or Keats he refused to make any effort to come to terms with it, since he felt that to do so would be at once hypocrisy and a betrayal. If the vision is man's last best hope in a corrupted and treacherous world, then there can be no possibility of any reconciliation. In *Alastor* the poet's vision is represented by a beautiful maiden, who is his own truest and best self:

> He dreamed a veiled maid
> Sate near to him, talking in low solemn tones.
> Her voice was like the voice of his own soul
> Heard in the calm of thought; its music long,
> Like woven sounds of streams and breezes, held
> His inmost sense suspended in its web
> Of many-coloured woof and shifting hues.
> Knowledge and truth and virtue were her theme,
> And lofty hopes of divine liberty,
> Thoughts the most dear to him, and poesy,
> Herself a poet.

To the poet this vision is irresistible, engulfing, powerfully erotic; but at the very moment when he endeavours to seize it he loses consciousness and awakens to vacancy and a sense of irreparable loss:

> Lost, lost, for ever lost,
> In the wide pathless desert of dim sleep,
> That beautiful shape.

In *Alastor* we are introduced to what is to become a familiar figure in Shelley's poetry, the poet as sufferer and victim. Alastor is the unknown poet:

> There was a poet whose untimely tomb
> No human hands with pious reverence reared,
> But the charmed eddies of autumnal winds
> Built o'er his mouldering bones a pyramid
> Of mouldering leaves in a waste wilderness.

It seems excessively paradoxical of Shelley to lament the fact that no poet uttered any word of regret at Alastor's death when his own poem is devoted precisely to a celebration of this mythical unknown poet; but Shelley is determined to enforce a recognition on the part of the reader that the lot of the poet

is one of suffering, loneliness and neglect. Shelley believed
that the poet had a crucial social role to play, but he did not
thereby delude himself into the supposition that this was a role
they actually filled. *A Defence of Poetry* is filled with intimations
of the exclusion of poetry from the world, so that the sense of
his title is stronger than that of Sir Philip Sidney: poetry is to
be not so much supported as protected from extinction.
Poetry in his own age struggles against the dominance of
practical and pragmatic knowledge, the power of wealth and
the prevalence of exploitation; the poet has been forced
'to resign the civic crown to reasoners and mechanists'.[31] So
Alastor, the poet as wanderer and outcast, embarks on a
quest for the recovery of vision that can only end in death:

> The boat fled on
> With unrelaxing speed. – 'Vision and Love!'
> The Poet cried aloud, 'I have beheld
> The path of thy departure. Sleep and death
> Shall not divide us long!'

In this poem the idea of the poem itself affords no consolation, since it is the vision itself that defines and determines the
existence of the poet. Before the loss of vision art itself must be
silent:

> Let not high verse, mourning the memory
> Of that which is no more, or painting's woe
> Or sculpture, speak in feeble imagery
> Their own cold powers.

The phrase 'that which is no more' focuses the way in which
poet and vision have become entangled; for it could refer to
either: without his vision the poet is nothing but a doomed and
accurst wanderer whose life has been deprived of all meaning.
Shelley's poem becomes the celebration of a multiple absence:
of the unremembered poet and the loss of hope, creativity,
vision, so that there is not simply a lack of remembering but a
lack that has to be remembered! The poet becomes an unacknowledged vacuum of mankind, a man who takes upon
himself the burden of mystery and desolation and who
thereby pays a terrible price. He is a martyr to the quest for
meaning.

A related sense of the poet as wanderer and outcast pervades Shelley's 'Lines Written among the Euganean Hills' – surely one of the most eloquent of all his poems – which also shows how that condition stems from the opposition between vision and history. For the poet, looking down on the 'sun-girt city' of Venice, is made to think of the transitory existence of that city itself, of the death of many 'sacred' poets, and of the endless repetitions in history, by which the spark of freedom has glowed into existence and been extinguished. Although the poem concludes with the wish that the earth would 'grow young again', it does so against the background of the concluding lines of *Hellas*:

> The world is weary of the past,
> Oh, might it die or rest at last.

'Lines written among the Euganean Hills' casts an ironic light on Shelley's statement in *A Defence of Poetry* that 'Poetry is the record of the best and happiest moments of the happiest and best minds',[32] in that, although it is indeed a record of such a happy moment in Shelley's life, the poet deliberately sets it in the most dispiriting and oppressive context. Life is seen as an endless journey on a dark, violent and obscure sea, alleviated by only the occasional landfall at some 'flowering isles'. Even when Shelley is possessed by his vision at its fullest intensity it nevertheless remains under a shadow:

> Noon descend around me now:
> 'Tis the noon of autumn's glow,
> When a soft and purple mist
> Like a vaporous amethyst,
> Or an air-dissolvèd star
> Mingling light and fragrance, far
> From the curved horizon's bound
> To the point of Heaven's profound,
> Fills the overflowing sky;
> And the plains that silent lie
> Underneath, the leaves unsodden
> Where the infant Frost has trodden
> With his morning-wingèd feet,
> Whose bright print is gleaming yet;

And the red and golden vines
Piercing with their trellised lines
The rough, dark-skirted wilderness;
The dun and bladed grass no less,
Pointing from this hoary tower
In the windless air; the flower
Glimmering at my feet; the line
Of the olive-sandalled Apennine
In the south dimly islanded;
And the Alps, whose snows are spread
High between the clouds and sun;
And of living things each one;
And my spirit which so long
Darkens this swift stream of song, –
Interpenetrated lie
By the glory of the sky:
Be it love, light, harmony,
Odour, or the soul of all
Which from Heaven like dew doth fall,
Or the mind which feeds this verse
Peopling the lone universe.

The invocation of noon is unexpected. Noon 'descends', although noon is normally thought of as the high point of the
day, and it is immediately linked with autumn, which is the
waning season that carries with it the imprint of the evanescent. So that the descent of noon in a soft and shimmering
glow is simultaneously apprehended as a timeless, suspended
moment and as one that must necessarily pass. For a brief moment the poet loses consciousness of his own sorrows and his
own separate identity and feels totally interconnected with the
world about him. The poem itself is a representation of this
moment and of its absence, a stream rushing out of the darkness of the poet's grief-laden existence momentarily into the
sunlight, only for it to be carried once more away, as in a more
ominous vein 'Noon descends' once more. Thus, for Shelley,
the visionary is always under a cloud; no matter how vivid or
intense the experience, it carries with it the threat of deprivation, the return into a world of pain and suffering.

In 'The Sensitive Plant' the loss of vision is allegorised as a
fall. The 'companionless Sensitive Plant' growing in a beauti-

ful garden is the figure of the isolated poet, who is defined in neo-Platonic terms – not as a possessor of the beautiful but as one who desires it and who, in desiring it, necessarily lacks it:

> For the Sensitive Plant has no bright flower;
> Radiance and odour are not its dower;
> It loves, even like Love, its deep heart is full,
> It desires what it has not, the Beautiful!

The beautiful is represented by the maiden who tends the garden, who brings intense pleasure but who, nevertheless, is intangible even in the moment of her presence:

> Her step seemed to pity the grass it pressed;
> You might hear by the heaving of her breast,
> That the coming and going of the wind
> Brought pleasure there and left passion behind.
>
> And whenever her aery footstep trod,
> Her trailing hair from the grassy sod
> Erased its light vestige, with shadowy sweep,
> Like a sunny storm o'er the dark green deep.
>
> I doubt not the flowers of that garden sweet
> Rejoiced in the shadow of her gentle feet;
> I doubt not they felt the spirit that came
> From her glowing fingers through all their frame.

Thus the presence of the beautiful has an invisibility that is only revealed through its absence; in this way the loss of the visionary though an everyday state of affairs appears in the light of the *abnormal*, an intolerable banality. This figures in the third section of the poem, where the garden on the death of the maiden becomes 'cold and foul', infected, blighted, overgrown with fungi and weeds. Shelley addresses himself to the loss and eclipse of vision in his conclusion, where he suggests that, since life is temporal and since we are 'the shadows of a dream', the sense of deprivation itself may only be an illusion, caused by our inability to apprehend the beautiful with sufficient intensity:

> That garden sweet, that lady fair

> And all sweet shapes and odours there,
> In truth have never passed away:
> 'Tis we, 'tis ours, are changed; not they.

The conclusion renders problematic what Shelley has depicted in the poem itself; for 'The Sensitive Plant' shows a vision and then brackets it by suggesting that it cannot persist in the real world – the world of thistle, nettles and 'plants, at whose name the verse feels loath'. But the conclusion brackets the bracketing.

Structurally the poem is a return from the ideal to the real, but, since this conclusion is unacceptable to Shelley, offering as it does no basis for hope, he switches back to the standpoint of the ideal. But this ideal is not identical with that of the garden itself. The vision of the maiden is framed within the vision of a garden subject to temporal metamorphosis, but the garden is itself framed by the philosophical reflection that beautiful forms are eternal. Thus, the poem in its entirety becomes a device whereby Shelley can shift from a sense of the transitoriness of the visionary to the conviction that that which the visionary apprehends is not subject to change. The poet shuttles back and forth between the eternal and the mutable tormented by discontinuity but nevertheless convinced of the reality of the beautiful that is desired.

All of Shelley's visionary poetry is tinged with pessimism, but the most affirmative is certainly *Epipsychidion*, despite its mournful dedication by the poet as 'verses addressed to the noble and unfortunate lady, Emilia V—, now imprisoned in the convent of——.' *Epipsychidion* depicts the same compulsive alternation between the presence and absence of vision that was the theme of Keats's *Endymion*, a parallel that Shelley seems to acknowledge by a reference to the mythological Endymion within the poem. But, whereas the moment of vision in 'Lines Written among the Euganean Hills' is set with a context of absence, in *Epipsychidion* the moments of loss are to be seen from the standpoint of Shelley's intense love for Emily. Shelley relates how he early saw a maiden, representative of his visionary consciousness, how he lost it – and, like Orpheus, desperately sought it through the world. Believing he had recovered it he almost instantaneously lost it again, only to recover it with Emily/Emilia:

I knew it was the Vision veiled from me
So many years – that it was Emily.

Emily is associated with the eternal world of Forms, situated
far beyond the temporal and the actual:

Thou Moon beyond the clouds! Thou living Form
Among the Dead! Thou Star above the Storm!

Not only the subject-matter of poetry, she becomes the
embodiment of the very spirit of poetry itself:

The glory of her being, issuing thence,
Stains the dead, blank, cold air with a warm shade
Of unentangled intermixture, made
By love and motion: one intense
Diffusion, one serene Omnipotence,
Whose flowing outline mingles in their flowing,
Around her cheeks and utmost fingers glowing . . ..

Emily is the principle of coloration in the world, a sign
simultaneously of vitality, of the interrelation of all things, of a
purity that is nevertheless radiant and complex, the one in the
many, the many in the one. It is precisely this that poetry
endeavours to represent – to show interrelatedness not as
a theoretical postulate but to re-enact it and recreate it in
language as living and vital: 'that Beauty furled/Which pen-
etrates and clasps and fills the world'. As always with Shelley,
the imagery is highly erotic and carries with it the implication
of possession in the fullest sense. Yet the theoretical incompatibility between the visionary and the real is not to be
evaded. In this sense the particular circumstances, Emilia
herself even, are incidental: the argument has to be worked out
in terms of the rigorous visionary problematic. Although
Shelley does envisage a consonance between desire and the
object of desire, between the poet and his vision so that they
become one, he also recognises that this is not possible in terms
of the real world, for a union in the real world would cancel the
meaning that the union is destined to signify. So death becomes
the ultimate goal because only there is mutability suspended:

> Like flames too pure and light and unimbued
> To nourish their bright lives with baser prey
> Which point to Heaven and cannot pass away:
> One hope within two wills, one will beneath
> Two overshadowing minds, one life, one death,
> One Heaven, one Hell, one immortality,
> And one annihilation.

What Shelley seems to acknowledge in *Epipsychidion*, if only obliquely, is that no attainment of the visionary is actually possible. The fulfilment of the visionary is necessarily a contradiction of the actual, and the poet, as mediator, like Endymion, disappears into the vision.

In *Adonais* the note of lamentation at the world's loss of a poet/hero is renewed. For Shelley, Keats is his own double: the poet as martyr and victim who has created, yet suffered, at the hands of the world. Unlike *Alastor*, which had the character of a theoretical description, *Adonais* is a response to a real situation. Shelley's sense of desolation and loss is the more convincing because he does not confine himself to decorous expressions of regret but, in violation of the canons of appropriateness, makes it clear that he is grieving as much for himself as for Keats. Furthermore, the poem must be understood as a poem about the death of a poet; it is for fulfilling this noble yet arduous role that Keats is to be remembered, and therefore it is only natural that Shelley should be conscious of his own situation also. Shelley's appearance at the graveside of Adonais, where he

> Made bare his branded and ensanguined brow,
> Which was like Cain's or Christ's – oh! that it should be
>   so

is symbolically crucial; for poets live and are immortalised only through their own mutual recognition: each must certify the authenticity of the other's vision and recall the world to a recognition of the transcendent. Shelley's predicament as he here presents it is that he really belongs to the spiritual other world and yet is compelled to live on in exile in this world. He is a *revenant* from the visionary,

> A phantom among men; companionless

As the last cloud of an expiring storm
Whose thunder is its knell

haunted both by the world and by his own internal conflicts.
Shelley is a victim of the intermittence of the visionary – he
characterises himself through images that articulate the
co-presence of presence and absence:

A pardlike Spirit beautiful and swift –
A Love in desolation masked; – a Power
Girt round with weakness; – it can scarce uplift
The weight of the superincumbent hour;
It is a dying lamp, a falling shower,
A breaking billow; – even whilst we speak
Is it not broken? On the withering flower
The killing sun shines brightly: on a cheek
The life can burn in blood, even when the heart may
    break.

The poet *is* powerful, through his contact and commerce with
the visionary, but 'Girt round with weakness', because it is so
ephemeral. Keats is fortunate because he has been delivered
not only from 'the contagion of the world's slow stain' but also
from the agonies of intermittence, the external pressure, the
internal fragmentation. For Shelley the poet is essentially
passive and receptive, open to impressions, driven and
impelled by forces over which he has no control – but we must
be careful to acknowledge that this is generated by Shelley's
analysis of the poet's situation and his understanding of the
visionary problematic. It is intellectually vulgar to interpret
Shelley's poetry so exclusively in terms of his own personal
'weakness', whatever that is supposed to mean. In a poet
weakness may be strength and *vice versa*. The poet is crucially
dependent on his moments of vision, which are the things that
make him a poet; but, as they can never be willed, since the
mind that creates is 'incapable of accounting to itself for the
origin, the gradations, or the media of the process',[33] he can
never be anything other than a desperate wanderer, searching
and hoping for the recovery both of the vision and himself. It
is for this reason that Shelley writes at the end of the poem:

The breath whose might I have invoked in song
Descends on me; my spirit's bark is driven,

> Far from the shore, far from the trembling throng
> Whose sails were never to the tempest given;
> The massy earth and sphered skies are riven!
> I am borne darkly, fearfully afar;
> Whilst, burning through the inmost veil of Heaven,
> The soul of Adonais, like a star,
> Beacons from the abode where the Eternal are.

The poet cannot escape his mission. He does not chose it but is chosen by it. Yet he is never at rest. The burden of the poet is a double exile: from the world of men and from the visionary, which beckons, dazzles and tantalises from afar.

Shelley met death by drowning in 1822, only a year after Keats and the writing of this poem. With the death of Byron two years later at Missolonghi in Greece there is a definite sense of closure as far as English Romanticism is concerned. Byron is both the summation of the Romantic movement and at the same time the writer who most seems to reach beyond it. Byron's European popularity is often regarded as an oddity; but this continuing tendency to underrate Byron is hazardous, not simply because it is tantamount to the loss of one of Romanticism's most representative figures but also because it enables an impoverished understanding to persist both of what Romanticism historically was and, equally significantly, what it was to represent for future generations.

Byron's poetry is inescapably connected with his creation of that distinctive figure, who recurs from work to work in a variety of guises that nevertheless exhibit a common underlying structure, the eminently recognisable 'Byronic hero'. Byron initially purported to disown any connection between his hero and himself. He claimed that Childe Harold was 'the child of imagination' and subsequently appended an addition to the Preface to Cantos I and II of *Childe Harold* in which he referred to his 'vagrante Childe' 'whom notwithstanding many hints to the contrary, I still maintain to be a fictitious personage'.[34] But the relation of Byron to his own fictions was transparent from the start, as his own comment indicates and as the confidence of the reviewer in the *British Critic* for December 1816 suggests: 'The hero of the poem is, as usual, himself: for he has now so unequivocally identified himself with his fictitious hero, that even in his most querulous moods,

he cannot complain of our impertinence in tracing resemblance.'[35] Byron could not complain because in his
Preface to *The Corsair* (1814) he had virtually confessed by
writing,

> With regard to my story, and stories in general, I should
> have been glad to have rendered my personages more
> perfect and amiable, if possible, inasmuch as I have been
> sometimes criticised, and considered no less responsible for
> their deeds and qualities than if all had been personal. Be it
> so – if I have deviated into the gloomy vanity of 'drawing
> from self', the pictures are probably like since they are
> unfavourable: and if not, those who know me are unde-
> ceived, and those who do not, I have little interest in
> undeceiving.[36]

Byron's tone has all the haughty indifference of his hero,
Conrad.

In Byron's verse we find the most consistent and thoroughly
worked out literary persona in any writer since Sterne. But to
labour with all the earnestness of the 'New Criticism' the
distinction between author and persona is rather to miss the
point. The Byronic hero is undoubtedly a literary construct,
whose parentage can be traced back through Scott's Marmion
to Gothic precursors such as Montoni, Schedoni and Fer-
dinand Count Fathom to Milton's Satan, but simply to invoke
these names is also to suggest how easily the Byronic hero
might have reeked not of autobiography but of the lamp, as a
striking cut-out of cardboard villainy. If this is not the case it
is because Byron interprets the stereotype in a highly em-
pathetic manner, always presenting him to the reader sympathetically, and showing him in an attractive, even glamorous, light. The Byronic hero has all the psychological complexity of the Gothic hypocrite but redeems himself precisely
because he is not one – as Byron writes of Conrad, the
Corsair:

> He knew himself a villain – but he deemed
> The rest no better than the thing he seemed;
> And scorned the best as hypocrites who hid
> Those deeds a bolder spirit plainly did.

For Byron boldness is a redeeming virtue. The Byronic hero is simultaneously mysterious and contradictory; thus of Conrad:

> His features' deepening lines and varying hue
> At times attracted, yet perplexed the view,
> As if within that murkiness of mind
> Worked feelings fearful, and yet undefined.

The Byronic hero is not be be read like a book, because external and internal do not correspond; his complex inner life, his tortuous struggles do not immediately reveal themselves but are disclosed progressively, if obliquely. Byron's adoption of discursive narrative forms and of rhyming couplets apparently looks back to the eighteenth century, but we should not miss the new uses to which they are put: the discursive form, as in *Don Juan*, permits an apparent focus on narrativity while the crucial emphases fall in parenthetical asides; the balance of the heroic couplet is ideally suited to the articulation of contradictions. The Byronic hero is cynical yet vulnerable, with a heart 'formed for softness'. He is fiery yet calm, bitter yet smiling, noble yet debased, villainous yet full of generous impulses, solitary and committed to isolation yet longing for love and companionship, enigmatic yet open, frank and free from guile. The origins of the figure in Milton's Satan becomes transparent in *The Giaour*:

> But sadder still it were to trace
> What once were feelings in that face:
> Time hath not yet the features fixed
> But brighter traits with evil mixed;
> And there are hues not always faded,
> Which speak a mind not all degraded
> Even by the crimes through which it waded:
> The common crowd but see the gloom
> Of wayward deeds, and fitting doom;
> The close observer can espy
> A noble soul, and lineage high.

Yet it is reformulated and given new meaning through the

stress on doubleness. The distinction between what is manifest and what is latent becomes critical. The persona is a lure constructed for the multitude that betrays and does not betray the nobler and deeper identity that lurks beneath. It is as if he is a villain for the very reason that he does not wish to be known; that he eagerly grasps at possibilities of misrepresentation and misconstruction – as Byron himself latched onto the scope of being construed/misconstrued as the Byronic hero. Thus the Byronic hero incorporates its own critique of the Byronic persona: the doublesidedness of its being like/ unlike Byron to which Byron alluded in conceding that the negative aspects of the portrait might all be autobiographical, is enigmatic and self-cancelling, since behind the gloomy, self-indulgent and haughty façade is concealed a pure and pristine figure, like a masterpiece overlaid with prenticework adornment, the truth both of the Byronic hero and of Byron himself. Thus Byron cannot escape the Byronic hero nor the Byronic hero Byron. They are bound together in an inescapable couple of veiling and unveiling, concealment and disclosure. The Byronic hero is and is not Byron in precisely the same mode that he is and is not what he seems. Indeed, the assurance of a real Byron as source of the Byronic poems gives the Byronic hero a greater plausibility, since we might otherwise query the aesthetic significance of the contradictory stereotype. So long as that contradiction is located purely within the poem itself it may be seen as propounding a conundrum beyond the power of the poem itself to resolve; it is only when read off as a gap between the work and the author that it points to contradictions in the mind of the author himself and that the device becomes aesthetically expressive. What the reader responds to in Byron's poetry is the interface between the Byronic hero and the poet's own meditative consciousness. Byron, like Wordsworth, is writing about himself, yet the effect is different because of the constant switching of codes – we are made to feel the plenitude and expressivity of the Byronic persona but in the moment of vacancy in which the persona is deflated we become conscious of Byron as author. In the rhythm of alternation Byron is always there before the reader's gaze, yet there and not there in a different mode, as follows:

PRESENCE   PRESENCE

Byronic Hero   Byron the Poet

Byron the Poet   Byronic Hero

ABSENCE   ABSENCE

    The Byronic hero synthesises many of the characteristic features of Romantic discourse. As wanderer, outcast and solitary – often with the added characteristic of being, as with the Corsair, a free and colourful figure from an earlier age – he has affinities with the heroes of the historical genre. As mysterious and contradictory, with a complex inner life riddled with contradictions and combining sympathetic with sinister traits, he represents a reworking of the Gothic hypocrite; while Byronic heroes such as Childe Harold articulate the theme of the lost vision, so characteristic of Romantic poetry. In Byron's poetry the crucial moment is always past and beyond recovery. The hero, having enjoyed ideal love, becomes, like Shelley, a desolate wanderer, ever searching for the recovery of a lost vision of beauty and happiness. As Manfred says to the Phantom of Astarte, 'I have wandered o'er the earth, / And never found thy likeness.' The facility with which Byron deploys these multiple resonances is significant both in constituting a poetic complexity and as constituting Byron himself as a quintessential synthesising figure of the Romantic movement.

    The Byronic hero invariably carries traces of the super-human. He is a cosmic rebel, who refuses to accept either the world as it is or his own place within it. He refuses to be judged by others or to accept any verdict other than his own. His project, his existence is one of self-definition. It moves beyond conventional schemas and value judgements. Since the hero is mysterious to everyone but himself, since his feeling and emotions lie hidden, only he can know and evaluate. Manfred's intransigent denial of any external tribunal, even that of Heaven itself, is but the apotheosis of Byron's insistence on the autonomy of the self. Byron is the first intellectual writer whom we can situate with confidence, and without either vulgarity or anachronism as well within the problematic of

Existentialism as that of Romanticism, since the one generates
the other and Byron himself marks an overlap between the
two. The hero is thrown into existence, into a world he never
made and did not choose, and is always placed in a position
where givenness overpowers the application of a conventional
morality. For morality implies a choice between alternatives,
but in Byron there are only states of feeling presented as
inescapable facts: to ask the hero why he feels as he does is
really neither here nor there, for, even if he were able to
answer, justify or explain, that state of consciousness would
nevertheless be there as the most irreducible and inescapable
datum. The hero is removed from the binary set of good and
evil, the application of which can only take the form of
irony – the irony of the Byronic poems – for his predicament
is rather a nullity that menaces for the very reason that it
cannot be so situated or defined. Morality is a kind of theatre
that passes over it and melodramatises it, but which can never
grasp the psychic reality, both because it is external and
because the psychological does not enter into its calculations.
Though sources and origins appear of the very essence, since
to know how the hero came to be what he was would be to
render him morally transparent, it is a solution that Byron
carefully excludes. The Byronic hero is not cause but consequence: he is always encountered *after* – a perennial fifth-
act Hamlet or Macbeth. The unravellable nature of the
Byronic world is epitomised by these words of Ulric in *Werner*:

> We have done
> With right and wrong; and now must only ponder
> Upon effects, not causes.

Hazlitt, in the course of a generally unsympathetic and slightly
obtuse discussion of *Childe Harold*, nevertheless showed himself acute in diagnosing the ominously self-referential nature
of Byron's poetry: 'He volunteers his own Pilgrimage, –
appoints his own penance, – makes his own confession.'[37]
This is all too apt. Byron's poetry creates a nightmare of
closure – not simply the closure of possibilities in the sense
that there could never be anything further that could actually
make an aesthetic closure possible (and what is this, after all, if
not *Don Juan*?), nor even the exhaustion of possibilities
whereby no further experience would signify, since the hero

has already gone through and used up all possibilities of
self-definition, but rather the closure of the poetic world itself
so that Byron in all his writing can never escape from the
malignant double of himself as arbiter. Byron is his own
hound of heaven, a tiger chasing his own tail, who pursues
himself endlessly and wearily yet unrelentingly through the
days and nights of his verse.

Childe Harold's Pilgrimage should therefore be seen as
nothing less than a quest for oblivion, for forgetfulness of self.
Childe Harold begins in the mode of a parody of *The Rime of the
Ancient Mariner*, but the parallel is all too close, for Childe
Harold too is a tormented soul, though, unlike Coleridge's
hero, without possibility of blessing. Stanza iv of the Third
Canto emphasises the paradoxical relationship between the
poet and his theme:

> Since my young days of passion – joy or pain –
> Perchance my heart and harp have lost a string –
> And both may jar: it may be that in vain
> I would essay, as I have sung, to sing:
> Yet, though a dreary strain, to this I cling;
> So that it wean me from the weary dream
> Of selfish grief or gladness – so it fling
> Forgetfulness around me – it shall seem
> To me, though to none else, a not ungrateful theme.

So the writing of the poem is seen by Byron as a forgetting;
but, in so far as it concerns a Byronic persona whose very
pilgrimage is a similar forgetting, it also necessarily involves
an act of remembering – the endless reduplication of what,
ostensibly, was to be expunged. And when Byron sang of one
who was 'The wandering outlaw of his own dark mind', that
person he sang of was also himself, perhaps even in a happier
time. So the theme of the Byronic hero is multiply ironised,
because, while the poet continues to repeat his theme, that
theme is no longer what it was, because of changes in the poet
and his attitude towards his own subject; so that the gloom
becomes less and less of an attitude and more and more of a
truth, though it is a truth made banal through the very process
of repetition. Thus, though Byron has created his own cliche
and stereotype, his deepest feelings are nevertheless aroused

and agitated as he sits with pen in hand confronting the page, reflecting on the reflection of a reflection. In the act of repeating he has turned his own feelings into an obsession:

> Yet must I think less wildly: – I *have* thought
> Too long and darkly, till my brain became,
> In its own eddy boiling and o'erwrought,
> A whirling gulf of fantasy and flame.

His sense of severance is total. He is cut off from other men, from his own self, from a movement of human history which seems another dismal cycle of repetition in which the attempts of men to free themselves from injustice and tyranny are themselves ironised as freedom generates its opposite and reaction triumphs again. The wandering of Childe Harold is the medium for describing this mode of consciousness; he stands 'A ruin among ruins' coming *after* both himself and the world, inserted incongruously and too late – too late to find any way of expressing himself through action. Byron did in fact find such a course of action in going to Greece to fight for Greek independence, and his poetry must be read in that light. It nevertheless does show how crucial it was for Byron to find something to which he could wholeheartedly commit himself and which would lift the mood of worldweariness which his poetry evoked and which found such an echo. For Byron more than anyone registered the stifling oppression and emptiness of the age of Metternich, which for many seemed the era of the exhaustion of all possibilities, the possibilities which Romanticism itself was bound up with. In the final canto of *Childe Harold* Byron bitterly parodies the language of Milton's Paradise:

> Alas! our young affections run to waste,
> Or water but the desert! whence arise
> But weeds of dark luxuriance, tares of haste,
> Rank at the core, though tempting to the eyes,
> Flowers whose wild odours breathe but agonies,
> And trees whose gums are poison; such the plants
> Which spring beneath her steps as Passion flies
> O'er the world's wilderness, and vainly pants
> For some celestial fruit forbidden to our wants.

For despite Byron's great admiration for Milton his own orientation could not have been more different. Milton is the great poet of origins, looking back to a Paradise which, because it existed, determines everything that follows as vision, benchmark and source. Byron has little faith in causes and explanations and, lacking Milton's faith in an obscure yet rigid structure to history, confronts desolation as an irreducible fact. For Byron, the ideal, the visionary, is something that one is torn between remembering and forgetting in an intimidating choice of demoralisations. *Childe Harold* nevertheless has its consolations. There is stoicism in survival itself, which together with a love for nature and the blessing of solitude, can ease the pain of existence. But the real goal of Byron's poetry is oblivion. When the Seven Spirits appear to Manfred and ask him what he desires, he asks for forgetfulness, for 'Oblivion – self-oblivion'. Byron's attitude to the visionary is thus rather different from Shelley's. Shelley always sought to recover the visionary. Byron, recognising that the visionary has been irremediably cancelled, seeks only to cancel the recognition that it is so.

This is the meaning of the quest of *Don Juan*. *Don Juan* can, of course, be read as social satire, which it undoubtedly is, but it can also be seen as a discourse on the loss of vision. Don Juan's idyll with Haidée is the visionary become real, the real become visionary. It is Byron's equivalent of the Paradise in *Paradise Lost* and nothing can happen to it other than that it can be lost. The love of Juan and Haidée is eternal and timeless, but it is Juan's fate to have to go on living after Haidée dies. He has relationships with many other women, but inevitably no one can be like Haidée, the child of innocence and nature – the difference between her and Adeline is like that between 'a flower and a gem'. Juan himself can never be the same. For Shelley the loss of vision can never be escaped or evaded. For Byron, on the other hand, poetry itself constitutes precisely such an evasion and process of forgetting – an endless disgression, a *quète sans fin*, a game of the poet with himself, a goalless quest. Byron is a perpetual prisoner whose sense of freedom is ceaselessly replenished by stone walls and iron bars. Byron is most truly a hero as poet, writing.

Notes

CHAPTER 1

1. Thomas Holcroft, *The Adventures of Hugh Trevor*, ed. S. Deane (London, 1973), p. 290.
2. Edmund Burke, *On Government, Politics and Society*, ed. B. W. Hill (Hassocks, 1975), p. 354.
3. Thomas Paine, *The Rights of Man*, (London, 1954), p. 32.
4. Ibid., p. 47.
5. William Godwin, *Enquiry Concerning Political Justice*, ed. I. Kramnick (London, 1978), p. 644.
6. Ibid., p. 501.
7. Ibid., p. 490.
8. Paine, *Rights of Man*, p. 33.
9. Godwin, *Political Justice*, p. 646.
10. Ibid., p. 646.
11. Charlotte Smith, *Desmond* (London, 1972) vol. III, p. 71. She also refers to 'usurped and abused authority' (ibid., p. 42).
12. Anne Radcliffe, *The Mysteries of Udolpho*, ed. B. Dobrée (London, 1966), p. 263.
13. Ibid., p. 227.
14. Ibid., p. 228.
15. Ibid., pp. 381–2.
16. Paine, *Rights of Man*, p. 265.
17. Michel Foucault, *Madness and Civilisation* (London, 1967), pp. 203–4.
18. Charlotte Smith, *Emmeline*, ed. A. H. Ehrenpreis (London, 1971), p. 79.
19. Ibid.
20. Ibid.
21. Ibid., p. 311.
22. Ibid., p. 442.
23. Radcliffe, *The Mysteries of Udolpho*, p. 4.
24. Ibid.
25. Jean-Paul Richter, *Titan*, trs. C. T. Brooks (Boston, Mass., 1868), p. 11.
26. Ibid., p. 135.
27. Thomas Holcroft, *Anna St Ives*, ed. P. Faulkner (London, 1970), p. 292.
28. Charlotte Smith, *Celestina* (London, 1791) vol. IV, p. 290.
29. Charlotte Smith, *The Old Manor House*, ed. A. H. Ehrenpreis (London, 1969), p. 361.
30. Ibid., p. 444.
31. Anne Radcliffe, *The Romance of the Forest* (London, 1882), p. 189.

32. Ibid., p. 262.
33. Robert Bage, *Hermsprong*, ed. V. Wilkins (London, 1951), p. 73.
34. Ibid.
35. Ibid., p. 237.
36. Radcliffe, *Romance of the Forest*, p. 312.
37. Ibid., p. 323.
38. Ibid., p. 419.
39. Radcliffe, *The Mysteries of Udolpho*, p. 510. Valancourt's corruption is particularly shocking because he has not been exposed to the depravity of the capital – St Aubert earlier remarks (p. 36), 'this young man has never been at Paris'.
40. Ibid., p. 585.
41. Ibid., p. 652.
42. Bage, *Hermsprong*, p. 11.
43. Holcroft, *Anna St Ives*, pp. 474–5.
44. Bage, *Hermsprong*, p. 243.
45. Ibid., p. 196.
46. Holcroft, *Anna St Ives*, p. 153.
47. Ibid., p. 261.
48. Ibid., p. 121.
49. Ibid., p. 480.
50. Ibid. Similarly, Hermsprong is described as 'soaring out of reach of common minds' (*Hermsprong*, p. 156).
51. Bage, *Hermsprong*, p. 98.
52. Holcroft, *Anna St Ives*, pp. 57–8.
53. Ibid., p. 401.
54. Ibid., p. 480.
55. Ibid., p. 479.
56. Ibid., p. 262.
57. Ibid., p. 274.
58. Bage, *Hermsprong*, p. 247.
59. Holcroft, *Anna St Ives*, p. 264.
60. Ibid., p. 194.
61. Ibid., p. 264.
62. Bage, *Hermsprong*, p. 97.
63. Holcroft, *Anna St Ives*, p. 108.
64. Ibid., p. 332.
65. Ibid., p. 364.
66. Ibid., p. 411.
67. Ibid., p. 390.
68. Ibid., p. 480.
69. Ibid., p. 364.
70. Ibid., p. 198.
71. Ibid., p. 255.
72. Ibid., p. 178.
73. Ibid., p. 367.
74. Marilyn Butler, *Jane Austen and the War of Ideas* (Oxford, 1975), p. 32.
75. Holcroft, *Hugh Trevor*, p. 254.
76. Ibid., p. 413.

77. Smith, *Desmond*, vol. II, p. 136.
78. Holcroft, *Hugh Trevor*, p. 414.
79. Ibid., p. 254.
80. Ibid., p. 365.
81. Ibid., p. 31.
82. Ibid., p. 315.
83. Ibid.
84. Ibid., p. 307.
85. Ibid., p. 487.
86. Ibid., p. 212.
87. Ibid., p. 489.
88. Ibid., p. 428.
89. William Godwin, *Caleb Williams*, ed. D. McCracken (London, 1970), p. 1.
90. Godwin, *Political Justice*, p. 114.
91. Godwin, *Caleb Williams*, p. 117.
92. Ibid., p. 181.
93. Ibid., p. 182.
94. Godwin, *Political Justice*, pp. 677–8.
95. Godwin, *Caleb Williams*, p. 305.
96. Ibid., p. 271.
97. Godwin, *Political Justice*, p. 104.
98. Ibid., p. 186.
99. Ibid., pp. 188–9.

CHAPTER 2

1. Matthew Lewis, *The Monk*, ed. H. Anderson (Oxford, 1973), pp. 345–6.
2. Ibid., p. 89.
3. Ibid., p. 124.
4. Ibid., p. 132. Similarly, Beatrice is described (p. 183) as displaying 'the incontinence of a prostitute'.
5. Ibid., p. 397.
6. Ibid., p. 12.
7. Ibid.
8. Ibid., p. 201.
9. Ibid., p. 203. Note also 'The blush of pleasure' (p. 32) and 'the blushing trembler' (p. 262).
10. Ibid., p. 18.
11. Ibid., p. 39.
12. Ibid.
13. Ibid., p. 80.
14. Ibid., p. 240.
15. Ibid., p. 237.
16. Ibid., p. 7.
17. Ibid., p. 297.
18. Ibid., p. 379.

19. Ibid., p. 383.
20. Ibid., p. 382.
21. Ibid., pp. 231–2.
22. Anne Radcliffe, *The Italian*, ed. F. Garber (London, 1968), p. 58.
23. Ibid., p. 34.
24. Ibid., p. 173.
25. Ibid., p. 198.
26. Ibid., p. 52.
27. Ibid., p. 130.
28. Ibid., pp. 121–2.
29. Ibid., p. 30.
30. Ibid., p. 40.
31. Ibid., p. 181.
32. Ibid., p. 62.
33. Ibid.
34. Ibid., pp. 62–3.
35. Ibid., p. 63.
36. Ibid., p. 90.
37. Ibid.
38. Ibid., p. 123.
39. Ibid., p. 255.
40. Ibid., p. 288.
41. Ibid., pp. 288–9.
42. Ibid., p. 292.
43. Ibid., p. 201.
44. Ibid., p. 78.
45. Ibid., p. 378.
46. Ibid., p. 411.
47. E. T. A. Hoffmann, *The Devil's Elixirs*, trs. R. Taylor (London, 1963), pp. 196–7.
48. Ibid., p. 165.
49. Ibid., p. 187.
50. Ibid., p. 59.
51. Ibid., p. 286.
52. Ibid., p. 206.
53. Ibid., p. 178.
54. Ibid., p. 240.
55. Ibid., pp. 6–7.
56. Ibid., p. 168.
57. Mary Shelley, *Frankenstein*, ed. M. K. Joseph (London, 1969), p. 41.
58. Ibid.
59. Ibid., p. 42.
60. Ibid., p. 47.
61. Ibid., p. 48.
62. Ibid.
63. Ibid.
64. Ibid., p. 54.
65. Ibid., p. 77.
66. Ibid., p. 68.

67. Ibid., p. 56.
68. Ibid., p. 88.
69. Ibid., p. 90.
70. Ibid., p. 139.
71. Ibid., p. 146.
72. Ibid., p. 160.
73. Ibid., p. 97.
74. Charles Robert Maturin, *Melmoth the Wanderer*, ed. D. Grant (London, 1968), p. 28.
75. Ibid., p. 58.
76. Ibid., p. 6.
77. Quoted by Douglas Grant, ibid, p. xiii.
78. Ibid., p. 107.
79. Ibid., p. 85.
80. Ibid., p. 118.
81. Ibid., p. 280.
82. Ibid., p. 91.
83. Ibid., p. 99.
84. Ibid., p. 141.
85. Ibid., pp. 250–1.
86. Ibid., pp. 290–1.
87. Ibid., pp. 278–9.
88. Ibid., p. 293.
89. Ibid., p. 266.
90. Ibid., p. 302.
91. Ibid., p. 343.
92. Ibid.
93. Ibid., p. 362.
94. Ibid., p. 371.
95. Ibid., p. 298.
96. Ibid., p. 189.
97. Ibid., p. 358.
98. Ibid., p. 436.
99. Ibid., p. 538.
100. Ibid., p. 484.
101. Radcliffe, *The Italian*, p. 34.
102. James Hogg, *The Private Memoirs and Confessions of a Justified Sinner*, ed. J. Carey (London, 1969), pp. 146–7.
103. Ibid., p. 204.
104. Ibid., p. 205.
105. Ibid., p. 114.
106. Ibid., p. 113.
107. Ibid., p. 107.
108. Ibid., p. 135.
109. Ibid., p. 140.
110. Ibid., p. 154.
111. Ibid., p. 182.
112. Ibid., p. 227.
113. Ibid., p. 187.

114. Ibid., p. 116.
115. Ibid., p. 233.
116. Maturin, *Melmoth the Wanderer*, p. 78.
117. Godwin, *Political Justice*, p. 637.
118. Ibid., p. 570.
119. Ibid., p. 571.
120. Ibid., p. 317.
121. Ibid.

CHAPTER 3

1. Friedrich Schiller, *On the Aesthetic Education of Man*, ed. and trs. E. M. Wilkinson and L. A. Willoughby (Oxford, 1967), p. 61.
2. C. L. de Secondat Montesquieu, *The Spirit of the Laws*, trs. T. Nugent (New York, 1949), vol. i, pp. 114–5.
3. Ibid., p. 122.
4. Ibid., p. 140.
5. Ibid.
6. Ibid., p. 23.
7. Ibid., p. 24.
8. Ibid., pp. 25–6.
9. Voltaire, *The Age of Louis XIV*, trs. and ed. J. H. Brumfitt (New York, 1963), p. 145.
10. Ibid., p. 144.
11. Ibid., p. 229.
12. Ibid., pp. 223–4.
13. Montesquieu, *Spirit of the Laws*, vol. i, p. 161.
14. Ibid., vol. ii, p. 171.
15. Adam Ferguson, *An Essay on the History of Civil Society*, ed. Duncan Forbes (Edinburgh, 1966), p. 65.
16. Ibid., pp. 105–6.
17. J. G. Herder, *On Social and Political Culture*, trs. and ed. F. M. Barnard (Cambridge, 1969), p. 103.
18. Ibid., p. 181.
19. Friedrich Schiller, *Naive and Sentimental Poetry and On the sublime*, trs. J. A. Elias (New York, 1966), p. 149.
20. Gotthold Ephraim Lessing, *Hamburg Dramaturgy*, trs. H. Zimmern (New York, 1962), p. 99.
21. G. W. F. Hegel, *Aesthetics*, trs. T. M. Knox (Oxford, 1975), vol. i, p. 196.
22. Walter Scott, *Poetical Works*, vol. xii (Edinburgh, 1880), p. 529.
23. Ibid., pp. 563–4.
24. Ibid., p. 564.
25. Ibid., p. 482.
26. Friedrich Schiller, *Works*, vol. vi (London, 1903), p. 17.
27. Schiller, *Naive and Sentimental Poetry*, p. 101.
28. Hegel, *Aesthetics*, vol. i, p. 195.
29. Schiller, *Works*, vol. vi, p. ix.
30. See Dushan Bresky, 'Schiller's Debt to Montesquieu and Adam Ferguson', *Comparative Literature*, xiii (1961) 239–53; and Benno von Wiese,

Friedrich Schiller (Stuttgart, 1959), pp. 76–82. See also M. H. Abrams, *Natural Supernaturalism* (London, 1971), pp. 210–11.

31. Ferguson, *History of Civil Society*, p. 50.
32. Ibid., p. 51.
33. Ibid., p. 183.
34. Ibid., p. 185.
35. Schiller, *Aesthetic Education*, pp. 35–7.
36. Schiller, *Works*, vol. vi, p. 168.
37. Ibid., p. 177.
38. Ibid., p. 229.
39. Ibid., p. 250.
40. Ferguson, *History of Civil Society*, p. 230.

CHAPTER 4

All references to the Waverley novels are to the Border edition with introductions and notes by Andrew Lang (London, 1900).

1. Walter Scott, *Poetical Works*, vol. xii (Edinburgh, 1880), p. 447.
2. Georg Lukács, *The Historical Novel*, trs. H. and S. Mitchell (London, 1962), p. 34.
3. Ferguson, *History of Civil Society*, p. 4.
4. Ibid., p. 19.
5. Scott, *Old Mortality*, pp. 83–4.
6. Ibid., pp. 85–6.
7. Scott, *The Bride of Lammermoor*, p. 14.
8. Ibid., p. 18.
9. Scott, *Guy Mannering*, p. 70.
10. Scott, *The Fortunes of Nigel*, pp. xxv–xxvi.
11. Sir Uvedale Price, *Essay on the Picturesque*, ed. Sir T. Lauder (Edinburgh, 1842), p. 117.
12. Richard Payne Knight, *An Analytical Inquiry into the Principles of Taste* (London, 1808), p. 197.
13. Ibid., pp. 197–8.
14. Ferguson, *History of Civil Society*, p. 161.
15. Ibid., pp. 161–2.
16. Ibid., p. 188.
17. Ibid., pp. 263–4.
18. Ibid., p. 29.
19. Scott, *A Legend of Montrose and The Black Dwarf*, p. 68.
20. Ibid., p. 258.
21. Ibid., p. 263.
22. Ibid., p. 13.
23. Ibid., p. 3.
24. Ibid., p. 143.
25. Ibid., p. 152.
26. Ibid., p. 217.
27. Ibid., p. 283.

28. Scott, *The Antiquary*, p. vii.
29. Scott, *Guy Mannering*, pp. 54–5.
30. Ibid., p. 61.
31. Ibid., p. 60.
32. Ibid., p. 352.
33. Scott, *The Antiquary*, p. 495.
34. Ibid., p. 489.
35. Scott, *The Heart of Midlothian*, p. 27.
36. Scott, *Rob Roy*, p. 17.
37. Ibid., p. 350.
38. Ibid., p. 504.
39. Ibid., p. 342.
40. Scott, *The Bride of Lammermoor*, p. 25.
41. Ibid., p. 55.
42. Ibid., p. 416.
43. Scott, *Guy Mannering*, p. 54.
44. Scott, *Waverley*, p. 164.
45. Scott, *The Antiquary*, p. vii.
46. Scott, *Waverley*, p. 648.
47. Ibid., pp. 647–8.
48. Ibid., p. 648.
49. Ibid., p. 601.
50. Scott, *The Heart of Midlothian*, p. 216.
51. Scott, *Waverley*, pp. 42–3.
52. Scott, *Redgauntlet*, p. 221.
53. Ibid., p. 442.
54. Ibid.
55. Scott, *The Heart of Midlothian*, p. 777.
56. Ibid., p. 173.
57. Ibid., pp. 777–8.
58. Scott, *Rob Roy*, p. 582.
59. See David Daiches, *Literary Essays* (Edinburgh, 1956), p. 119; A. N. Wilson, *The Laird of Abbotsford* (Oxford, 1980), p. 60; *Scott's Mind and Art*, ed. A. N. Jeffares (Edinburgh, 1969), pp. 89–91; Marion H. Cusac, *Narrative Structure in the Novels of Sir Walter Scott* (The Hague, 1969), p. 101.
60. Scott, *The Abbot*, p. 609.
61. Scott, *Waverley*, p. 649.
62. Scott, *Quentin Durward*, p. 264.
63. Scott, *The Pirate*, p. xxv.
64. Ibid., p. 597.
65. Scott, *The Fortunes of Nigel*, p. 484.
66. Scott, *The Fair Maid of Perth*, p. 403.
67. Scott, *Quentin Durward*, pp. 540–1.
68. Scott, *The Abbot*, pp. 192–3.
69. Scott, *Peveril of the Peak*, p. 805.
70. Scott, *St Ronan's Well*, p. 143.
71. Ibid., p. 621.
72. For another discussion of Scott which also employs this Nietzchean

term, see Wolfgang Iser, *The Implied Reader* (Baltimore, 1974), pp. 81–100, although Iser sees this primarily as a stylistic device that seeks to achieve 'an enhanced vividness'.
73. Scott, *The Fair Maid of Perth*, p. xvi.

CHAPTER 6

1. I. Day, *Scenes for the Young* (London, 1807), p. 21.
2. Anthony Ashley Cooper, Third Earl of Shaftesbury, *Characteristics of Men, Manners, Opinions, Times*, ed. J. M. Robertson (Indianapolis, 1964), vol. I, p. 131.
3. Jean-Paul Richter, *Flower, Fruit and Thorn Pieces*, trs. A. Ewing (London, 1877), p. 167.
4. Scott, unsigned review of *Childe Harold's Pilgrimage*, Canto III *The Quarterly Review*, vol. XVI (Oct. 1816) p. 186.
5. Ibid.
6. *Coleridge: The Critical Heritage*, ed. J. R. de J. Jackson (London, 1970), p. 329.
7. *Blake: The Critical Heritage*, ed. G. E. Bentley (London, 1965), p. 66.
8. 'On the Cockney School of Poetry: No. I', *Blackwood's Edinburgh Magazine*, vol. II (Oct. 1817) p. 39.
9. *Romantic Bards and British Reviewers*, ed. J. O. Hayden (London, 1971), p. 43.
10. Ibid., p. 52.
11. Ibid.
12. Thomas de Quincey, *Confessions of an English Opium-Eater* (London, 1949), p. 2.
13. Thomas Carlyle, *Critical and Miscellaneous Essays* (London, 1869), vol. V, pp. 255–6.
14. John Brown, *History of the Rise, Union and Power, the Progressions, Separations and Corruptions of Poetry and Music* (New York, 1971), p. 181.
15. *The Letters of John Keats*, ed. H. E. Rollins (Cambridge, Mass., 1958), vol. I, pp. 223–4.
16. *The Poetical Works of William Wordsworth*, ed. E. de Selincourt, 2nd edn (Oxford, 1952) vol. III, p. 331.
17. *Collected Letters of Samuel Taylor Coleridge*, ed. E. L. Griggs (Oxford, 1966), vol. II, p. 714.
18. Coleridge, *Biographia Literaria*, ed. J. Shawcross (Oxford, 1907), vol. II, p. 12.
19. *Shelley's Critical Prose*, ed. B. R. McElderry Jr (Lincoln, Nebr., 1967), p. 30.
20. Ibid., p 31.
21. Ibid.
22. Ibid., p. 11.
23. Ibid., p. 36.
24. Ibid., p. 35.
25. Ibid., p. 10.
26. Ibid., p. 6.

27. Ibid., p. 18.
28. John Brown, *History*, p. 181.
29. *Shelley's Critical Prose*, p. 19.
30. Shelley, *Poetical Works*, ed. T. Hutchinson, revised G. M. Matthews (London, 1970), p. 157.
31. *Shelley's Critical Prose*, p. 26.
32. Ibid., p. 31.
33. Ibid.
34. Byron, *Poetical Works*, ed. F. Page; corrected J. Jump (London, 1970), p. 179.
35. Theodore Redpath, *The Young Romantics and Critical Opinion 1807– 1824* (London, 1973), p. 222.
36. Byron, *Poetical Works*, p. 277.
37. *Byron: The Critical Heritage*, p. 132.

Index